# The Novels of Toni Morrison

## A Study in Race, Gender, and Class

*Books are not spun in mid-air by incorporeal creatures, but are the work of suffering human beings and are attached to grossly material things like health and money and the houses we live in.*

**Virginia Woolf**

*It seems to me that the best art is political and you ought to be able to make it unquestionably political and irrevocably beautiful at the same time.*

**Toni Morrison, "Rootedness"**

# The Novels of Toni Morrison

## A Study in Race, Gender, and Class

K. Sumana

PRESTIGE

*Published by*
Prestige Books
3/28, East Patel Nagar
New Delhi 110 008

1998

ISBN: 81-7551-048-X

*Photo Typesetting by*
Pivot Computers
Delhi 110 006
Ph. 2934490

*Printed at*
Chaman Offset Printers
New Delhi 110 002

# Contents

Dedicated
to

Sri Vuppala Gopala Rao

***a committed writer and a social worker***

**in deep gratitude and affection**

# Preface

Toni Morrison's recent naming as winner of the 1993 Nobel Prize for Literature compels us to recognize her not only as a writer of international stature, and thus of "universal" significance, but also as an African-American woman writer, and thus writing out of racial, gendered, class, and national specificity. Like Thoreau in *Walden*, Morrison delves deep into the particular in order to reach the universal. Our scholarship on her should, therefore, delve deeply into the specificities to facilitate our understanding of a multi-cultural plurality of her voices.

No doubt, Toni Morrison has received a good deal of critical attention since 1985 when Bessie Jones and Audrey L. Vinsons' *The World of Toni Morrison: Explorations in Literary Criticism* came out. Since that first book, four others—Karla Holloway and Stephanie Demedrakopolous' *New Dimensions of Spirituality: A Biracial and Bicultural Reading of the Novels of Toni Morrison* (1987), Nellie McKay, ed., *Critical Essays on Toni Morrison* (1988), Wilfred D. Samuels and Clenora Hudson Weems' *Toni Morrison* (1990) and Harold Bloom, ed., *Modern Critical Views: Toni Morrison* (1990)—have been published, almost yearly, until 1990. Since then, seven more critical studies— Trudier Harris' *Fiction and Folklore: The Novels of Toni Morrison* (1991), Barbara Rigney's *The Voices of Toni Morrison* (1991), Doreatha Drummond Mbalia's *Toni Morrison's Developing Class Consciousness* (1991), Patrick Bryce Bjork's *The Novels of Toni Morrison: The Search for Self and Place within the Community* (1992), Karen Carmen's *Toni Morrison's World of Fiction* (1993), Henry Louis Gates Jr., and K.A. Appiah, eds., *Toni Morrison: Critical Perspectives Past and Present* (1993), Denise Heinze's *The Dilemma of "Double-Consciousness": Toni Morrison's Novels* (1993)—on Toni Morrison have been brought out. This amply illustrates the growing range of Morrison scholarship.

These critical studies on Toni Morrison, in quick succession, have generally placed her within one of five contexts—race, gender, class, comparative American/Western literature,or universal paradigms. Critics of African-American literature have demonstrated Morrison's aesthetic and thematic use of black cultural traditions. If feminist critics have focused on how gender shapes Morrison's texts and Marxist critics have dwelt on Morrison's class consciousness and cultural redefinitions, comparativists have discussed Morrison's debt to great writers such as Faulkner, James Joyce, Ellison, Virginia Woolf and Shakespeare, universalists have delineated patterns such as christian myth or archetypal psychology in Morrison's novels. These variegated critical approaches to Toni Morrison's fiction are by no means mutually exclusive of one another, or exhaustive of all possibilities.

One of the possibilities is to make a critical study of the interrelationship of race, gender, and class in the novels of Toni Morrison. As it stands now, only four critics—Gloria Wade-Gayles, Barbara Christian, Elliott Butler-Evans and Doreatha Drummond Mbalia—have made a study of the fiction of African-American women writers including Toni Morrison, keeping in mind the problems of racism, sexism, and classism. Gloria Wade-Gayles deals only with the issues of race and gender in her critically acclaimed book, *No Crystal Stair: Visions of Race and Sex in Black Women's Fiction* (1984). Her approach is feminist in that she tends to see racism and sexism from the female perspective. She takes up for study only two novels of Toni Morrison—*The Bluest Eye* and *Sula*. In her path-breaking study, *Black Women Novelists: The Development of a Tradition 1892-1976* (1980), Barbara Christian describes the various realities in the fiction of black women novelists with special reference to race and gender. But, the focus is not directly or exclusively on racism and sexism. Like Wade-Gayles, she too discusses only the first two novels of Toni Morrison. Butler-Evans' purpose in his book, *Race, Gender and Desire: Narrative Strategies in the Fiction of Toni Cade Bambara, Toni Morrison and Alice Walker* (1989) is to fill what he describes as a void in Houston Baker's and Henry Louis Gates' "racial discourse" which generally downplayed the ideological issues generated by the representations of black women in the narratives of black males. If these three writers sporadically touch upon race and gender in select novels of Morrison, Doreatha Drummond Mbalia, in her significant book, *Toni Morrison's Developing Class Consciousness* (1991), argues that Morrison's novels move in chronological order closer to a Marxist view that capitalism is the primary enemy of blacks in white America.

From this brief survey of the Toni Morrison scholarship, it is clear that no single critic has so far examined the interaction of race, gender, and class, taking into consideration the entire Morrison canon. Hence the need for a full-length critical study of the interconnection of race, gender, and class in the novels of Toni Morrison.

The present book aims at making an in-depth study of the interrelationship of race, gender, and class in the novels of Toni Morrison with a view to establishing an evolutionary pattern in the Morrison canon, thereby revealing that Morrison's fictional art, in her own terms, is "unquestionably political and irrevocably beautiful," inasmuch as she succeeds in her attempt to combine political consciousness with aesthetic sensibility. The purpose is to show how Morrison is essentially a fictional artist despite her deep commitment to a pan-Africanist view involving the total liberation and unification of Africa. It is hoped that an analysis of the interrelatedness of race, gender, and class in Morrison's novels will help us gain fresh insights into her fictional art.

The book is divided into eight chapters. The introductory chapter seeks to place Toni Morrison in the literary tradition of black women's writings and establish the interconnectedness of race, gender, and class which, as systems of societal and psychological restrictions, have critically affected the lives and conscience of African-American women. The chapter also details the various factors, including different literary influences, that have contributed to Toni Morrison's developing social, political, and aesthetic consciousness and have helped her forge her fictional art.

The second chapter deals with Toni Morrison's first novel, *The Bluest Eye* (1970), in which the emphasis is on racism. She investigates the devastating effects of the beauty standards of the dominant culture on the self-image of the African female adolescent. The role of class is only relevant insofar as it exacerbates the self-image of the African female. However, the novel serves as proof of Morrison's low level of gender and class consciousness at the beginning of her writing career when she thought that racism was the main form of oppression of blacks in white America.

The third chapter is concerned with *Sula* (1973) where Morrison's primary focus is on gender, especially the individualism of the African woman. Morrison is interested in the struggle for individual rights, in general, and woman's rights, in particular, rather than the rights of African people as a collective group. The concept of gender and its relation to race and class is very much a part of the novel. The concerns of class, whether of the capitalists or the masses, rank third after gender and race.

The fourth chapter is devoted to a study of *Song of Solomon* (1977) in which class, in relation to race and gender, becomes more focal. Since Morrison has now become more aware of the dialectical relationship between capitalism, racism, and sexism, she subordinates sexism to both racism and capitalism, realizing that the exploitation of the African woman by the African man is the result of his national and class oppression.

The fifth chapter is about *Tar Baby* (1981) in which the thematic emphasis is on class struggle—the struggle between the ruling class and the subject class. Racism is presented as a coequal, but consequential cause of the African's oppression. Sexism gets little of the author's attention. In other words, racism and sexism, although equally oppressive, are treated as by-products of capitalism. Dealing as it does with individual class struggle against capitalism, *Tar Baby* reflects Toni Morrison's increased consciousness as revealed in her ability and commitment to explore the cause-and-effect relationship between class, race, and gender. Furthermore, it explores the tensions between the Euro-American and Afro-American understanding of shared myths thereby adapting Toni Morrison's folk sensibility to the is-ness of the African-American experience.

The sixth chapter concerns itself with Toni Morrison's masterpiece, *Beloved* (1987), which expounds the theme of collective class struggle against capitalism. It examines a critical period in the history of African people in order to demonstrate that the economic source of both gender and class oppression is unobscured in slavery. Gender oppression is considered a visible problem, not as it exists between African men and women, but as it exists within the context of the economic relationship between master and slave. Like gender oppression, race oppression is examined as a consequence to the economic exploitation of African people. Exploring the dialectical relationship between problem and solution, Morrison suggests that eradication of capitalism ensures eradication of racism and sexism.

The seventh chapter pertains to Toni Morrison's latest novel, *Jazz* (1992), which adds a new dimension to the solution arrived at in *Beloved*, with its thematic emphasis on gender solidarity through women bonding. However effective the collective class struggle against capitalism may be, it will not, in Morrison's view, fully solve the problem of African women because it is only they who experience the triple oppression of race, gender, and class. Hence the need for women bonding as a viable solution to gender oppression which is peculiar to African women. Morrison achieves her objective by transposing jazz—the music that springs out of her people and expresses their joys and sorrows, their beliefs and their psyche—into another medium, novel, thereby making fiction do what the black American music used to do in telling the whole world the ongoing story of her people.

While offering a summing-up of the main argument of the book, the last chapter shows how an evolutionary pattern emerges as Toni Morrison, with her increasing commitment and heightened consciousness, treats, in the course of her novels, race, gender, and class as the sources of oppression of black people in white America. While each of her novels concentrates on a different but related factor of the oppression of the African people, all are symbiotically related. Toni Morrison's treatment of the interrelationship of race, gender, and class reveals that she is at once a deeply committed novelist and a highly conscious artist. By combining political consciousness with aesthetic sensibility, Morrison succeeds in her attempt to elevate the beautiful, that is, the reclaimable in the human condition through her superb fictional art. It is concluded that Toni Morrison's writing, although emerging as it does from a specific political, economic, social, and cultural experience, reaches out to the entire world, and has a good deal of relevance to the postcolonial situation in India.

"I owe debts I cannot pay—nor do they dress me" thus goes an African-American folk song which sums up my feelings of gratitude to the institutions and individuals who made it possible for me to successfully complete my work. It is hoped that the present book, perhaps the first one on Toni Morrison by an Indian, would be of considerable interest and use to the students and teachers of African-American literature. And, as a comprehensive study of not much explored aspects of Morrison's fiction in a fairly original, critical perspective, the book is also expected to offer fresh insights to Morrison scholars and critics the world over.

University of California
Los Angeles

**K. SUMANA**

# CHAPTER I

## Introduction

> The Act of writing requires a constant plunging back into the shadow of the past where time hovers ghostlike.
>
> Ralph Ellison, *Shadow and Act*

> To read is to find meaning and to find meaning is to name them; but these named meanings are swept away toward further names; names invoke each other . . . I name, I unname, I rename.
>
> Ronald Barthes, *s/z*

In his now famous essay, "Blueprint for Negro Literature," Richard Wright asserts that a Marxist black male-oriented aesthetic and politic against racism and capitalism should be the all consuming perspective of the Negro writer.[1] Accordingly, the central character in all his novels and stories is a young black male, ensnared in the nightmare of a white racist, capitalistic world. Furthermore, the masculine perspective itself, concerning the manhood of the black race, has always occupied centre stage in the drama of African-American literature. The African-American male writers have been machoistic in their treatment of black women as fully debased creatures, evil castrators and immoral beings. They also portrayed black women as sex-objects or merely an extension of the male ego with no autonomous individual self. In other words, black male writers have been no different from their white counterparts in their treatment of black women.

It is this hegemony of the masculine perspective, along with its male-centered aesthetic, that is now being challenged in and through the writings of Black American women. Black women in America being at once black, female and poor, have been victimized by the mountains of racism, sexism, and capitalism, not only from the white world but also from the men of the black world. Black women are bearers of what Barbara Smith calls "geometric oppression."[2] They are, therefore, bearers of a triple consciousness—race, gender and class.

Small wonder, therefore, if a black feminist perspective pervades contemporary African-American literature. Happily, the perspective governs the aesthetic and the aesthetic informs the landscape and the vision. The status of the black women writers is no longer relegated below the status of the males. Instead of being secondary to the literary dominance of black males, the literature of black women is expansive and, what is more, liberating. Unlike in the past when women were supposed to be seen but not heard, the women of today are recognized writers in all fields and genres. Most importantly, black women are dealing with the political machinations of the racial and sexual beliefs, feelings and actions that black men writers have maintained towards black females, in the street, in the family, and in the bedroom. Their perspective, which is consistent with the aesthetic, is faithful to the actual experiences of black women in America. As a result, we have in their works a woman-to-woman approach rather than a woman-to-man approach. It is, in brief, a black feminist aesthetic in which the form, language, syntax, sequence and metaphoric rendering of experience are markedly different and expansive in comparison to the male-authored literature. This can be meaningfully witnessed in the works of Toni Morrison, the richly deserving recipient of the Nobel Prize for literature for 1993.

Toni Morrison is, perhaps, the most formally sophisticated novelist in the history of African-American literature, whose work has been described as "amazingly high." She astutely describes aspects of the blacks' lives and especially of blacks as the people they are. There are many writers who are willing to describe the ugliness of the world as ugly, but the uniqueness of Toni Morrison lies in revealing the beauty and the hope beneath the surface of black America. Combining the aims of the Black Freedom Movement and Women's Liberation, she seeks to produce literature which is irrevocably and indisputably black. But the artistic excellence of Morrison's fiction lies in achieving a balance between writing a truly black literature and writing what is truly universal literature. Although firmly grounded in the cultural heritage and social concerns of black Americans, her work transcends narrowly prescribed conceptions of ethnic literature, exhibiting universal mythic patterns and overtones. To put it in Faulkner's phrase, her novels "grieve on universal bones."

The signal accomplishment of Toni Morrison as a writer is that she has managed uncannily to invert her own mode of literary representation. Her themes are often those expected of naturalist fiction—the burdens of history, the determining social effects of race, gender or class—but they are also the great themes of lyrical modernism—love, death, betrayal, and burden of individual responsibility for her or his own fate. Like Golding's, her novels have a fabulistic quality as she has been directly influenced by Afro-American folktales. Like George Eliot she has a rare gift for characterization. She can compel her readers to learn about themselves by experiencing through her characters, states of mind which they would ordinarily disavow. Morrison's extraordinary distinction as a novelist also lies in restoring the language the black people speak to its original power.

As a result of her literary and artistic abilities and competence, Toni Morrison stands in the vanguard of contemporary writers of fiction, transcending both her racial identity and gender. Her acclaim is international as her novels are translated into many languages. Scholars and doctoral candidates the world over critique and assess her works, seeking to unravel the complexity that Morrison prides herself upon. An astute scholar as well as a uniquely creative writer, Morrison has won the deepest respect and admiration of both her fellow writers and populace at large. In addition to the feature coverage she has received from the popular media, from major national magazines and journals, she has been the recipient of several honorary degrees, literary awards, and domestic recognitions. The numerous awards she has received, culminating in the Nobel Prize awarded to her in 1993 for her distinctive writing, bear testimony to her genius as a writer. With her powerful narratives set against a historical as well as mythical backdrop, Morrison has captivated the hearts of the common reader as well as scholars of literature. She enjoys today the unique distinction of being both a popular writer and an outstanding literary figure.

## II

But, in order to really understand the remarkable achievement of Toni Morrison as a novelist, one must go back and appreciate the black women's literary tradition to which she belongs and the conflict of images with which her foremothers have had to contend. For, what African-American women have expressed as part of the self is greatly affected by various other complex issues. As Barbara Christian rightly observes, "To be able to use the range of one's own voice, to attempt to express the totality of self, is a recurring struggle in the tradition of those writers from the nineteenth century to the present."[3]

Black women literary tradition can be traced back to Phillis Weatley in the eighteenth century down to the boom period— the seventies and the eighties with its remarkable talented writers like Paule Marshall, Alice Walker and Gloria Naylor, encompassing the pioneering work of Zora Neale Hurston in the forties. Barbara Christian calls it the "Development of a Tradition" meaning that it has been a continuously evolving process, if one can trace the development of the black women's self from its infantile stage of invisibility to its present stage of self-definition and self-assertion. A survey of black women writers tradition reveals that women writers could discover the positive-self in women and give a true picture of womanhood in all its density and complexity.

Women writers took it up as their bounden duty to discover black women's self entrapped in the white society. The urge to discover one's self and its relation to the world have become the important thrusts of these novelists. About this Alexis De Veau says: "I see a greater commitment among black women writers to understand self multiplied in terms of the community, the community multiplied in terms of the world."[4]

Barbara Christian explains how difficult it has been for them to achieve such "an overtly self-centered point of view", because of the way in which they have been conceptualized by black as well as white society. She says: "The extent to which Afro-American woman writers like Alice Walker, Paule Marshall, Gloria Naylor, Alexis De Veau, in the seventies and eighties have been able to make a commitment to an exploration of self, as central rather than marginal, is a tribute to the insights they have called in a century or so of literary activity.[5] Their predecessors were not permitted to contemplate and express their views on their self, because their self was not their own but something gravely affected by other complex issues. They had to struggle hard to evolve a self which was deeply afflicted by racism and sexism. They found it even harder to give self-expression to the unheard voice of their self.

Early African-American women novelists like Frances Harper, Jessie Fauset, Nella Larsen and Ann Petry indicate their stated intentions and their primary reasons for writing their works. Frances Harper in her preface to Iola Leroy makes her purpose clear when she writes that "her story's mission would not be in vain if it awakens in the hearts of our countrymen a strong sense of justice and a more Christian like humanity."[6] Harper, thus, pleads for the justice for African-Americans, who, in the 1890s, were being lynched, burned out, raped, and deprived of their rights as citizens in the wake of the failure of Reconstruction. However, her intention is to impress and to please the white readers by creating a lady-like version of the heroine, Iola Leroy, whom the Americans are expected to respect even though she is black. Jessie Fauset (1884-1961), a woman novelist of the Harlem Renaissance, also writes with a craving for white acceptance. She wants to correct the impression most white people have about black people. In her preface to *The Chinaberry Tree* (1931), she says that her novel is about "those breathing spells in-between spaces where coloured men and women work and live and go their ways in no thought of the problem."[7] Both Harper and Fauset were thus aware of the negative images of the black people that predominated in the minds of white Americans. Nella Larsen (1893-1963) too creates such heroines who wish to 'pass' for whites. They look like whites and act like whites. She felt that creation of assimilated women and a new bourgeois class in the black community would take the race closer to power and white acceptance. For example, her heroine, Helga Crane in *Quicksand* (1928), identifies herself with the white value structure so much so that she gets herself alienated from the common Negro mass socially and culturally. Ann Petry (1908) continues the tradition of the heroines who want to 'pass' for white. For example, Lutie Johnson in *The Street* (1946) is frustrated and alienated from self because she tries to live by the female version of the American Dream as pure, protected and well-provided for. However, Petry's contribution to the development of black women's literary tradition is that she presents women and mothers struggling against the social and economic hostilities stacked against them.

We have, however, one notable exception to this trend in early African-American women writers' works in Zora Neale Hurston's *Their Eyes Were Watching God* (1937). It appeared eight years after Nella Larsen's *Passing* and new winds began to blow across the black women's fictional landscape. Hurston was not only the group's best woman writer, but one of the first black women writers to attempt serious study of the black folklore and folk history. The major themes that emerge in the novels of Hurston are search for black woman's self-fulfillment through community, quest for the ideal relationship between man and woman, black sisterhood, and significance of fidelity in interpersonal relationships.

Hurston not only preserves black folk culture but even contributes to the definition of woman's selfhood. Like Jessie Fauset or Nella Larsen, Hurston does not employ the 'passing' theme or the white emulative motif, nor does she show crude bitterness toward the white society, nor any extrovert reaction to the external forces, but rather an "opposition to various forms of repression which are more generally human, and sometimes self-manufactured."[8] Unlike her predecessors' heroines, Hurston's women continually quest for personal freedom and self-love by placing themselves in relation to the community they live in. By presenting black women with all the ordinariness of their lives, their aspirations, their dreams, Hurston not only rescues them from the stereotypical upper middle-class bourgeois traps, but comes close to probing the dimensions representing the general female condition as well. Thus, in its radical envisioning of the self as central, and "in its use of language as a means of exploring the self as female and black, *Their Eyes Were Watching God* is a forerunner of fiction of the seventies and eighties."[9] A 'transitional' writer, Hurston, shows considerable talent in revising the preceding models of black womanhood and leading the way a bit further up. Her writings signalled that the dawn was not far off and the 'new black woman' would soon knock at the doors of African-American literature.

But, the attempt on the part of Hurston to present positive images of black woman did not result in any improvement in her image or in her condition. On the other hand, refutation of negative images created a series of contradictions between the image that black women could not attain and the reality of their existence. That kind of tension increased throughout the first half of the century till the 1940s when the destruction it created becomes apparent in the fiction written by black women. The heroines in the fiction of the forties like Lutie Johnson in Ann Petry's *The Street* (1946) and Cleo Judson in Dorothy West's *The Living Is Easy* (1948) are defeated both by social reality and by their black self-knowledge.

However, there was a definite shift in the African-American women's writings towards the process of self-definition beginning with Gwendolyn Brooks' *Maud Martha* (1953). The protagonist of the novel, a very ordinary black woman, manages to transform her 'little life' into something significant in spite of the limitations set by her husband, her family, her race, her class and by society in general. She manages to be her own creator. Thus, while presenting a young black girl coming into womanhood, Brooks never employs the stereotypes used by her predecessors. For the first time in African-American literature, we come across a black female character who is neither a tragic victim consumed by the deterministic socio-economic conditions, nor a pariah obsessed by any cult. Barbara Christian critiques Brooks' protagonist:

> She [Maud Martha] is no Iola Leroy. Nor is she, like Fauset's heroine, merely conventional. . . . Nor is Maud Martha a beautiful Lutie Johnson, tragically destroyed by her environment. . . . It is just that she is not reduced to a stereotype either in the grand heroic style or the mean downtrodden mode.[10]

Thus, signifying the end of an era of 'contradictory instincts' characterized by the malady of suspendedness and soul-stifling black bourgeoism, *Maud Martha* heralded the long awaited moment in African-American literary history which was to establish the authenticity of black woman's true self by placing her life in the context of black culture and community.

The African-American women's literary tradition took a qualitative leap into the world of ontological transmutation of black women's existential conditions in America with Paule Marshall's first novel, *Brown Girl, Brownstones* (1981). The novel opened the creative floodgates and black women's words poured forth from the depths of their souls in an undiminished stream. The creative outpouring indicated the coming of age of black women's literary tradition. The novel clearly demonstrates black women's determination to revise history, to carve out a place for themselves and to announce to the whole world their existence as "a person and as a presence, as someone autonomous and as someone responsible to a community."[11] Unlike her predecessors, who spoke to others, Marshall's women speak to their own self and try to articulate that self with a great force.

Paule Marshall meaningfully engaged herself to the task of reconstructing black womanhood. She is the first black woman novelist who sculpts black female characters in relation to their culture and community. Barbara Christian writes: "She [Marshall] veers sharply away from much of the preceding literature, which emphasized advancement for black women in terms of white American values."[12] One of the reasons why she felt impelled to write *Brown Girl, Brownstones* was also to seek corrective measures against the prevalent derogatory image about black woman. In her interview with Sabine Brock, Paule Marshall states: "One of the reasons I wanted to write the story of a Selina Boyce was to give an answer to the prevailing image, to say that she was not a topsy, she was not any of the characters . . . or any of the stereotypes. . . . I wanted Selina to be a departure from all that."[13] Marshall charges that such a truthful reflection of black women's realities was not chronicled both in American and African-American literature.

Paule Marshall, thus, stands out as a pioneer of the black women's renaissance. Until her arrival on the literary scene, most writers approached the major themes like history, colonialism, slavery, racism from a male perspective. Marshall is the first black woman writer who treated these ideas from a black feminist point of view. Helene Christol writes that Marshall's *Brown Girl, Brownstones*, became "the starting point for the contemporary black women writer's thrust forward to a courageous revision of American history, society and literature from a black feminist perspective."[14]

During the sixties there was a perceptible change in the attitude of writers on account of the cultural renaissance. For a long time, many blacks deliberately attempted to forget their painful past or leave it to the deliberations of the white writers. But, after the cultural upheaval,

African-American literary traditions took a new direction. Writers started making conscious attempts to go to the roots and re-link the present with the past. This radical change in the attitude of the writers in the late sixties manifested especially in the works of Alice Walker.

Alice Walker prefers to call herself a 'womanist' because 'womanism,' in her opinion, expresses women's concerns better than 'feminism.' It appreciates "women's culture, women's emotional flexibility . . . and women's strength."[15] As a womanist she is certainly concerned with the liberation of all womankind from the psychology of oppression. But as an African-American woman writer she is more "committed to exploring the oppressions, the insanities, the loyalties, and the triumphs of black women."[16] This is made clear when, in an interview with John O'Brien, she unequivocally expresses: "I am preoccupied with the spiritual survival, the survival of whole of my people. But beyond that, I am committed to exploring the oppressions, the insanities, the loyalties and the triumphs of black women."[17]

What Alice Walker professes in theory is practised in her novels. *The Third Life of Grange Copeland* (1970), for instance, demonstrates that the violence that the men and women and children of the Copeland family inflict on each other is the direct outcome of the internalization of racist hatred. The basic principle that Walker highlights is that the change in a person is linked with the change in the society. Walker gives expression to the tension that prevailed between the need for black man's self-love and his sense of shame. Her masterpiece, *Meridian* (1976), is about a woman protagonist who gradually awakens from her subordinate status as a black female, daughter, wife, and mother to her own self and tries to become the maternal provider of the larger black community. She finally rejects the status of a biological mother, but tries to become the community's mother.

Thus, by the mid-seventies, African-American women writers like Paule Marshall, Alice Walker, Toni Cade Bambara, Gayle Jones and Toni Morrison had not only defined their cultural context as a distinctly African-American one, but also probed many facets of the interrelationship of racism, sexism, and classism in their society. They not only demonstrated the fact that these three sources of oppression existed in black communities but also challenged the prevailing definition of woman in male-dominated American society, especially in relation to motherhood and sexuality. Furthermore, they insisted on the centrality of black women to African-American history as well as on their pivotal significance to the contemporary social and political developments in America. Their novels invariably look at ways in which the quality of black women's lives is affected by the interrelationship of racism, sexism and classism. Race, gender and class are not separate entities, at least in America, but closely linked with each other. As Barbara Christian observes, "like the images of a kaleidoscope, these elements are so organically connected that one must understand their interrelationship in spite of their ever-shifting appearance."[18]

III

Racism, sexism and classism signify the traumatic conditions under which African-Americans lived in white America. They are systems of societal and psychological restrictions that have critically affected the lives of blacks, in general, and African-American women, in particular. Right from the days of slavery, the blacks, irrespective of sex had realised the cruel reality of racism. Judged from the white man's standards of life and beauty, the black man's life became unbearable. Sexism, more oppressive physically and mentally was cause of grievance to the black women who were sexually exploited by both the black and white men. Just as blacks as a group were relegated to an underclass by virtue of their race, so were women relegated to a separate caste by virtue of their sex. Confronted on all sides by racial and sexual discrimination, the black woman has no friends but only liabilities and responsibilities. Responsible for their own and their children's well-being and future, these women had to face daily the reality of their relationships with white men, with white women, and, above all, with black men. But, within the separate caste, a standard of woman was designed in terms of a class definition. The ideal southern lady image of eighteenth century America has been one of the dominant factors in America's conception of woman. She was expected to be beautiful in an ornamental way, chaste, pious, married, and eventually, a mother. She was obviously a white, beautiful and rich woman who did not work. The ideal concept of woman in the society, then, is not only racist and sexist but also classist. And because black women were, by nature of their race, conceived of as lower class, they could hardly approximate the norm: "They had to work; most could not be ornamental or withdrawn from the world; and, according to the aesthetics of this country, they were not beautiful. But neither were they men. Any aggressiveness or intelligence on their part, qualities necessary for participation in the work world, were constructed as unwomanly and tasteless."[19] Thus, African women could not achieve the standard of womanhood on the one hand and on the other, they were biologically females, with all the societal restrictions associated with that state.

So, to be black and female is to suffer from the twin disadvantages of racial discrimination and pronounced gender bias. Possibly no other social group has been subjected to such an unedifying spectacle of human debasement and depravity. Being black, the African women suffered from racism; being females they were the victims of sexual atrocities at the hands of the white patriarchs as well as the blacks and being former slaves, the white establishment forced them to live on meagre resources and were compelled to remain poor. In short, the black women in America were made victims of triple jeopardy—racism, sexism, and classism.

As sources of oppression of blacks, racism and sexism are allied and have a parallel existence. They are mutually interdependent and hence they arise from the same set of circumstances. Gloria Wade-Gayles explains this interesting phenomenon through the imagery of circles:

> There are three major circles of reality in American society, which reflect degrees of power and powerlessness. There is a large circle in which white people, most of them men, experience influence and power. Far away from it there is a smaller circle, a narrow space, in which black people, regardless of sex, experience uncertainty, exploitation and powerlessness. Hidden in this second circle is a third, a small, dark enclosure in which black women experience pain, isolation, and vulnerability. These are the distinguishing marks of black womanhood in white America.[20]

What we see here is the omnipresent, all-embracing reality of racism as a common factor in the lives of all blacks, irrespective of sex. The black man faced with the hard fact, and cruel reality, of racism realised right from the days of slavery that his colour and physiognomy were terrible handicaps, and as such would mark him off as evil, despite all claims to the contrary. Judged by the white man's standards of life, behaviour and beauty, his life became unbearable. Universal codes of social and psychological praxis as laid down by the dominant white culture were forcibly thrust upon him.

Thus began the oppressive story of racism in America. It brought with it pain, sorrow, bloodshed, death and, above all, the negation of an entire race. The African-American race was ghettoized, persecuted and viciously outlawed from all avenues of decency, hope, progress and livelihood. Racism, as a life-threatening, non-nurturing force, exists even today, thus becoming the forum for all types of discussion.

Racism, as a man-made phenomenon, may be defined according to Hernton as "all of the learned behaviour and learned emotions on the part of a group of people towards another group whose physical characteristics are dissimilar to the former group; behaviour and emotions that compel one group to . . . treat the other on the basis of its physical characteristics alone, as if it did not belong to the human race."[21] The basic myth of racism, in other words, is that white skin brings with it cultural superiority—that the white are more intelligent and more virtuous than the black by the mere fact of being white. On the psychological level, whiteness is automatically equated with beauty and culture and blackness with ugliness and slavery.

Racism started in America when white masters of the land brought the first Africans in chains and used their labour to enrich their coffers. As a result, black people soon ceased to exist as human beings in the white world. In an illuminating study of the origin of racism in the United States, Joel Kovel says that the white master "first reduced the human self of his black slave to a body and then the body to a thing; he dehumanised his slave, made him quantifiable, and thereby absorbed him into a rising world market of productive exchange."[22]

All that was left to blacks was their African soul which was also taken away by imposing white values on them. With the breakdown of their native values, they lost their authentic self and almost invariably fostered feelings of inferiority. Whites created the institutions which blacks were finally ready to live by. This covert form of racism, Plakkoottam correctly maintains, "was doubly injurious to the black race in that not much notice was taken of its invisibly corrosive nature."[23] No wonder, it proved most devastating in its ultimate repercussions. Such was the first step toward the establishment of racism as an inseparable part of white American civilization.

Sexism, with its accompanying horrors, mutilated the backs and minds of slave women and defiled their sexual beings and scarred them psychologically for all time. Suffering at the hands of both black and white men, the African-American woman had to fight for survival both inside and outside her house. Thus, her story, even in modern America, is fraught with the perils of navigating between the Scylla of racism and the Charybdis of sexism. Impeded from attaining social, political and economic independence and prosperity, black women have had to fight hard for just the basics. With emancipation and induction at the lowest levels of the work force, these women have selected education as their one strong weapon for integration. Despite gradual progress, they are still far behind black men and white women. Racism and sexism should be blamed for this hapless situation.

Gloria Steinem, in her introduction to *Outrageous Acts and Everyday Rebellions*, states this equation very tersely thus: "Just as male was universal but female was limited, white was universal but black was limited."[24] A sense of inferiority and inadequacy was being cultivated by the white dominant group to deprive blacks of their genuine potential. Thus, race and gender, that is, 'black' and 'female' were juxtaposed against 'white' and 'male,' in the process creating a subjugated microcosm within a dominating microcosm. Just as racism deprived a group of people of their growth and happiness, so too sexism. Racism and sexism grew out of the same stultifying atmosphere of prejudice, discrimination and condescension. In the case of racism, discrimination was based on the differences of race and color, in the case of sexism, on that of gender. But in spite of these differences, they create the same kind of negative currents which even today cause great harm. On the whole, it was the black woman who had the greater cause for grievance, being oppressed as both a black and a woman. It is her story which more vividly describes this horrendous tale and its accompanying woes. The entire African-American community was condemned to endless suffering, yet the black woman's condition was much worse than the black man's because "To be black and Female was to be in Double Jeopardy."[25]

There has ever been an unholy nexus between racism and sexism. They, in fact, originated from the same set of circumstances: "both are motivated by similar economic, social and psychological forces, it is only logical that those who sought to undermine Blacks were also most virulent anti feminists. The means of oppression differed across race and sex lines, but the wellspring of that oppression was the same."[26] Because of her ability to do man's work and her extraordinary reproductive capacity, the black woman was treated by her white master as an indispensable commodity. Miscegenation played a vital role in their relationship during the days of slavery. White mercenary planters saw profit in it. The children born out of such a sordid union would be their sole property and, therefore, could be used to further their economic interest. The black woman was also seen as a wanton creature easily available for instant sexual gratification. Thus, she became the double victim of racist and sexist oppression including lynching and rape.

The other side of the coin tells of the disgrace the black woman suffered at the hands of her own man. Despite all sympathy for his abused wife, the black man gradually developed a kind of aversion to her. He also began to see her as a loose woman who preferred extramarital adventures to marital permanence. The stigma attached to the black woman by her white slaver ironically received the black man's sanction. He felt sexually neglected and took his woman to be his enemy. The white man's clever manipulation of the social situation thus escaped black man's attention. On the other hand, one discovers the latter's helplessness. Being a slave himself, he was absolutely powerless to question the scheme of things. Either way, "the black woman was deprived of a strong black man on whom she could rely for protection." [27] So, her awful predicament continued.

But then, the alternate voices of the oppressed are not those of race and gender alone. Class exploitation is, perhaps, the greatest source of oppression of blacks in white America. After the Civil War, during which blacks were liberated, there was some improvement in the condition of their lives. But the First World War again hit them hard as it precipitated a global crisis. The Great Depression posed further threats to the African-American population. As a matter of fact, to millions of common people in America, irrespective of race, nothing seemed so urgent as survival in a world of unemployment and economic collapse. Yet, blacks were worst affected as racial discrimination reached its apex.

Even if it is true that the class struggle has not been a major theme in the history of the African-American freedom movement, we cannot possibly negate the class issue. Nor can we agree with critics like Wade-Gayles who see class "not as urgent as race and sex in black women's reality for class oppression cuts across racial and sexual lines and is, therefore, not unique to black women."[28] Even if we do not see ethnicity as a mask behind which people conceal their class position both from each other and from themselves, even if we realise the importance of racial and ethnic values, we cannot ignore the class issue—capitalism.

Capitalism is an economic system characterised by the concentration in a few hands of the ownership of the means of producing wealth and by unequal distribution of the products of human labour. Thus, it is a system which "divides society into classes [sections of people who get their living in the same way], one which carries out the actual process of production [slave, serf, wage-worker], while the other [slave-owner, lord, capitalist employer] enjoys a part of the product without having to work to produce it."[29] The class that owns and controls the means of production is called the ruling or capitalist class. To rule society simply means organising it to serve the interests of only one class of people and imposing the will of this group on all other groups, whether they agree or not. Ultimately, the objective of the ruling class is to convince others that its rule is the most just. If the objective is accomplished, the ruling class secures its place in the society and thus continues its exploitation with few opposing disturbances. In any society in which the interests of only a small sector of the population are considered, gross injustices are present. Under capitalism, for example, there exists a permanent sector of unemployed people, and periodic economic crisis: "incredible poverty in the midst of wealth and wastage, deviant behaviour based on placing individual interests above group interests and racism.[30]

There is ample evidence to prove that racism is a by-product of capitalism. Walter Rodney refuses the myth that racism was the initial cause of the enslavement of African people and, by doing so, effectively negates the argument of those nationalists who say that the racism and sexism are the primary causes of their oppression today. According to Rodney, Africans were enslaved "for economic reasons, so that their labour power could be exploited."[31] Thus resulted racism, the doctrine based on the assumption that psychological traits and capacities are determined by biological race. In his words, "[After] having been utterly dependent on African labour, Europeans at home and abroad found it necessary to rationalise that exploitation in racist terms as well. Oppression follows logically from exploitation, so as to guarantee the latter."[32] The economic system of slavery, an early form of capitalism, was the cause of racism and sexism rather than the result of it. Kwame Nkrumah confirms Rodney's analysis when he writes: "It was only with capitalist economic penetration that the master-servant relationship emerged, and with it, racism, colour prejudice and apartheid."[33]

Eric Williams, an economist, offers indisputable facts to illustrate that racism was the result of the exploitation of the African's labour. He points out that the enslavement of the African had everything to do with the cheapness of labour, not the colour of the labourer's skin: "racial differences made it easier to justify and rationalise Negro slavery. . . . Finally, and this was the decisive factor, the Negro slave was cheaper. The money which procured a white man's service for ten years could buy a Negro for a life."[34] Williams substantiates this premise by examining the rise of capitalism. Offering convincing facts, he proves that the early European capitalists were willing to exploit the labour power of any group of people, even their own, to make a handsome profit. All these factors, according to Williams, confirm that racism stems from class exploitation.

However, to state that racism was the consequence of the European's quest for greater profits is not to imply that racism did not ultimately become a concomitant reason for oppressing African people. According to Rodney, "Oppression of African people on purely racial grounds accompanied, strengthened and became indistinguishable from oppression for economic reasons."[35] Nkrumah, too, believed that the African suffered from a nation- class oppression. In analysing the African's plight in United States, he wrote: "Race is inextricably linked with class exploitation; in a racist-capitalist power structure, capitalist exploitation and race oppression are complementary, the removal of one ensures the removal of the other."[36] Rodney and Nkrumah agree, however, that while the African suffers equally from both—racism and sexism—racism cannot exist under a non-exploitive economic system.

Since race, sex and class have been so interrelated in the history of America, it is not surprising that when black women published novels, they necessarily reflected on that relationship, whether they intended to or not. From Harper's *Iola Leroy*, published in 1892, to Toni Morrison's *Beloved*, published in 1987, the tradition of African-American women novelists as an entirety is a stunning expression of various configurations of social definitions that have been inflicted on the black women. The novels of black women from 1892 to the present have had to react to the elements of race, gender, and class as the factors upon which the societal definition of the black woman is based.

## IV

Black women have been victimised not only by racist, sexist, and classist assumptions but also by scholarly neglect. Yet they have tried down the ages to present their case through various media, especially through literature. Black women novelists of the twentieth century have openly portrayed in their works their experiences of exploitation—political, racial, sexual and emotional. Driven by an overriding impulse towards self-assertion, which can be traced back to the cultural ethos of the 1960s, they have later succeeded in turning their identity into a source of strength. Their works of fiction, published over the last two decades, reflect their version of American experience that was excluded from both black male and white female writings. They strive to present the black woman's quest for total freedom as a human being. A look at some of the novels of African-American women writers would take us through many a chapter in black woman's life in America and help see her rise gradually from passivity to consciousness.

Frances E.W. Harper's *Iola Leroy* or *Shadows Uplifted* is historically important as the first novel by a black woman to treat racism and sexism. It portrays a young Christian octoroon who, being totally unaware of the Negro blood in her veins, thinks herself white and behaves exactly like a racist. Deluded by her apparent skin colour, she feels proud of her parentage and justifies slavery as a necessity of plantation life. It is highly ironical that a person of her stock should advocate white values which shows the reversal of Iola's fortune. Because of her black ancestry, however remote it may be, she too is finally thrown into slavery. Her racist assumptions radically change as she herself faces racial polarity. She feels the pain of all blacks and looks on her own plight as a kind of penance for her past sins. Racism is then well combined with sexism to focus on another facet of black suffering. Sex-crazed white men pursue Iola, although she successfully resists their advances. With her awareness, Iola wants to live and struggle as a black woman. She recreates herself in the light of her actual experience. The ending implies that American society cannot be transformed until white supremacy is understood and attacked by full-blooded whites.

Nella Larsen's *Quicksand* presents a mulatta's awareness of her true identity and her determination not to imitate white values. Helga knows that to embrace such values would simply mean falling into the white trap. She is equally aware of sexual polarity in the form of white, male dominance in American society. Helga's dignified appearance and bearing would easily qualify her as a true lady. She could surely marry a white man and enjoy great honour. But she rightly thinks that she would, in that case, disgrace her black blood and a chance revelation of her mixed parentage might also knock her off her pedestal. So, she marries a travelling minister instead, who takes her to rural Alabama. Yet, Helga cannot realise herself because there she sinks into the quicksand of poverty and continual childbearing. To her horror, she discovers that her gender, no less than her race, has left her vulnerable to exploitation. The novel, thus, records the simultaneity of racial and sexual discrimination faced by African-American women.

Zora Neale Hurston's *Their Eyes Were Watching God* articulates the black woman's plight in unambiguous terms. Remarkable is the following extract:

> de white man is de ruler of everything as fur as Ah been able tuh find out. So . . . (he) throw down de load and tell de nigger man tuh pick it up. He pick it up because he have to, but be don't tote it. He hand it to his women-folks. De nigger woman is de mule uh de world so far as Ah can see.[37]

Hurston was one of the foremost black thinkers to attack American capitalism for creating a tier of socio-economic classes that ranks the black woman at the bottom. At this point, it is interesting to note how Gloria Wade-Gayles later depicts the syndrome through the imagery of "circles":

> There are three major circles of reality in American society, which reflect degrees of power and powerlessness. There is a large circle in which white people, most of them men, experience influence and power. For away from it there is a smaller circle of sex, experience . . . exploitation and powerlessness. Hidden in this second circle is a third . . . in which black women experience pain, isolation and vulnerability.[38]

Janie, the protagonist of the novel, is a beautiful mulatta who is treated by the men around as a trophy to be fought over and won. Marriage jeopardizes her self-identity all the more and abandons her to anonymity. Her first husband, Logan, wants her to work like a mule for him and the second one, Jody, considers her an exotic possession. In either case, Janie has to live up to the irrational expectations of her man and suffer humiliation. Janie's sense of deprivation is coupled with a feeling of utter isolation as she is eventually cut off from the local black community. With Janie stepping out of her small, dark enclosure, Hurston's delineation of black womanhood takes a new turn. The woman shakes off her marital bonds and becomes free to choose the course of her own life. She meets another man, Teacake, who treats her as a human being and helps her realize her self-worth. His death leaves her sad, yet his fond memory gives her the strength to live on. Sexism plays a more important role than racism in this novel.

Ann Petry's *The Street* shows how racial discrimination renders blacks jobless and how poverty, in turn, exposes the African-American woman to sexual exploitation. Lutie Johnson, a lower class black woman, has been abandoned by her husband for her obsessive desire for 'a comfortable life.' Alone with a small child, she has to come out on the streets of a big city for her livelihood. Petry portrays with remarkable clarity the social and economic problems faced by black women in urban areas. With all her decency and moral integrity, Lutie is labelled a whore by her neighbours because they cannot accept a single black woman with trust or dignity. Deprived of the basic necessities of life, Lutie encounters overwhelming odds in rearing her child. Unable to find a job, she desperately tries to get established in the entertainment world by becoming a singing woman. This leaves her more vulnerable to the ugly demands of the urban society. Frustrated and lost in the sea of crowds, she painfully realises that if she cannot sell her talent she must sell her body. Petry points out that her people "were so damn poor they didn't have time to do anything but work and their bodies were the only source of relief from the pressure under which they lived."[39] However, Lutie still refuses to buy happiness at the cost of her moral values. She murders her prospective employer as he tries to rape her. In fact, the black woman experiences the threat of rape not only from the dominant group, but from within her own. Lutie's final action, which is a definite sign of rebellion, speaks of her resilience and her inviolable sense of self-dignity.

Paule Marshall's first novel, *Brown Girl, Brownstones*, as has already been pointed out, ushered in a new period of female characters in African-American literature. It prefigured the major themes of black woman's fiction in the 1970s: "the black woman's potential as a full person and necessarily a major actor on the social, cultural and political issues of our times."[40] Marshall gave new meaning to black womanhood by transforming abused creatures into self-conscious rebels who meet the challenges of the world and seek to define their identity within the context of their own culture.

*Brown Girl, Brownstones* centers around Selina, a girl child of first generation—Barbadian immigrant, who pass from a traumatic childhood to womanhood. With a psyche damaged by the racist and sexist ideology, she initially judges her self-worth by the white standards of feminine beauty. She suffers from a sense of inadequacy as she does not have blond hair, blue eyes and white skin. Selina's craving for white elegance and refinement, in fact, alienates her further from her native value system. Fostering a debased self-image and subordinating herself to the beautiful white people around, she only confirms her invisibility and worthlessness. Black psychiatrists analyse the crippling effects of such double-consciousness on the black woman: "[Her] blackness is the antithesis of a creamy white skin, her lips are thick, her hair is kinky and short. She is, in fact, the antithesis of American beauty. . . . There can be no doubt that she will develop a damaged self concept and an impairment of her feminine narcissism which will have profound consequences for her character development."[41] We do find black women in fiction as well as in real life. We have incorporated a white ideology into the fabric of their consciousness and consequently failed to realize their authentic self. But Marshall believes that it would be suicidal for the black woman to accept white values. Selina, who initially failed to grasp the truth, later becomes aware of her misconceptions and revolts against the distorted image of the black woman which white America carefully keeps alive in order to hold her in perpetual enslavement. Selina also disabuses herself of her false belief in male supremacy, which she inherited from her black father. The girl who was once proud of being called 'Deighton's Selina,' now identifies herself with her long-suffering mother. She tells her, "Everybody used to call me Deighton's Selina but they were wrong. Because you see I'm truly your child. Remember how you used to talk about, how you left home and came here alone as a girl of eighteen . . . ? I love hearing that. And that's what I want."[42] She takes her mother, Silla, as the symbol of black womanhood and becomes her daughter.

Consequently, Selina discovers her close affinities with all the oppressed black women in their struggle for human rights. Moreover, she realises that they cannot change the present without a search for roots. Selina finally decides to go back to Barbados, the centre of her life. It is no escape, but rather a conscious choice to restore the self and the community, a spiritual return back over history in order to have a sense of total experience. Selina's tossing of her bangle high into air before departure is symbolic of her ultimate emergence as a black woman determined to seek out a more truthful identity.

Alice Walker's *Meridian*, one of the most celebrated novels, reflects her strong belief in the black womanist tenets. It tells the story of the black woman in a period of transition, the story of a coming to consciousness and a subsequent development of self and search for authenticity. The first part of the novel describes Meridian's initiation into adulthood and the beginning of her search for her black woman self. The second part focuses on her renunciation of her child and active participation in the Civil Rights Movement. The third and final part deals with her release from sexual bonds with an accent on her great preoccupation with the 'survival whole' of her people. Meridian's quest for black womanhood finally turns into a concern for the survival and wholeness of the entire black community. She finds the real meaning of her life in her very attempt to change the present social system for the benefit of all blacks, male and female. The transformation she insists on is possible not through violence but through a spiritual awakening. Meridian, thus emerges as a liberated black woman with a hard-won insight into the riddles of life. Evidently, the novel creates an image of the African-American woman with her complexity, diversity and depth.

Like other black woman novelists of the contemporary period, Toni Morrison analyses the relationship between race, gender and class assumptions. In each of her novels she explores some aspect of the oppression afflicting African people. Titled as a 'Black Woman Writer' committed to survival and wholeness of entire black people, male and female, Morrison has also been called a 'womanist' by Alice Walker. Though most of the stories of her novels are revealed through the eyes of black women, she does not adopt the kind of political feminism associated with women's movement of the 1970s. Rather, she writes in the tradition of black women writers like Hurston and Paule Marshall as a cultural feminist, celebrating the strengths of black women against the heavy odds of racism, sexism and classism by developing the necessary political, social and aesthetic consciousness.

## V

A number of factors contributed to Toni Morrison's developing social, political and aesthetic consciousness—environment, familial background, community, African-American folklore, her educational background and early professional life, her Random House experience and literary works by great writers. These factors helped her become more conscious of the nature of the African's dilemma, the crisis of the African personality, the cause and effects of it, and her increasing commitment to help solve it in terms of fictional art, thereby combining her political consciousness with aesthetic sensibility.

Toni Morrison's personal landscape—the environment in which she was born and brought up—has been at once colourful and complex like that of many of her fictional characters. She was born on 18 February 1931 in Lorain, Ohio, a small midwestern steel-mill town located twenty-five miles west of Cleveland. Situated far from the madding crowd—the hustle and bustle of NewYork's inner city, as well as from the noisy highways—the salubrious atmosphere of Morrison's home provided important insights into the life of this significant African-American woman writer. Wilfred Samuels and Clenora Hudson-Weems highlight the complexity and subtlety of life this pastoral setting offers, ensuring the privacy and gateway to the past, when they put it:

> Permanently docked off the Hudson River, it looks toward a horizon of infinite possibilities that seems oblivious to and unbound by the city's skyline or the wired mesh of a towering bridge in the foreground. The pier off the patio appears to serve as a runway, offering passage and passport to a world of known and unknown realities; fact, fiction, fantasy; mystical and magical realms that converge in the world that Morrison creates.[43]

Morrison's early years in the steel-mill town of Lorain, Ohio during the Depression years created within her a sensitivity toward the struggling masses in general and the African people in particular. As a child, she experienced enough poverty, hatred and racism to last a lifetime. From her parents, George and Rahmah, Southern migrants who left the deep South in search of improved social, political, economic and educational opportunities for their family, whose profound and positive influence is still borne by her, Morrison learned many lasting lessons relevant to race, gender, and class. They firmly believed that "black people were the humans of the globe."[44] Their diverse personalities gave Morrison, the second of their four children, wherewithal not only to live in America but to do so successfully.

From her father, a shipyard welder, who was a stickler for excellence, Morrison gained a garvy-like perspective on whites as he believed that all African people were morally superior to Europeans. She admits: "My father was a racist. As a child in Georgia, he received shocking impressions of adult white people, and for the rest of his life felt he was justified in despising all whites, and that they were not justified in despising him."[45] Her father, thus, impressed upon her a positive self-image while instilling in her the tools for combating what Carolyn Gerald calls "the zero image."[46] Her mother, who was ever optimistic in her belief that the future would bring better race relations, unyieldingly handled offensive landlords and insidious social workers. Though on relief during Great Depression, she was self-assured enough to belong to a Black woman's club and was bold enough to write to president Roosevelt when the meal received during the Great Depression as dole was bugridden. Furthermore, the hair-raising ghost tales told by her parents, particularly her father who told her the scariest folktales "would become the genesis of the mysticism and magic that permeates Morrison's fiction."[47] Her father told such thrilling terrifying ghost stories that Morrison confesses, "We were always begging him to repeat the stories that terrified us most."[48] Small wonder if Morrison said, "we were intimate with the supernatural."[49]

Morrison's grandparents also made their impact on her. Her grandmother Ardelia, made her greatest impact during Morrison's childhood, by acquainting her with the blacklore that now permeates her fiction. Similarly, her grandfather Solomon, influenced her as a writer with his skilled craftsmanship as a carpenter and his superb artistry as violinist. Thus, all her early life Morrison absorbed the black lore, music, language and rituals that give her prose its special flavour and tone. And, as Jean Strouse observes: "Morrison's world, like the world of her novels, was filled with signs, visitation, and ways of knowing that reached beyond the five senses."[50]

Morrison's foundation and sense of self were also strengthened by the cohesiveness of the small black Lorian community which parented and nurtured her for seven years. Morrison considers this community a 'neighbourhood'—a life-giving and sustaining compound, where myth abounds as a "concept of truth or reality a whole people has arrived at over years of observation."[51] Like the community in which Pecola of *The Bluest Eye* finds herself, it was a place that cared if someone was in difficulty. This is made clear when Morrison, in her interview, tells Robert Stepto how people were taken care of: "If they were sick, other people took care of them; if they were old, other people took care of them; if they were mad, other people provided a small place for them, or related to their madness or tried to find out the limits of their madness."[52] It is this family background that convinced Morrison that there are no boring black people and, what is more, interested her in 'scratching the surface' to discover the complexity and subtlety in their lives as clearly revealed in her novels.

African-American folklore is arguably the basis for Morrison's fiction as for most Black American literature. As Trudier Harris observes, "The link to orality is one of the keys to unlocking African-American literary history."[53] In a country where, as late as the 1830s, there were laws prohibiting the teaching of slaves, it was necessary for the oral tradition to carry the values which the group considered significant. Transmission by word of mouth took the place of pamphlets, poems, and novels. Themes such as the quest for freedom, the nature of evil, and the powerful verses of the powerless became themes of African-American literature. For instance, William Wells Brown's slaves in his *Clotel* (1853) verbalize the disparity in riches and their exploitation:

> The big bee flies high,
> The little bee makes the honey;
> The black folk makes the cotton
> And the white folk gets the money.[54]

This folk rhyme encapsulates the history of black and white interaction in the United States and, what is more, it epitomizes the sentiments expressed in protest literature.

The African-American folklore has wielded a tremendous influence upon the characters and worlds that Morrison creates, as well as upon the very shape of her novels. Her awareness of the inseparability of oral forms and effects from written media in African-American culture informs her writing throughout her career. In her use of folklore, Morrison is fascinated by the magic of fairy tales and intrigued with the horrors to be found in monsters, or at least in monstrous behaviour. Her famliarity with African-American folk communities and with other oral traditions enables her to develop her themes, shape the structure of her novels, and delineate the characters. Furthermore, like Zora Neale Hurston, Morrison exhibits a fascination for patterns of black folk speech and uses folk metaphors so authentically engaging that they compete with theme and character in most of her novels. Perceiving herself as a cultural activist, Morrison writes from a folk aesthetic that is much like the one that informs Ralph Ellison's theoretical assertion that folklore is the basis of all great literature:

> For us [black Americans] the question should be, what are the specific forms of that humanity, and what in our background is worth preserving or abandoning. The clue to this can be founhd in folklore, which offers the first drawings of any group's character. It preserves mainly those situations which have repeated them-

> selves again and again in the history of any given group. It describes those rites, manners, customs, and so forth, which insure the good life, or destroy it; and it describes those boundaries of feeling, thought, and action which that particular group has found to be limitation of the human condition. It projects this wisdom in symbols which express the group's will to survive. . . . These drawings may be crude but they are nonetheless profound in that they represent the group's attempt to humanize the world. It's no accident that great literature, the product of individual artists, is erected upon his humble base.[55]

Morrison's educational background and early professional life has helped her a good deal in moulding herself into a creative writer with social and political consciousness. Her precocity was detected very early when she was in the first grade as she was "the only black in the class and the only child who could read."[56] Eventually, literature became her favourite subject and reading her fondest pastime. Moreover, she studied Latin for four years before graduating with honours from Lorain High in 1949. After receiving a Bachelor of Arts degree in English from Cornell University in 1955, she embarked on a teaching career as a member of the English faculty at Texas Southern University in Houston. Her fascination for books especially the classics, continued though she showed no real interest in writing fiction.

Morrison's years at Random House where she served as an editor, went a long way in stimulating her developing consciousness. By editing some of the significant works written by Africans, she was exposed to the thoughts of those who were more conscious than she was of the nature of the plight confronting her people. One such African, Chinweizu, must have had a considerable impact on her. After the edition of his book, *The West and the Rest of Us*, which is one of the most insightful works that explore the nature of African oppression, expounding the theory that economics precedes racism, Morrison's own works would reflect a qualitative leap in the author's consciousness, not only of the race and gender oppression of Africans, but also of the primacy of class exploitation. The major premises of *The West and the Rest of Us* that the primary problem confronting Africans is capitalism and that the solution lies in the unity of African people would become major themes in works such as *Tar Baby* and *Beloved.* Morrison has also been influenced by a pictorial she edited—*The Black Book* (1974), a compendium of news clippings and advertisements chronicling the life of African people in the United States from slavery through the Civil Rights Movement, in her concern about the significance of place, history and myth, and especially in writing *Beloved.* She got here the kernel of her novel—the ex-slave mother so devastated by her own oppression and exploitation in slavery that she murders one of her children to prevent it from experiencing that life.

Morrison gained social consciousness not only by reading and editing historical works of pan-African writers such as Chinweizu, and *The Black Book*, but also by reading literary works by such writers as Ralph Ellison, Alex Haley, Toni Cade Bambara, Henry Dumas and Jean-Paul Sartre. The bits and pieces that she borrowed from the monumental works of art of these writers have a significant impact on her. Ellison, who burst the seams of traditional fiction in context and form, and synthesized myth and reality, folklore and history, in his effort to recreate the world from the perspective of the crisis-ridden African, served as a strong role model for her. Morrison was greatly impressed by Ellison's world in which Africans can live a life of visibility underground and invisibility above ground.

As regards Alex Haley, Morrison learned from his *Roots* the dialectical relationship between discovering one's ancestral roots and discovering one's self. Morrison seems to have greatly liked Haley's pertinent remark: "The memories of the mouths of the ancient elders was the only way that early histories of mankind got passed along . . . for all of us today to know who we are."[57] This idea of the interconnectedness between past and present impressed Morrison, and it forms the theme of *Song of Solomon.* Clearly, the underlying premise of both books—*Roots* and *Song of Solomon*—is that discovering one's roots is a precursor to discovering oneself.

Morrison is indebted to Toni Cade Bambara for the concept of the 'African Spirit.' Evidently, this concept of a haunting collective of African women who offer advice to the female protagonist, Velma Henry, in Bambara's work, had a tremendous impact on Morrison. She uses it in *Tar Baby* in which a group of African women direct the female protagonist, Jadine, toward her African, woman self, in their effort to prevent her from becoming the model of a European female. And, like Bambara's Velma Henry, Jadine rejects the sister-women's advice to be what she is—African and woman.

Morrison has been influenced by Henry Dumas in developing her commitment to write about African people in ways that would capture the positive essence of their lives and thereby help them to reclaim the African personality. She seems to have readily joined Dumas when he says: "I am very much concerned about what is happening to my people and what we are doing with our precious tradition."[58] Morrison has such a great admiration for the brilliant works of Dumas that she extracted several key concepts and names like 'Sweet Home,' ' Heyboy' (the dog in one of Dumas' most impressive stories, "Ark of Bones") which figure prominently in *Beloved.* Sweet Home, Dumas' hometown, becomes Sweet Home plantation in *Beloved.* Similarly Heyboy in Dumas' "Ark of Bones" becomes Here Boy in *Beloved.*

Morrison also seems to have been considerably influenced by Jean-Paul Sartre, the French existentialist, who professes that "man is nothing but what he makes of himself" but that in his freedom he "carries the weight of the world on his shoulders."[59] This is evident when Toni Morrison tells Gloria Naylor: "The point is that freedom is choosing your responsibility. It's not having no responsibilities, it's choosing the ones you want."[60] Morrison's protagonists who express either the 'effort of will' or a 'freedom of will' live richer, although their lives may be said to be dangerously free. The danger emerges from the nature of what is an existential perspective. For, it is freedom that is not without responsibility for the neighbourhood, involving angst.

Thus, Toni Morrison's familial, educational, cultural and literary background with an ambience of historical and social consciousness, mysticism, master craftsmanship and a love of excellence and work must have gone a long way in shaping and moulding her as a committed novelist. The various factors of influence further provide us with the subtle and profound insights into the human condition in general, and black life in particular, that Morrison has carefully woven into the landscape of her fictional world. In other words, Morrison's fiction emerges from within the universe of her mind which has been shaped by the African-American culture of her childhood, expanded by a formal education in English and the classics at Harvard and Cornell Universities, and forged by her own experiences as an African-American woman.

## VI

Although Toni Morrison is among the foremost African-American women novelists today, it is interesting to note, she never wanted to become a writer in her lifetime. As a studious adolescent, Morrison read Jane Austen and the great Russian novels like Dostoevsky's *Crime and Punishment* and Tolstoy's *War and Peace*, and remarked:

> Those books were not written for a little black girl in Lorain, Ohio, but they were so magnificently done that I got them anyway—they spoke directly to me out of their own specificity. I was not thinking of writing then—I wanted to be a dancer like Maria Tallchief.[61]

Not intending to become a writer, Morrison started writing as a therapeutic means of dealing with loneliness when she lived in Syracuse. Although at the point of going to Syracuse, Morrison had no real interest in writing as a vocation, she was still haunted by a need for greater fulfilment of her own creative talents and better direction of her creative energies.[62] In Syracuse, she decided to return to her short story about a little black girl who longed for blue eyes which she had jotted down when she was thirty. She was soon encouraged by Allen Rancler, then an editor at MacMillan to expand it into a full-length novel. This is how Morrison became a writer. She says: "I realised in the process of *The Bluest Eye* that writing had become a compulsion so I became a writer. . . . I will always be a writer."[63] Although Morrison confesses to writing both *The Bluest Eye* and the next novel, *Sula* because they were books she was interested in reading but had not been able to find, writing for her became "the most extraordinary way of thinking and feeling—it became one thing that I was doing that I had no intention of living without"[64]. In short, as Morrison told Thomas LeClair, "writing became a way to become coherent in the world."[65]

Black writing did not come into being as a result of some black persons' desire to exercise the "inspirational muse." What motivated blacks to write was the condition of the oppression, and what they desired of their writing was to ameliorate their condition. By virtue of its origin, nature and function, black writing is mission-conscious. From the beginning, black writers have written a literature of social protest and human enlightenment. Being a black writer is an ennobling exigency in black literature and it constitutes one of the supreme enrichments of black life and black culture. This has been and is the burden as well as the heritage and the legacy of every black writer in white America. Toni Morrison has not only participated in the evolving canon of Black American literature but has done much to influence, expand and solidify the place created by its vanguard, including Phillis Wheatly, Fredrick Douglass, Langston Hughes, Richard Wright, Zora Neale Hurston, James Baldwin and Ralph Ellison.

Toni Morrison made her debut as a novelist in 1970 with *The Bluest Eye* and soon gained attention for her epic power, poetic imagery, fabulistic quality, richly expressive depictions of black America, and the wonderful richness and vitality of her language. Set in a small midwestern town in Lorain, Ohio during the Depression, *The Bluest Eye* tells the story of Pecola Breedlove, who, hating her black self, yearns for blue eyes which she believes will make her white, extinguish her position as pariah, and give her the love and security that are desperately missing from her life.

By 1973 Morrison's career as a novelist soared as the publication of *Sula*, her second novel, clearly marked her as a significant literary voice in America. This seminal work reflected the shift in the mood of society at large where the emphasis had veered from the mass struggle for black consciousness, to the personal struggle for self-realization and affirmation. Just after the publication of *Sula*, Morrison in 1974 stated: "What we [blacks] have to do is to reintroduce ourselves to ourselves. We have to know the past so that we can use it for now."[66] This statement foreshadows the theme of *Song of Solomon* (1977),—truth compels one to get in touch with his or her heritage in order to comprehend and appreciate one's true self and establish a higher quality of existence. *Song of Solomon*, which would receive both the 'National Book Critics Circle Award' and the 'Friends of American Writers Award' established Morrison as a major American writer.

Morrison's fourth novel, *Tar Baby* (1981), mirrors the eighties in which "individuals increasingly sought to tap their sixth sense to unravel the mysteries of the universe."[67] It is a truly public novel about the condition of society, examining the relationships between blacks and whites, men and women and civilization and nature. Filled with allusion to African-American folklore and mythology, *Tar Baby* won accolades and recognition from all critical corners, putting the author on the cover of *Newsweek* magazine. Toni Morrison had entered the mainstream of American literature and her name had become a household word.

With her fifth novel, *Beloved* (1987), Morrison's place in American literature has been expanded as it won the Pulitzer Prize for fiction. Six years in the making, *Beloved* artistically dramatizes a haunting amalgam of the past and present experiences of an escaped female slave, tracing the heroine's quest for meaning and wholeness in slavery and in freedom. Critics have been nearly unanimous in acclaiming *Beloved* as Morrison's finest work to date. Meeting the criteria for greatness in many arenas, *Beloved* was considered by one reviewer "a milestone in the chronicling of the black experience in America,"[68] and by another "a stunning and lasting achievement (which) transforms the sorrows of history into the luminous truth of art."[69] Such spectacular praise represents not just a hallmark in Toni Morrison's career, but quite possibly in the history of African-American writers in American literature.

Before readers had caught their breath from *Beloved*, Morrison launched *Jazz* (1992), her sixth novel, which met with generally positive reviews and solidified her prominence as "one of the finest contemporary writers in America."[70] For instance, David Gates, in a review of *Jazz*, calls Morrison "the last classic American writer, squarely in the tradition of Poe, Melville, Mark Twain and Faulkner."[71] A luminously literary rendering of an art of composition that Duke Ellington perfected sometime in the summer of 1926, *Jazz* represents an advance in her work. While many black writers have used musicians and music as theme and metaphor for their writing, none have attempted to drop on jazz as the structuring principle for an entire work until Toni Morrison's new novel, *Jazz*. Morrison has used the mode of jazz to depict the experience of black community in the city of New York during the 1920s, a decade itself known as the Jazz Age. Through a meticulous use of the jazz idiom, Morrison relates the story of Joe Trace and his wife Violet, both of whom had train-danced to the City, leaving behind all the traumas of their childhood. With Jazz, Morrison has established herself as one of the truly original novelists at work in the world today.

Released simultaneously with *Jazz* was Morrison's *Playing in the Dark: Whiteness and Literary Imagination* (1992), a scholarly work based on a lecture series she delivered at Harvard University. It reveals Morrison's deeper analytical talents as she diagrams the presence of the Africanist personae in the works of white writers, while probing the problem of living in a rationalised society with its democratic egalitarianism, on one hand, and its ideological dependence on racialism, on the other.[72] Morrison argues that the African presence in America, which shaped the entire nation, has had no significant place in the country's literature. She feels that a contemplation of the black presence is essential to any understanding of the nation's literature. Morrison writes with a clarity and simplicity which can attract a general audience. Her discerning discussion on Africanism in major works of white American fiction enlivens debates on the function of literary criticism and alternative constructions of the Africanist character in African, African-American and related interdisciplinary studies. It is bound to alter our reading of the so-called classics in white American literature. The very fact that Harvard University Press decided to run twenty five thousand initial copies of *Playing in the Dark*, instead of the traditional number of fifteen hundred, is clearly indicative of Morrison's stature as a great American novelist. Morrison has also written several essays which have a bearing on her fictional art. They include "What the Black Woman Thinks about Women's Lib" (1971), "Behind the Making of the Black Book" (1974), "City Limits," "Village Values: Concepts of Neighbourhood in Black Fiction" (1981), "Recitalif" (1983), "Rootedness: The Ancestors as Foundation" (1984), "Memory Creation and Writing" (1984), "A Knowing so Deep" (1985), "The Site of Memory" (1987), "Unspeakable Things Unspoken" (1989), and a collection of essays which include "Racing Justice," "En-gendering Power," essays on Anita Hill, Clarence Thomas and "The Contribution of Social Reality"

(1993).

Morrison has also to her credit a play, *Dreaming Emmett* (1986), which is based on the life of the young boy, Emmett Till, who was killed by a lynch mob in Mississippi in 1954. The play was written in honour of the first national observance of the birthday of Dr. Martin Luther King Jr. It was performed by the Capital Repertory Theatre of Albany, New York on January 4, 1986. The play reveals that Morrison has many literary gifts—her instinct for storytelling, her free-standing characters and her astute ear for language and observation of human gesture—to offer the theatre. Even more important, however, is her focus on the historical and psychological complexities in the lives of ordinary black women and men. And, as Margaret Wilkerson in her brilliant critical essay, "The Dramatic Voice in Toni Morrison's Novels," points out the richness of language and perception that Morrison brings to her subject matter "should be brought to the stage so that there itself many learn from her dramatic voice."[73] The dramatic voice is strong in Morrison's novels. Her characters are complex and well developed. Conflict is sharply defined as in any powerful play. Above all, her dialogue is crisp, concise and revealing.

## VII

It seems appropriate to end this excursion into the world of Toni Morrison by having her speak for herself so as to know of her views regarding her function and goal as a writer. In an interview with Steve Cannon and Ntozake Shange, Toni Morrison offers a candid insight into her goal as a writer. She says: "My attempt, although I never say any of this, until I'm done . . . is to deal with something that is nagging me, but, when I think about it in a large sense, I use the phrase 'bear witness' to explain what my work is for."[74] Here, Morrison refers to the act of rememory, of tapping into the deepest recesses of consciousness, and of ripping the veil so that one's interior life and history can surface. She defines the role of the writer as witness bearer—an idea that will be repeated throughout her career. The ability to bear witness is closely tied to her concept of prophecy that has sacred undertones. This prophecy, or bearing witness, in her fiction is essential to her belief that the future is inextricably linked up with the past.

In her conversation with LeClair, Morrison envisions herself writing what is called village literature. She glories in writing peasant literature for her people. She declares: "I write what I recently began to call village literature, fiction that is really for the village, for the tribe. Peasant literature for my people, which is necessary and legitimate but which also allows me to get in touch with all sorts of people."[75] The function of novels in village literature is to clarify the roles that have become obscure and to identify those elements from the past that are useful and give nourishment to the people in the present. Morrison believes in the need to bring forth the meanings and lessons of the past into the present. She takes up this mission as a writer as a challenge against forgetfulness: "I think long and hard about what my novels should do. They should clarify the roles that have become obscured, they ought to identify those things in the past that are not and they ought to give nourishment."[76] She does not seek a historical rendering of facts, but endeavors to incorporate into the action, values, feelings and emotion that accompanied events in black life which she believes contains the lesson for survival.

In a 1984 interview, Toni Morrison comments that she tries to incorporate into her fiction one of the major characteristics of Black art, that is,

> the ability to be both print and oral literature; to combine those two aspects so that the stories can be read in silence, of course but one should be able to hear them as well. It should try deliberately to make you stand up and make you feel something profoundly in the same way that a Black preacher requires his congregation to speak, to join him in the sermon to behave in a certain way, to stand up and to be and to cry and to accede or to change and modify—to expand on the sermon that is being delivered.[77]

These functions were once culturally performed by black music, but are no longer. This is made clear when Morrison states: "For a long time, the art form that was healing for black people was music. That music is no longer exclusively ours. . . . So another form has to take that place."[78] What she suggests here is that the African-American novel is that form. She believes that the black writer can bring something unique—approximating the profound depths of black music—to fiction, "an ineffable quality that is curiously black."[79] As a black woman writer, this is what Toni Morrison seeks to do in her fiction. This is driven home to us when Morrison herself proclaims: "I am not like James Joyce; I am not like Thomas Hardy; I am not like Faulkner. I am not like that in that sense. . . . My effort is to be like something that has probably only been fully expressed in black music. . . . Writing novels is a way to encompass this—this something."[80] Morrison's explanation of the affinity between her writing and black music defines her strong sense of tradition. From the foregoing statements of Morrison it is clear that what she seeks to do in her fiction is what others in the past have done in black music.

To accomplish this, Morrison offers a solution to restore the power of African-American language to the people—the 'nommo' or power that exists in language and has the potential to reshape reality. She says: "I don't like to have someone call my books 'poetic,' because it has the connotation of luxuriating richness. I wanted to restore the language that black people spoke to its original power. That calls for a language that is rich but not ornate."[81] Morrison succeeds brilliantly in restoring the language of black people to its original power by turning it into "a musical instrument that trumpets the desires, disappointments, and triumphs of African-Americans."[82] As Dannile Taylor-Guthrie points out, "she writes and rewrites and rewrites, and, if necessary rewrites again and again until the language achieves a high level of exactness."[83] It is this labour that she enjoys most. Morrison says: "It must appear effortless! No matter what the style, it must have that. I mean the seams can't show!"[84] Morrison's novels, constituting as they do village literature, portray an exotic, fantastic world in which even the everyday black life of ordinary Midwestern towns comes alive in folklore, magic, superstition, fable, poetry, song, and myth.

In her interview with Mel Watkins, Morrison discusses two related major concepts regarding her writing. First, for her, writing is a "way of thinking," and a process. She says: "It [writing] stretches you, makes you think the unthinkable, project yourself into people you even dislike, people I couldn't stay in a room with for 20 minutes. It makes you stay in touch with yourself; I guess it's like going under water for me, the danger, yet I'm certain I'm going to come up."[85] Secondly, she is a writer who works from images. She must have an image of a scene in her mind before she can write it. She is fascinated by the techniques of painters—their ability to re-create interpreted images to usual forms. As a writer she seeks to transform the visual to the aural via language, so that readers can create pictures in their own mind.

Morrison proudly presents herself as a branch on ancient tree of black assertiveness and self-definition that is richly and deeply rooted in the folk culture. As a Black Cultural Nationalist, she "validates black culture, and reaffirms its adaptive survival power, its creativity amidst oppression, life-affirming qualities, as well as its ancient wisdom and humanity and its capacity for survival."[86] She unapologetically declares herself to be a 'black woman writer.' Like Faulkner she wants to write regional literature, which is at once specific and universal, and have it published all over the world. In other words, she delves deep into the particular in order to reach the universal. This is made clear when she says:

> If I tried to write a universal novel, it would be water. Behind this question is the suggestion that to write for black people is somehow to diminish the writing. From my perspective, there are only black people. When I say "people," that's what I mean. Lots of books written by black people about black people have had this "universality" as a burden. They were writing for some readers other than me.[87]

Much of what Morrison writes individually as a black woman writer eventually leads back to the universal condition of being human. Morrison's ability to transform the individual into universal forces and idiosyncrasies into inevitabilities has led some critics to call her the "D.H. Lawrence of the black psyche."

Unlike other black artists—Gwendolyn Brooks, Clarence Major, and Albert Yound—who use art for strictly political purposes, Morrison realizes that strict adherence to political dogma would be insufficient to promote the aesthetic qualities of art. She, therefore, chooses to subordinate the political in order to "establish a positive black identity and to reorder racial consciousness through serious exploration and rediscovery of the black community's unique cultural heritage: its own particular beauty, its rich and varied oral tradition, its private joys and agonies, as well as its communal trials and tribulations."[88] Though she validates the aesthetic qualities of the black community, Morrison is anything but apolitical. She unequivocally declares: "The work must be political. It must have that as its thrust. . . . The best art is political and you ought to be able to make it unquestionably political and irrevocably beautiful at the same time."[89] There is no contradiction in Morrison's belief that art is political, that it must have aesthetic qualities and that ideally it must be committed to its people. For, by combining political consciousness with aesthetic sensibility, she achieves a very delicate balance. Without directly denouncing white society, she illustrates the demise of blacks who have adopted the corrupting influence of the white community. While valorizing the black community and igniting both blacks and whites into political action, she wishes to elevate, through art, the beautiful in the human condition.

It is but natural that Toni Morrison, with her political commitment to her people and her aesthetic responsibility to her art of fiction, is sensitively concerned with race, gender and class as three major forms of oppression of blacks in America. Morrison's novels document the author's awareness and concern for the historical conditions that sparked the national struggle of African people against oppression and exploitation, thereby revealing her heightened consciousness of the interrelationship of race, gender and class.

Though all the three elements—race, gender and class—are present in all the novels of Toni Morrison, the emphasis on them varies from novel to novel. *The Bluest Eye*, her first novel, examines racism as a primary source oppression of the Africans. *Sula* lays emphasis on gender oppression and *Song of Solomon* on the importance of knowing one's history to determine one's identity. *Tar Baby* is about class contradictions that keep African people divided and *Beloved* is about the solution—collective class struggle—that will help solve the exploitation and oppression of African people. *Jazz*, her last novel, focuses on gender solidarity through women bonding. Certainly, no one could choose and develop such themes as racism, gender oppression, identity crisis, class contradictions and class exploitation within the African race, as well as collective class struggle and women bonding, without herself having a commitment to struggle for African people. And, certainly no one would be concerned enough to shape her works into narrative structures that enhance the themes, without herself being interested in turning theory into practice, as demonstrated in the following chapters.

## NOTES

1. Richard Wright, "Blueprint for Negro Literature," *Challenge*, 1937.
2. Barbara Smith, "Doing Research on Black American Women," *Women Studies Newsletter*, 4 (Spring 1976), 4, 5,7.
3. Barbara Christian, "Trajectories of Self-definition: Placing Contemporary Afro-American Women's Fiction," *Conjuring: Black Women, Fiction and Literary Tradition*, ed. Pryse Marjorie and Hortense J. Spillers (Bloomington: Indiana University Press, 1985), 234.
4. Alexis De Veau, *Black Women Writers at Work*, ed. Claudia Tate (New York: Continuum, 1983), 55.
5. Barbara Christian, "Trajectories of Self-definition," 234.
6. Frances Harper, *Iola Leroy, Shadows Uplifted*, 3rd ed. (Boston: James H. Earle, 1895), 281.
7. Jessie Redmon Fauset, *The Chinaberry Tree* (New York: Fredrick A. Stokes, 1931), ix.
8. Mckay Nellie, "Ann Petry's *The Street and the Narrow*: A Study of the Influences of Race and Gender on African-American Women's Lives," *Diedrich and Fisher Hornung*, 139.
9. Barbara Christian, "Trajectories of Self-definition," 236.
10. Barbara Christian, *Black Women Novelists: The Development of a Tradition 1892-1976* (West Port, Connecticut: Greenwood Press, 1980), 70-71.

11. Selwyn R. Cudjoe, "Maya Angelou and the Autobiographical Statement," in *Evans*, 7.
12. Barbara Christian, "Trajectories of Self-definition," 239.
13. Brock Sabine, "Talk as a Form of Action," *Lenz* 1984, 206.
14. Christel Helene, "Paule Marshall's Bajan Women in *Brown Girl, Brownstones*," *Diedrich and Fischer-Hormong*, 141.
15. Alice Walker, *In Search of Our Mother's Gardens: Womanist Prose* (New York: Harcourt, 1983), xi.
16. John O'Brien, *Interviews with Black Writers* (New York: Liveright, 1973), 192.
17. *Ibid.*
18. Barbara Christian, *Black Feminist Criticism: Perspectives on Black Women Writers* ( New York: Pergamon Press, 1985), 79.
19. *Ibid.*, 72.
20. Gloria Wade-Gayles, *No Crystal Stair: Visions of Race and Sex in Black Women's Fiction* (New York: The Pilgrim Press, 1984), 3-4.
21. Hernton Calvin, *Sex and Racism in America* (New York: Grove Press, 1965), 175.
22. Joel Kovel, *White Racism: A Psychohistory* (New York: Columbia UP, 1984), 18.
23. A.J. Plakkoottam, "Racial and Gender Discrimination in Fiction by Afro-American Women," *Indian Journal of American Studies*, 20, 1 (1990), 13.
24. Gloria Steinem, *Outrageous Acts and Everyday Rebellions* (London: Fontana, 1984), 7.
25. Beal Frances, "Double Jeopardy: To be Black and Female," *The Black Women: An Anthology* (New York: Signet, 1970), 90.
26. Giddings Paula, *When and Where I Enter: The Impact of Black Women on Race and Sex in America* (New York: Morrow, 1984), 6.
27. Lerner Gerda, *Black Women in White America* (New York: New American Library, 1969), xxiii.
28. Gloria Wade-Gayles, *No Crystal Stair*, 7.
29. Emile Burns, *An Introduction to Marxism* (New York: International Publishers, 1966), 54.
30. Walter Rodney, *How Europe Underdeveloped Africa* (Dar es Salaam: Tanzania Publishing House, 1972),16.
31. *Ibid.*, 99-100.
32. *Ibid.*, 100.
33. Kwame Nkrumah, *Class Struggle in Africa* (New York: International Publishers, 1970), 29.
34. Eric Williams, *Capitalism and Slavery* (New York: G.P. Putnam's, 1944), 18-19.
35. Walter Rodney, 100.
36. Kwame Nkrumah, *Class Struggle in Africa*, 27.
37. Zora Neale Hurston, *Their Eyes were Watching God* (New York: Fawcett, 1937), 29.

38. Gloria Wade-Gayles, *No Crystal Stair*, 7.
39. Ann Petry, *The Street* (Boston: Houghton, 1946), 206.
40. Barbara Christian, *Black Feminist Criticism*, 103-5.
41. William H. Grier and Price M. Cobbs, *Black Rage* (New York: Bantam, 1968), 33.
42. Paule Marshall, *Brown Girl, Brownstones* (New York: Avon, 1959), 252.
43. Wilfred D. Samuels and Clenora Hudson-Weems, *Toni Morrison* (Boston: Twayne, 1990), 3.
44. Toni Morrison, "Slow Walk of Trees . . . ," *New York Times Magazine*, 4 July 1976, 152.
45. Jean Strouse, "Toni Morrison: Black Magic," *Newsweek*, 30 March 1981, 52.
46. Carolyn F. Gerald, "The Black Writer and His Role," *The Black Aesthetics*, ed. Addison Gayle, Jr. (New York: Anchor Books, 1970), 349-56.
47. Samuels and Hudson-Weems, *Toni Morrison*, 4.
48. Colette Dowling, "The Song of Toni Morrison," *New York Times*, 20 May 1971, 42.
49. Jean Strouse, "Toni Morrison: Black Magic," 54.
50. *Loc. cit.*
51. Toni Morrison, "Behind the Making of *The Black Book*," *Black World*, 23 (1974), 88.
52. Robert Stepto, "Intimate Things in Place: A Conversation with Toni Morrison," *Chant of Saints*, ed. Michael S. Harper and Robert Stepto (Urbana: University of Illinois Press, 1979), 214.
53. Trudier Harris, *Fiction and Folklore: The Novels of Toni Morrison* (Knoxville: The University of Tennessee Press, 1991), 1.
54. William Wells Brown, *Clotel or The President's Daughter* (1853, rpt. New York: Collier, 1970), 108.
55. Ralph Ellison, *Shadow and Act* (New York, 1953), 172.
56. Doreatha Drummond Mbalia, *Toni Morrison's Developing Class Consciousness* (Selingrove: Subsquehanna University Press, 1992), 105.
57. Alex Haley, *Roots: The Saga of an American Family* (New York: Dell, 1976), 10.
58. Henry Dumas, *Goodbye, Sweetwater* (New York: Thunder's Mouth Press, 1988), xiv.
59. Jean-Paul Sartre, *Existentialism and Human Emotions* (Secaucus, N.J.: Castle, n.d.) 15, 52.
60. Gloria Naylor and Toni Morrison, "A Conversation," *Southern Quarterly*, 21 (1985), 573.
61. Jean Strouse, "Toni Morrison: Black Magic," 54.
62. Although kept busy by full-time teaching of English classics and Freshmen composition by her role as faculty advisor for the English Club at Harvard University, and by the obligations of familyhood, Toni Morrison remained somewhat unfulfilled.
63. Jessica Harris, "'Interview with Toni Morrison,'" *Essence* 7, 8 (1976), 54.

64. Mel Watkins, "Talk with Toni Morrison," *New York Times Book Review*, 11 September 1977, 50.
65. Thomas LeClair, "The Language Must Not Sweat: A Conversation with Toni Morrison," *New Republic*, 21 March 1981, 25.
66. Toni Morrison, "Behind the Making of *The Black Book*," 90.
67. Samuels and Hudson-Weems, *Toni Morrison*, 8.
68. Review of *Beloved* by Toni Morrison, in *Publishers Weekly* (17 July 1987), 53.
69. Merle Rubin, "Review of *Beloved* by Toni Morrison," *Christian Science Monitor*, 5 October 1987, 20.
70. Faye Chadwell, "Review of *Jazz* by Toni Morrison," *Library Journal*, 15 (April 1992), 122.
71. David Gates, "Review of *Jazz*, by Toni Morrison," in *Newsweek* (27 April 1992), 66.
72. See Toni Morrison, *Playing in the Dark: Whiteness and Literary Imagination* (London: Harvard University Press, 1992), 64.
73. Margaret B. Wilkerson, "The Dramatic Voice in Toni Morrison's Novels," *Critical Essays on Toni Morrison* (Boston: Hall, 1988), 189.
74. Ntozake Shange, "Interview with Toni Morrison," *American Rage*, November 1978, 52.
75. Thomas LeClair, "The Language Must Not Sweat," 25.
76. Elaine Showalter, *Modern American Women Writers* (New York: Charles Scribner's, 1991), 334.
77. Toni Morrison, "Rootedness: The Ancestor as Foundation," *Black Women Writers (1950-1980)*, ed. Mari Evans (New York: Anchor Books, 1984), 340.
78. *Ibid.*, 341.
79. *Ibid.*, 342.
80. Nellie Mckay, "An Interview with Toni Morrison," *Contemporary Literature*, 24, No. 4 (Winter 1983), 426.
81. Thomas LeClair, "The Language Must Not Sweat," 27.
82. Nancy J. Peterson, "Introduction: Canonizing Toni Morrison," *Modern Fiction Studies*, 39, 3 and 4 (Fall/Winter 1993), 476.
83. Dannile Taylor-Guthrie, ed., *Conversation with Toni Morrison* (Jackson: University Press of Mississipi, 1994), xi.
84. Jane Bakerman, "The Seams Can't Show: An Interview with Toni Morrison," *Black American Literary Forum*,12, 1978, 56-60.
85. Mel Watkins, "Talk with Toni Morrison," *New York Times Book Review*, 7 (11 September 1977), 49.
86. Harry Read, "Toni Morrison, *Song of Solomon* and Black Cultural Nationalism," *Centennial Review*, 32 (Winter 1988), 50.
87. Thomas LeClair, "The Language Must Not Sweat," 28.
88. Norris Clark, "Gwendolyn Brooks and a Black Aesthetic," *A Life Distilled: Gwendolyn Brooks, Her Poetry and Fiction*, ed. Maria K. Mootry and Gary Smith (Urbana: University of Illinois Press, 1987), 82.
89. Toni Morrison, "Rootedness: The Ancestor as Foundation," 340.

## CHAPTER II

# Race in Relation to Gender and Class: *The Bluest Eye*

> Her blackness is the antithesis of a creamy white skin, her lips are thick, her hair is kinky, and short she is, in fact the antithesis of American beauty . . . in this country she is ugly . . . when to her physical unattractivenessis added a discouraging, deprecating mother—family—environment into which she is born, there can be no doubt that she will develop a damaged self-concept and an impairment of her feminine narcissism.
>
> Calvin Hernton, *Sex and Racism in America*

> The attempt to become "white" intensifies rather than mitigates the Negro woman's frustration in white world. No amount of pain, powder, and hair straightner can erase all the things in the black woman's background that make her feminity and aesthetic appreciation of herself as a beauty capable of attracting men. The Negro woman becomes ashamed of what she is. . . .
>
> William Grier and Price Cobbs, *Black Rage*

In his turn-of-the century definition of double-consciousness, W.E.B. DuBois, in his book, *The Souls of Black Folk*, gauges the deleterious impact of racism on cultural self-consciousness and identity. The term, 'double-consciousness,' refers to two distinct realities—a psychological conflict between opposing cultural world views and debilitating resolution in which externally derived and distorted perceptions of the self constitute a single, but alienated self-consciousness. DuBois further notes: "It is a peculiar sensation, this double-consciousness, this sense of always looking at one's self through the eyes of others, of measuring one's soul by the tape of a world that looks on in amused contempt and pity."[1]

This observation illuminates the socio-political implications behind Toni Morrison's first novel, *The Bluest Eye* (1970). Inspired by the climate of revolution and evolving black consciousness of the sixties, a period characterized by an almost evangelical struggle for personal and racial identity, Morrison chooses, as the basic theme and subject of her first major work, the obsession of blacks with an American standard of beauty that seems both inescapable and destructive. And, as Morrison herself states, "the concept of physical beauty as a virtue is one of the dumbest, most pernicious and destructive ideas of the western world."[2]

*The Bluest Eye* is a tragic tale about a young, black girl's desire for the bluest eyes, the symbol for her of what it means to be beautiful and, therefore, worthy in society. The pivotal idea in the novel is the domination of blacks by the existing American standards of beauty—blue eyes, blond hair and white skin. It deals honestly and sensitively with the damaging influence of white standards and values on the lives of black people. It portrays in poignant terms the tragic condition of blacks in a racist America. It examines how the ideologies, perpetuated by the institutions controlled by the dominant group, influence the making of self-image of black women, thereby exposing the devastation caused by white cultural domination in the lives of African-Americans. As Elizabeth Jane Way observes, Morrison's "stunning insight reveals the disrupted emotions produced by living in a world where white standards and goals are presented to blacks as uniquely important and, at the same time, impossible for them to achieve."[3] In short, the novel lays bare the victimization of black people within the context of racist social order.

Although *The Bluest Eye*, at the core, is about the contradictions fostered by racism, sexism, and class distinctions affecting the black girls in white America, Morrison, at this stage of her literary career, considers racism the African's primary obstacle. For, as Doreatha Drummond Mbalia points out, when this novel was written "Morrison's level of consciousness about the primary cause of the nature of the African's oppression in the United States as well as in the rest of the world was considerably weak, for she not only subordinates the role of economics to racism, but also neglects to show a causal relationship between them, that an exploitive economic system gives rise to racist ideology."[4] Naturally, the whole emphasis of the novel is on racism which "abstracts the colour of the living body into non-colours of extreme value, black and white, within this organization; black represents the shade of evil, the devil's aspect, night, separation, loneliness, sin, dirt, excrement, the inside of the body, and white represents the mark of good, the token of innocence, purity, cleanliness, spirituality, virtue and hope."[5] *The Bluest Eye*, thus, makes one of the most powerful attacks on the relationship between western standards of female beauty and the psychological oppression of black women.

The thesis of the novel is that racism devastates the self-image of the African female in general, and African female child in particular. At the crux of the novel is the society's need for a pariah, the need of its members to have someone to look down upon and, therefore, enhance one's constantly threatened sense of worth. The novel succinctly expresses the vulnerability of poor black girls and how easily they can become the pariahs in a white society.

Furthermore, the novel reveals a consistency in Morrison's vision of the human condition, particularly in her preoccupation with the effect of community on the individual's achievement and retension of an integrated, acceptable self. In treating this subject, she draws recurrently on myth and legend for story pattern and characters, returning repeatedly to the theory of 'quest' as a motivating and organising device. Moreover, the theme of quest is always underscored by ironic insights and intensely evocative imagery. An exploration of these distinguishing qualities—technical and thematic—enhances one's appreciation of Morrison's achievement in her maiden attempt.

*The Bluest Eye* is not only the story of the destructive effects of intraracial prejudice upon impressionable black girls in the midwest, but also a succinct account of African-American folk culture in process. Through subtle ways, Morrison suggests that the vibrancy of the folk culture persists through the fortunes and misfortunes of the characters and that it serves to baptize them into kinship with each other. The novel is about cultural beliefs which are the essence of folkloristic transmission. The belief that black was not valuable or beautiful was, however, one of the cultural hindrances to black people throughout their history in America.

## II

This belief informs the tragedy of Pecola Breedlove who is at the centre of *The Bluest Eye*. Pecola comes from a poor family that is virtually cut off from the normal life of a community. The Breedloves despise themselves because they believe in their own unworthiness which is translated into ugliness for the women of that family. Pecola's mother, Pauline, who works as a domestic servant in a beautiful house, hates the ugliness of her house, her daughter, her family and herself and, what is worse, blames her sense of unworthiness on being black and poor. Having inherited the myth of unworthiness, the Breedloves can only live the outlined saga to its expected conclusion. The novel, therefore, becomes a myth that defines human worth and explores the potential greatness of the people who are waylaid by the beliefs they have adopted from outsiders.

The mythology Morrison explores in *The Bluest Eye* centres upon the standard of beauty by which white women are judged in America. They are taught that their blond hair, blue eyes, and creamy skins are not only wonderful but are the surface manifestations of the very best character God and nature ever moulded. Oral traditions bolstered by literature and other media have solidified their pedestalization. We see in the novel how Pecola is forced to long for blue eyes like those of white children, so that she would also be loved and accepted by both whites and blacks:

> Pecola Breedlove is a young black girl driven literally insane by the pressure toward absolute physical beauty in a culture whose white standards of beauty . . . are impossible for her to meet, though no less alluring and demanding. Surrounded by cultural messages that she is ugly by definition, she can achieve peace only by retreating into schizophrenia.[6]

Pecola's yearning for blue eyes—the white American standard of beauty—is an external manifestation of the internal need to be loved and accepted by the white community.

Pecola, who never considers herself beautiful, is all admiration for the eyes of the whites which she longs to possess through some miracle. Her obsession with physical beauty leads to disastrous consequences. Morrison says:

> When the strength of a race depends on its beauty, when the focus is turned to how one looks as opposed to what one is, we are in trouble. . . . The concept of physical beauty as a virtue is one of the dumbest, most pernicious and destructive ideas of the western world, and we should have nothing to do with it. Physical beauty has nothing to do with our past, present or future. Its absence or presence was only important to "them," the white people who used it for anything they wanted.[7]

But, Pecola never realises this, being as she has been under the spell of white cultural domination. All that she has experienced is repeated rejection and brutalization. Even more chillingly, her parents, who have never experienced nurturing love, do not know how to love, and so they cannot give their children a sense of worth. This predicament of her parents is also the outcome of racial injustice.

The racial predicament in which Pecola and her parents are placed is exquisitely expressed in the main body of the novel which is divided into four chapters named after four seasons—Autumn, Winter, Spring and Summer. And, we are prepared for this scheme by Claudia's introductory statement in which she relates the failure of the marigolds to sprout with the death of Pecola's baby. Nature images are constant throughout the book and help in organising its structure. Interspersed with this are the physical and psychological events that lead to the rape of Pecola by her father and to her ill-fated pregnancy. The division into seasons, beginning with autumn, charts the development of events that form the plot of the novel.

The use of names of seasons, intended to indicate the major parts of *The Bluest Eye*, aids Morrison in telling her story. By beginning the novel with autumn, she suggests to us that the world of the novel is topsy-turvy. Spring usually symbolizes the beginning of things, the time of birth and rebirth. Winter, in contrast, is the time of death and decay. And, summer, commonly associated with life in full bloom and ripeness, is a time of death, life in its final moments. These seasonal divisions help the reader in understanding the fundamental decadence of life of the Africans living in the United States. They help in telling Morrison's story of the warped psyche of an adolescent African female living in a racist society.

Morrison begins the novel most innovatively with a passage in the simplest possible language, the language of a prep school reader:

> Here is the house. It is green and white. It has a red door. It is very pretty. Here is the family. Mother, Father, Dick and Jane live in the green-and-white house. They are very happy. See Jane. She has a red dress. She wants to play. Who will play with Jane? See thc cat. It gocs mcow-mcow. Comc and play. Comc play with Jane. The kitten will not play. See Mother. Mother is very nice. Mother, will you play with Jane? Mother laughs. Laugh, Mother, laugh. See Father. He is big and strong. Father, will you play with Jane? Father is smiling. Smile, Father, smile. See the dog. Bow-wow goes the dog. Do you want play with Jane? See the dog run. Run, dog, run. Look, look. Here comes a friend. The friend will play with the Jane. They will play a good game. Play, Jane, play.[8]

The passage is subsequently but immediately repeated twice in two entirely different ways. The second version repeats the same passage exactly, but without capitals or punctuation:

> Here is the house it is green and white it has a red door it is very

pretty here is the family mother father dick and jane live in the green-and-white house they are very happy see jane she has a red dress she wants to play who will play with jane see the cat it goes meow-meow come and play come play with jane the kitten will not play see mother mother is very nice mother will you play with jane mother laughs laugh mother laugh see father he is big and strong father will you play with jane father is smilling smile father smile see the dog bowwow goes the dog do you want play with jane see the dog run run dog run look look here comes a friend the friend will play with the jane they will play a good game play jane play. (1)

In the third version, the wording of the paragraph is likewise unaltered, but without boundaries of spacing or punctuation:

Hereisthehouseitisgreenandwhiteithasareddooritisveryprettyhereisthe familymotherfatherdickandjaneliveinthegreenandwhitehousetheyar everyhappyseejaneshehasareddresssshewantstoplaywhowillplaywith janeseethecatitgoesmeowmeowcomeandplaycomeplaywithjanethek ittenwillnotplayseemothermotherisverynicemotherwillyouplaywith janemotherlaughslaughmotherlaughseefatherheisbigandstrongfathe rwillyouplaywithjanefatherissmilingsmilefathersmileseethedogbo wwowgoesthedogdoyouwantplaywithjaneseethedogrunrundogrunl ooklookherecomesafriendthefriendwillplaywiththejanettheywillpla yawillplaywiththejanetheywillplayagoodgameplayjaneplay. (2)

The passage which is completely run together like one long collection of consonants and vowels seeming to signify nothing, invariably reminds us of a similar but far longer passage in Beckett's play, *Waiting for Godot*, through which Lucky thinks.

The three versions of the unique opening paragraph of *The Bluest Eye* may be said to be symbolic of the three life styles that Morrison explores in the novel either directly or by implication. The first version of the paragraph indicates an alien white world, represented by the Dick-Jane family that intrudes into the lives of the black children. The second version represents the life style of the MacTeer family which survives the poverty and the racism that it encounters in Ohio. The third distorted run-on-version of the paragraph stands for the Breedlove family which lives in a deformed world being exploited by the ruling class. Thus, the simulated "here is the house" passage, with its variants, serves several purposes as Klotman points out: "First and foremost it serves as a synopsis of the tale that is to follow revealing the psychic confusion of the novel. It also serves as an ironic comment on a society which educated and unconsciously socializes its children like Pecola with callous regard for the cultural richness and diversity of its people."[9]

On top of that, in the third version of the paragraph the individual space between two words disappears as it does in the novel. The father intrudes on and violates the child's space. The clear structure of the story book world is wrecked as Pecola's life is wrecked. The cat and dog motif, for instance, appears in a sinister form in the novel. The black cat has blue eyes like Pecola which haunt her. And, the dog writhes as it dies of poison, the sign that Pecola must look for in order that her eyes become blue. The "friend" who comes to "play with Jane" is the invented friend who comes to play with Pecola as she enters the world of insanity. Jacqueline de Weever hardly exaggerates when, in her brilliant article, "The Inverted World of Toni Morrison's *The Bluest Eye* and *Sula*," she quips: "all the elements of the novel are here."[10]

In *The Bluest Eye*, there are three "minor" African families who, for their social status and economic and political advancement, exploit their own brethren in order to become close to the ruling class. One such family is the Peals. Although the reader is introduced to only one member of this family, Maureen, her appearance, behavioural patterns, and remarks offer sufficient glimpses of consciousness of the Peals. By dissociating itself from the African community, the second family, Geraldine Louis and Louis Junior also nurture the aspirations of the ruling class. They consider themselves to be 'coloured,' signifying some nebulous group of Africans who are neither European nor African: "Coloured people were neat and quiet; niggers were dirty and loud." (67) The third family, the Elihue Micah Whitcombs, are so obsessed with the physical appearances of Europeans that they jeopardize their mental stability by intermarrying, only to maintain some semblance of whiteness. Here Morrison seems to be more interested in developing the skin-colour conflict or race conflict than the gender and class conflicts.

III

Even though Morrison is conscious of the role class-aspirations play in the minor families, she often discusses these aspirations as if they were intraracial prejudices based on skin colour rather than class conflicts. Her discussions on class conflicts, which are couched within, are overshadowed by her discussions on racial prejudices. As a result, the focus in *The Bluest Eye* is on racism as a primary problem confronting African people.

There are many incidents in the novel which hurt Pecola into a feeling of isolation and pain because of her race. To mention but a few, her encounter with a fifty-two-year-old white storekeeper makes her aware that for many people, she does not really exist. Let alone the whites, even the black boys taunt her, at school. She becomes the scapegoat for their own humiliation and pain. Junior, a black boy, makes her the scapegoat for his own pain. Pecola's mother, who works as a housekeeper in a white family, lavishes all her love and affection on her employer's children, reserving her jibes and slaps for her own hapless daughter. The reason for the tendency of black people to harass other black people is, perhaps, self-hatred induced by white hegemony. White standards corrupted the minds of black people in such a way that black people have developed self-hatred:

> It was as though some mysterious all-knowing master has given each one a cloak of ugliness to wear, and they had each accepted it without question. The master had said, "you are ugly people." They looked about themselves and saw nothing to contradict the statement, saw, in fact, support for it leaning at them from every billboard, every move, every glance. (28)

The ultimate act of brutalization and betrayal for Pecola comes when Cholly, her own father, rapes her. Cholly's unnatural rape of Pecola could be interpreted "as a pathetic attempt to return to the heady days of first love when his very presence essentially created another human being."[11] Cholly turns to Pecola in hopes of rescuing her from the dehumanizing glare of all white people and a subsequently loveless existence. His tenderness and protectiveness, however, unfortunately slip into lust and rage which he directs at Pecola and all those like her "who bore witness to his failure, his importance. The one whom he had not been able to protect to spare to cover from the round moon glow of the flashlight." (119) Cholly's rape of Pecola is, thus, the distortion of his love for Pecola. Pecola's stillborn child is not only a symbol of his personal violation but of the fettered life she has been made to live.

In sum, Pecola is the central scapegoat of the novel, *The Bluest Eye*. For, she is not only made a scapegoat by her parents but also by the mulattos in the novel, and even by the narrator, Claudia, a once caring friend who shuns Pecola in the end. At the end of her assessment, Claudia recognizes Pecola's role as scapegoat:

> All of us—all who knew her—felt so wholesome after we cleaned ourselves on her. We were so beautiful when we stood astride her ugliness. Her simplicity decorated us, her guilt sanctified us, her

> pain made us glow with health, her awkwardness made us think we had a sense of humour. Her inarticulateness made us generous. Even her waking dreams we used—to silence our own nightmares. And she let us, and thereby deserved our contempt. We honed our egos on her, padded our characters with her frailty, and yawned in the fantasy of our strength. (163)

Clearly, Claudia maintains that Pecola is equally responsible for the role in which she is cast. In the end, she holds Pecola partially responsible for her unfulfilled life.

Thus, as a black girl, Pecola undergoes all the traumatic experiences. She wants to rise up out of the pit of her blackness and see the world with blue eyes, but the pity is that she is not allowed to. Excluded from reality by racial discrimination and inequality, Pecola goes mad, fantasizing that her eyes have turned blue and so fitted her for the world. She has lost her balance of mind. As Cynthia Davies points out, "Pecola is the epitome of the victim in a world that reduces persons to objects and then makes them feel inferior as objects."[12]

Morrison's purpose in showing us the psychic state and the resultant behaviour of Pecola under the pressure of white domination is to expose the vicious genocidal effects of racism on the black girls, thereby raising the question of what it means to be black in a racist society. As Shelby Steel puts it, "to be black was to be a victim; therefore not to be a victim was not to be a black."[13]

The experiences of black children growing up amid the standards of the larger, white society are conveyed through a number of images which are both grotesque and ordinary. Blue eyes, which are Pecola's unfulfilled dream, seem to stem from the background in surrealistic dominance: "Pecola Breedlove believes that exchanging her brown eyes for blue ones will make her beautiful and loved. The people who influence Pecola as she grows up are clearly the source for this harmful idea. As appearance approved by dominant white society, such people damage both themselves and others."[14] The tangible Shirley Temple doll, with which the girls play, has blue eyes. Furthermore, the little daughter of the employer of Pecola's mother has blue eyes. The image remains, in the same way like a painfully blinding light, an instrument of torture throughout the novel.

The Shirley Temple Cup and the Mary Jane candies allow Pecola to carry the image through her very being, to become one with it for short periods of time. However, she believes that seeking after and obtaining the bluest eyes, the most irreproachable feature in the world, will allow permanent union with those currently transitory features. Hating her black self, she yearns for blue eyes because she believes that will extinguish her position as pariah and give her love and security that are desperately missing from her life. Thus, Pecola sincerely believes that blue eyes are a panacea for all her ills:

> It had occurred to Pecola some time ago that if her eyes . . . were different . . . she herself would be different. . . . If she looked different, beautiful, maybe (her father) would be different, and (her mother) too. Maybe they'd say, why look at pretty-eyed Pecola. We must n't do bad things in front of those pretty eyes. (34)

The bluest eyes, thus become the metonymical representation of the myth. Having blue eyes means having everything—love, acceptance, friends, family—in short, a truly enviable place in the society.

The white baby dolls, so antithetical to negroid features are presented to little black girls like Claudia and, what is more, they are judged to be their most sought-after wish. Claudia muses: "Adults, older girls, shops, magazines, newspapers, window signs—all the world had agreed that a blue-eyed, yellow-haired, pink-skinned doll was what every girl treasured." (14) To the parents, dolls are unfulfilled longings of their own childhoods, and Mrs. MacTeer and other adults cannot understand Claudia's destroying of them. She tears them apart in an attempt to find the source of their loveliness and what makes the world treasure them.

To illustrate the depth of Pecola's motivation for the quest for blue eyes, Morrison uses several characters and incidents to depict the kind of world into which Pecola has been born and the effect of the myth upon her. We see how Pecola's own mother, Pauline, who is, in effect, a black mammy to the wealthy blonde girl doll who lives in a beautiful house, consciously and unconsciously passes on certain attitudes toward colour to her daughter. For instance, when Pecola comes, along with other black girls, to the kitchen of the white home where Pauline works to pick up wash, she drops a hot pan of blueberry pie and dirties the floor. Instead of comforting her daughter, who has been burnt, Pauline spits out words like "rotten pieces of apple" at the black girls and turns to hushing and soothing the tears of the little pink-and-yellow girl who is upset by the accident. Pecola is made to feel ugly and stupid beside the little white girl, who represents everything that is 'right.'

Pauline's dominant characteristic, however, is her overwhelming self-hatred, which precludes struggle of any kind. She is aware of the turning wheels of racial oppression in her life, but she makes no effort to stop the turning. Instead, she oils the axles and polishes the spokes so that the wheels turn more smoothly, more rapidly, and without interruption. She wears her maid's uniform with pride and bows low to the racist demands of the white Fisher family. She does not bemoan her lot in the house of whiteness and plenty. Rather, she smiles as she plays the role of surrogate mother for Fishers' young daughter, Polly. She struts as she surveys the results of her handiwork—an immaculate house filled with enticing aromas of home-made pies and other dishes the fishers enjoy. In her storefront house, irritating and melancholy in appearance, she is irredeemably ugly. In the Fisher home, she is beautiful and important, made so by the magic of service to white people.

We find resemblance between Pauline and the traditional image of the black mammy. The black mammy is a pervasive character in white American fiction. She appears as Disley in *The Sound and the Fury,* Calpurnia in Carson McCuller's *A Member of the Wedding,* Berenice in Harper Lee's *To Kill a Mockingbird*, and simply 'Mammy' in Margaret Mitchell's *Gone with the Wind.* Whatever her name, and whatever the artistic merit of the book that contains her, she is always "a dutiful black female servant, who attempts to keep white families from cutting their souls on the shattered pieces of their morally bankrupt lives, while able to place only a thin and soiled bandage on the open wounds of her own black family."[15]

## IV

The poignancy of Pecola's victimization emanates not only from the racism and resulting inter-racial conflicts, but also from the intraracial conflicts related to colour, firmly rooted in white racist myths. As damaging as the white criterion of beauty that denies Pecola a positive sense of self are the values of light-skinned Maureen Peal, whose sense of superiority is associated with her colour. Morrison's narrator is clear about how the Breedlove's appearance becomes problematic. It is not their ugliness, but their conviction of their ugliness that makes the difference.

Pecola experiences the greatest damage from intraracial prejudice, however, at the hands of her abusive, negligent parents. We are told that even her mother, Pauline, has decided at the time of Pecola's birth that she is an ugly child. To be sure, the onus of Pecola's negativity rests initially with her family's failure to provide socialization, identity, love and security that are essential for healthy growth and development. The emptiness of her parent's lives and their own negative self-images are particularly hurtful. Not only does their socio-economic status as poor blacks set them on the periphery of society, but their perception of themselves as ugly isolates them further, resulting in their self-hatred which is the most destructive element in their lives. Morrison's discourse, thus, strongly suggests that Pecola's alienation and sense of unworthiness emerge not solely from the 'others' definition but also from her own inability to transcend the resulting reification.

Morrison's condemnation of racism in *The Bluest Eye* is, thus, tempered by the recognition of the unnatural position of blacks in a racist society. At the end of the novel, Morrison does not suggest that the victim is to blame for all that happens, in every instance. She is, however, exploring a larger question of 'being' through the characters of this novel. In spite of the existence of "the other," what is important is each individual's willingness to take responsibility for his or her own life. Morrison does not suggest that external forces, such as racism and sexism, are unimportant. Neither the indictment of white society for its oppression of blacks nor the indictment of blacks for their treatment of women is her sole interest or focus. As W. Lawrence Trightly notes: "Morrison is concerned with the ontological structures and mythological thought systems that blacks develop to define and reinforce their definition of self and existence."[16]

## V

One should not, however, fail to note that Pecola suffers not only because of her race but also because of her gender. In other words,she suffers both as a black and a female. Just as blacks as a group are relegated to an underclass in America by virtue of their race, so are women relegated to a separate caste by virtue of their sex. "Just as white people have created and maintained a racist culture, so have men created and maintained a sexist culture."[17] The women fnd themselves in a double jeopardy of race and gender. As a racial being she is asked to relinquish her individual and cultural ways and follow white dictates and as a gender being she is socialized to subordinate her femininity and remain subsumed in the orbit of patriarchy. Morrison seems to move her examination of Pecola's life back and forth from the axis of race to that of gender.

Since black women find themselves in a double jeopardy of race and gender, any study on them must be related not only to their racial or colonial experience, but also to the experience arising out of their femininity. Having got to share oppression equally with both the groups, blacks and women, the black woman remains a victim of both racism and sexism. That is why Pecola in the novel experiences dependency, repression, internalization, alienation and all such neuroses not only as a racial being but as a woman as well. As a woman, she shares almost the same experiences and undergoes the same subjugation and marginalization which any other woman would experience under patriarchal imperialism.

Woman in a patriarchal society is the socially sanctioned 'other' and her psyche is the product of social constructs. As Simon de Beauvoir points out: "One is not born, but rather becomes woman. . . . It is civilization as a whole that produces this creature, intermediate between male and eunuch, which is described as feminine."[18] From the moment of birth, when the conventional first question is asked regarding the gender of the child, a female is constantly bombarded with social images, rewards, and punishments that are designed to ensure that she does not develop any quality associated with the other half of humanity. She must be "feminine" and restrict herself to a 'woman's place.' It is the patriarchal civilization that defines woman as a marginalized creature. Her definition and differentiation is always made in deference to man. A woman is never considered an autonomous self, but as just incidental, the inessential and an appendage to man.

In *The Bluest Eye*, black girlhood assumes tragic propensities when it borrows identity models from the mandates of white culture and from the malevolent parental mirrors as well. Like many other contemporary black women writers such as Maya Angelou, Gwendolyn Brooks and Paule Marshall, Morrison believes in the anxiety black girls and women feel about and what their mirrors tell them. For instance, Maud Martha, in Brooks' *Maud Martha*, is a woman who is aware of her own reality, and this is evident from what she understands of her husband's mind:

> . . . it's my color that makes him mad. I try to shut my eyes to that, but it's no good. What I am inside, what is really me, he likes okay. But he keeps looking at my color—which is like a wall. He has to jump over it in order to meet and touch what I've got for him. He has to jump away up high in order to see it. He gets awful tired of that jumping.[19]

Brooks has shown us a courageous, simple black woman who is able to make the best of her life, despite her race and sex.

Morrison too holds that girls growing up black and female in a white society often experience the malady of internalizing the belief that an aesthetically pleasing image is what constitutes the necessary precondition for receiving love and security. Clearly, sexism and racism are systems of societal and psychological restrictions that have critically affected the lives of African-American women. Since sex and race have been so interrelated in the history of America, it is not surprising that when black women published novels, they necessarily reflected that relationship.

From a feminist perspective, *The Bluest Eye* is a study of the various degrees of fulfilment women experience as women. Pauline is at one end of the spectrum. Other women characters are less obviously deprived, at least economically. Some are "comfortable" completely immersed in the motherhood and find peace in resignation to the limitations of their lives. Mrs. MacTeer, whose daughters befriend Pecola, is such a woman. She rears her family in rooms "peopled by roaches and mice" and open around windows and doors to the cold wind. She makes ends meet by taking in boarders and by "watching every possibility of excess." Like other women in the community, she dreads the "real terror of life," being put "outdoors," and "having no place to go." Claudia MacTeer explains the reality of her mother and other women in the community: "Being a minority in both caste and class we moved about . . . on the hem of life, struggling to consolidate our weakness and hang on, or to creep singly up into the major folds of the garment." (18)

The second group of women, whom Morrison calls the "sugar-brown mobile girls," lives in better neighbourhoods where everyone is employed and where there are fine houses with porch swings and sunflowers and pots of bleeding hearts. These women are poor imitations of what they believe whiteness to be. They have smooth hands and slim ankles. They wash with "orange-colored lifebuoy soap, dust themselves with Cashmere Bouquet and soften their skin with Jergen's Lotion." (68) Though they marry and have children, they find sex repulsive. At land-grant colleges and normal schools where they are educated, they learn "how to do the white man's work with refinement . . . how to instruct black children in obedience and how to develop thrift, patience, high morals, and good manners." (64) They are fake and frigid women who deny their blackness and their sexuality, who tried to get rid of the funkiness:

> The dreadful funkiness of passion, the funkiness of nature, the funkiness of the wide range of human emotions. Wherever it erupts, this Funk they wipe it away; where it crusts, they dissolve it; wherever it drips, flowers or clings, they find it and fight it until it dies. They fight this battle all the way to the grave. (64)

The third category of women Morrison depicts in the novel have no desire for prosperity or rootedness of any kind. These women are prostitutes, embittered and frigid in love-making because they choose to be.

And they choose to be prostitutes because they hated men, all men, without shame, apology, or discrimination. They abused their visitors with a scorn grown mechanical from use. Black men, white men, Puerto Racians, Mexicans, Jews, Poles, whatever—all were inadequate and weak, all came under their jaundiced eyes and were the recipients of their disinterested wrath. (43) Regardless of the category in which her women characters exist, they are removed from the possibility of self-knowledge, self-expression, and freedom.

VI

But, as Donald B. Gibson observes, "the novel has its class ramifications too."[20] Pecola suffers not only because she is a black and a female but also because she is poor. Pecola is poor and so too, may be slightly better off, is the MacTeer family which takes her in. The contrast between even the MacTeer house and the white house where Pauline works, is not just a contrast between blacks and whites but between poverty and affluence. Critics like Gloria Wade-Gayles see class "not as urgent as race and sex in black women's reality for class oppression cuts across racial and sexual lines, and is, therefore, not unique to black women."[21] Even if we do not see ethnicity as a mask behind which people conceal their class position both from each other and from themselves, even if we realize the importance of racial and ethnic values, we cannot ignore the class issue. No doubt, the African-American women writers—Frances Harper, Jessie Fauset, Nella Larsen, Zora Neale Hurston, Paule Marshall, Alice Walker, and Gloria Naylor—have dealt with it, but they and many of their critics lay more stress on race and gender than on class.

Although Morrison's class analysis is immature at this point, she is at least conscious of a limited role that economics plays in the exploitation of African people. It is Morrison's growing awareness of the inherent characteristics of capitalism that help her understand that racism is an integral part of the capitalist mode of production. There is ample evidence to prove that racism is a by-product of capitalism. However, to state that racism is the consequence of the European's quest for greater profits, is not to imply that racism has not ultimately become a concomitant reason for oppressing African people. In the words of Rodney, "oppression of African people on purely racial grounds accompanied, strengthened and became indistinguishable from oppression for economic reasons."[22]

Though Morrison has rightly understood the concept of beauty from an intellectual point of view, she could not understand that even this concept would change depending on the racial make up of the dominant class. Her misconception of class consciousness at this point in her writing career might be due to her lack of understanding of three important factors. First, the ruling class, whether of European, African or Asian descent, possesses the major instruments of economic production and distribution as well as the means of establishing its socio-cultural dominance. Second, possessing such means, the ruling class uses and promotes its own image as a measurement of beauty for the entire society. Third, the success of this promotion ensures the continual dominance of the ruling class. This is amply endorsed when Nkrumah says: "Race is inextricably linked with class exploitation; in a racist-capitalist power structure, capitalist exploitation and race oppression are complementary, the removal of one ensures/the removal of the other."[23]

## VII

Thus, Pecola Breedlove in the novel is oppressed not only racially, but also sexually and on the basis of class distinction. Associated with her condition is funk, violence, ugliness and poverty, symbolized by her storefront house. The mother's own internalization of the desirable woman as beautiful, well-taken-care-of and cuddled, results in Pauline's rejection of her own daughter, Pecola, who cannot possibly obtain such a standard not only because of her blackness but also because of her poverty. Nevertheless, Morrison's focus is on racism inasmuch as she considers, at the initial stage of her career, racism the primary obstacle of the Africans in America.

To conclude, a close study of *The Bluest Eye* from the viewpoint of the interaction of race, gender, and class reveals Morrison's low level of gender and class consciousness at the beginning of her literary career. Initially she thinks that racism is the only form of oppression of Africans in the white-dominated society. Though classism and sexism, the other primary causes of oppression, are also treated in the novel, they are overshadowed by Morrison's emphasis on racism.

# NOTES

1. W.E.B. DuBois, *The Souls of Black Folk* (New York: Avon Books, 1965), 14

2. Toni Morrison, "Behind the Making of *The Black Book*," *Black World*, 23 (1974), 89.
3. Elizabeth Janeway, ***Women's Literature***, in Hoffman (1979), 383.
4. Mabalia Doreatha Drummond, *Toni Morrison's Developing Class Consciousness* (Selinsgrove: Susquehanna University Press, 1991), 28.
5. Joel Kovel, *White Racism*: *A Psychohistory* (New York: Columbia University Press, 1984), 232.
6. Raymond Hedin, "The Structuring of Emotion in Black American Fiction," *Novel*: *A Forum on Fiction*, 16, 1 (1982), 49-50.
7. Toni Morrison, "Behind the Making of *The Black Book*," 89.
8. Toni Morrison, *The Bluest Eye* (London: Pan, 1970), 1.
9. Klotman Phyllis, "Dick and Jane and Shirley Temple Sensibility in *The Bluest Eye*," *Black American Literature Forum*, 13 (1979), 124.
10. Jacqueline de Weerer, "The Inverted World of Toni Morrison's *The Bluest Eye* and *Sula*," *CLA Journal*, 22 (1979), 21.
11. Denise Heinze, *The Dilemma of "Double-Consciousness"*: *Toni Morrison's Novels* (Athens and London: The University of Georgia Press, 1993), 74.
12. Cynthia Davis, "Self, Society and Myth in Toni Morrison's Fiction," *Contemporary Literature,* 23, 3 (1982), 330.
13. Steel Shelby, "Black Consciousness in Perspective," *The American Review*, 33, 1 (1989), 58.
14. Elizabeth B. House, "Artists and the Art of Living: Order and Disorder in Toni Morrison's Fiction," *Modern Fiction Studies*, 34, 1 (1988), 29.
15. Denise Heinze, *The Dilemma of "Double-Consciousness*," 72.
16. Hogue Lawrence, *Discourse and the Other* (Durham: Duke University Press, 1986), 133.
17. Calvin C. Hernton, *The Sexual Mountain and Black Women Writers* (New York: Anchor, 1987), 10.
18. Simon de Beauvoir, *The Second Sex* (London: Picador, 1988), 16
19. Brooks Gwendolyn, *Maud Martha* (New York: Harper, 1953), 87-88.
20. Gibson B. Donald, "The Text and Countertext in Toni Morrison's *The Bluest Eye*," *Literature and Interpretation Theory*, 1-2 (U.S.A: Gordon and Breach Science Publishers), 171.
21. Gloria Wade-Gayles, *No Crystal Stair*: *Visions of Race and Sex in Black Women's Fiction* (New York: The Pilgrim Press, 1984), 7.
22. Walter Rodney, *How Europe Underdeveloped Africa* (Dar es Salaam: Tanzania Publishing House, 1972 ), 100.
23. Kwame Nkrumah, *Class Struggle in Africa* (New York: International Publishers, 1970 ), 27.

**CHAPTER III**

# Gender in Relation to Race and Class: *Sula*

Man for the field and woman for the hearth;
Man for the sword and for the needle she;
Man with the head, and woman with the heart;
Man to command, and woman to obey;
All else is confusion.

Alfred Tennyson, "The Princess"

Man can think of himself without woman. She cannot think of herself without man. . . . She is defined and differentiated with reference to man and not he with reference to her; she is the incidental. . . . He is the subject, he is the Absolute—she is the 'other'.

Simon de Beauvoir, *The Second Sex*

When one endeavours to understand racism in America, one comes across the indispensability of the sexuality of American racism. Calvin Hernton, in his book, *Sexism and Racism in America* (1965), remarks: "The sexualization of racism in the United States is a unique phenomenon in the history of mankind, it is anomaly of the first order. In fact, there is a sexual involvement, at once real and vicarious, connecting white and black people in America that spans the history of the country from the era of slavery to the present, an involvement, so immaculate and yet so perverse, so ethereal and yet so concrete that all race relations tend to be, however subtle, sex relations."[1]

Toni Morrison seems to have realized this awful truth by the time she comes to write her second novel, *Sula* (1973). The major predicament that Morrison considers in this novel is, therefore, two-fold—the effect of racism upon black identity formation, and the effect of racism and sexism upon the identity formation of the black female. In an interview conducted by Colette Dowling, Morrison states that "blacks, if they are to succeed in American society, must leave their native communities, and in so doing, cut themselves off from their old lives."[2] This amounts to double isolation, since the doors to the white American mainstream generally remain closed to blacks.

In *Sula* Morrison captures most profoundly the way concepts of good and evil are related to societal definitions of woman. For the Bottom, a Black community located in the hills above the fictional town of Medallion, Ohio, that definition has much to do with the status of black people within the larger society, which ironically is the basis for the adventure and rebellion that Sula represents. What is equally important is that the Bottom characterizes all its women as a class, though not in terms of dependent beautiful ornaments. Because of this black community's vulnerability, the distinguishing characteristic of the class of woman, is that she insures the continuity of the community by bearing children and by supporting the beleaguered men either sexually, emotionally or financially.

In these, as well as other particulars, Sula opens up new literary and critical options, not only for the study of texts by African-American women, but for African-American literary study more generally. The novel certainly helps to set a new agenda for black women's social and narrative possibilities. Coming significantly on the heels of the Black Power Movement that rendered black women prone or the 'queens' of the male warrior, the narrative invites the reader to imagine a different script for women that transcends the boundaries of social and linguistic conventions. Further, it offers a useful model of self, of identity and identification in the reading process, a model that springs the traditional African-American critic from the rhetoric of opposition that has kept the discourse in arrest:

> Day and night are mingled in our gazes. . . . If we divide light from night, we give up the lightness of our mixture. . . . We put ourselves into watertight compartments, break ourselves up into parts, cut ourselves in two. . . . We are always one and the other, at the same time.[3]

To posit that "we are always one and the other at the same time" is to challenge effectively a fundamental assumption of Western metaphysics that has operated historically in African-American literature and criticism. In *Sula* Morrison complicates and questions that assumption, evoking the very oppositions on which it has tended to rest. What is more, she transgresses the boundaries separating black women from others, and rendering them, others to themselves.

Naturally, Morrison's focus in *Sula* is on gender. The concept of gender with its relation to race and class forms an integral part of the novel. The concerns of class, whether of the capitalists or the masses, rank third after gender and race. The issue of class is only incidental, the thrust being on sexism. This switch in thematic emphasis suggests that Morrison sees the lack of individual rights as the primary cause of the oppression of Africans.

Despite its periodic inclusion of racial concerns and its incidental incorporation of class-related issues, the novel begins and ends with an exposition of individual rather than group fulfilment. Sula, the protagonist of the novel, suffers not only at the hands of whites but also at the hands of blacks. That is why she rejects the traditional role ascribed to women in society. Here Morrison is interested in the struggle for individual rights, in general, and woman's rights in particular, rather than in the rights of African people as a collective.

Thus in *Sula*, Morrison's focus shifts to the black woman as an individual, struggling towards freedom and selfhood, as in Alice Walker's *Meridian*. Though their literary visions are shaped by different perspectives, Morrison and Walker speak a similar truth out of their "collective consciousness" and create women who are "spiritual sisters." Sula and Meridian are "spiritual sisters," though superficially no two women could be more different. Meridian is a young, pure, saintly woman of the South who has functioned in the roles of wife and mother. Sula, on the other hand, is a defiant woman of the Midwest who has been neither wife nor mother. What, however, they have in common is "intense desire to give birth to themselves as persons."[5] Their individual quests for selfhood are precipitated by different personal needs and reflect different attitudes toward the human condition. The stages of their journeys towards selfhood are decidedly different. But "the goals of their quests are the same—a cleaner understanding of self, and expanded room in which to hum their own melodies and sing their own lyrics."[6] Theirs is a formidable struggle, for they live in societies which censure individual expression especially for women. All the same, they flourish and evolve into a prototype for psychic wholeness and individual autonomy.

*Sula* is fundamentally a woman's novel in the sense that it concerns itself with the feeling and affairs of women and the roles they assume, whether by choice or force. It chronicles the fortunes of women in two matriarchal households within the black community whose lives represent the range of choices possible for black women in white America. Even though a good deal of the action of the novel derives from the consequences of male and female relationships, it is the self-perception of woman and her subsequent reactions to self-concept that are central to it. The male characters undergo no development, play no major roles, and they are important only because of the reactions they might prompt or provoke from the females. For the most part of the men are "superficial, immature, untrustworthy, and anonymous, as is suggested by their names—Jude (Judas), Green (naive), Boy-Boy (infantile), Chicken Little (fearful and diminutive), the Deweys (anonymous)."[7] The negative aspects of their names are most visible when juxtaposed with the empowering names of the women. The men's behaviour, including Ajax's, is less than heroic. Each man leaves a community of abandoned women. This abandoment becomes the impetus for Eva, the paradigmatic woman who rebounds through assertiveness and self-reliance after she and her children are deserted by her husband.

The oppression of African women in the United States, especially in the first quarter of the twentieth century, is documented throughout the novel. The manner in which Morrison chooses to explore the nature of the woman's oppression is unique. She creates two female characters—Nel and Sula—neither of whom is complete in herself. The idea that Nel and Sula represent two halves of one person reverberates throughout the novel. When Sula returns to Bottom, Nel thinks that her friend's return is like 'getting an eye back' and that talking to Sula has always been 'a conversation with herself.' Significant too is the authorial comment: "their friendship was so close, they themselves had difficulty distinguishing one's thoughts from the other's."[8] Nel and Sula, then, are separate facets or faces of one being. Morrison suggests that to attain an ideal and holistic personality, "the part embodied in Sula has to be wedded to the safe, conventional part represented by Nel."[9]

For Nel and Sula the problem of one's loss of identity is a direct result of the Bottom's limiting definition of women as subservient, self-sacrificing beings. Nel assumes the traditional role the community prescribes, and retains her social identity, though her personal identity is non-existent. Sula, by contrast, is a free-spirited woman whose determination to define herself places her at odds with the culturally rich black community. Hers is the psychological dilemma out of touch with the historic Black past. In their quests for wholeness both women find their world rife with contradictions and tensions. As M.L. Montgomery observes, Nel and Sula " experience a profound sense of alienation in a patriarchal world which evolves no terms for their existence."[10]

Morrison's most articulate statement regarding the degradation of the female comes in a passage that appears after the first meeting of Nel and Sula: "Because each had discovered years before they were neither white nor male, and that all freedom and triumph was forbidden to them, they had set about creating something else to be." (52) Within this statement are found both the dilemma of the novel and its solution. African women are oppressed and, to escape their oppression, they must become self-propagators. Accordingly, Sula rejects the traditional role ascribed to women. However, since her oppression as a woman is the result of an oppressive economic system, not men, Sula finds it impossible to escape all the traditionalisms associated with women.

II

As a contemporary novel about female friendship, Sula "offers a view of female psychological development that defies traditional male-centered interpretations of female development and calls out for an expansion of the woman-centered paradigm."[11] It is a deep study of friendship between the two black girls—Nel and Sula—growing into womanhood that serves as the periscope through which the tremendous contradictions of life are viewed. Their broken lives speak of the depth of their agony which is the result of the loss of identity at the cultural, gender, and racial planes: "Their broken friendship is a measure of their broken lives, lives that are cramped from the very start. As counterpoints, all the other women in this book (*Sula*) must either fit themselves into the place life has set for them or defy it with tragic circumstances proportionate to their degree of non-accommodation."[12] Nel and Sula seek solace in each other's company because they share the common bond of being young, black and female in a world that is commonly geared to meet the designs of mature, white males. From drastically different social backgrounds, Nel and Sula are bound by factors much stronger than those which might tend to separate them.

Sula develops her intense friendship with Nel at the age of twelve. Each girl receives from the other security, love and identity blatantly denied to them in their homes. Barbara Smith writes that the friendship between Nel and Sula is an example of "the necessary bonding that has always taken place between Black women for the barest survival. Together the two girls can find the courage to create themselves."[13] Together Sula and Nel enter puberty, together they discover boys and together they become aware of their own sexuality.

The intense friendship between Nel and Sula invariably reminds us of a similar kinship between Rosalind and Celia in Shakespeare's *As You Like It.* Though Rosalind and Celia are cousins, they are more like bosom friends so closely attached to each other. The attachment between them is driven home to us when the banishment of Rosalind as a traitor by Federick provokes Celia to protest against it saying: "If she be a traitor, why, so am I; We still have slept together, Rose at an instant, learn'd, play'd, eat together; And wheresoe'er we went, like Juno's swans, Still we want coupled and inseparable." (I, iii, 68-72 ) Naturally, Nel recognizes Sula as her alter ego. In the words of Naana Banyiwa-Horne, "Sula is to Nel as Mr. Hyde is to Dr. Jekyll in Robet Louis Stevenson's classic novella, *Dr. Jekyll and Mr. Hyde*."[14]

Nel and Sula represent the two sides of the coin that stands for the total human personality. Both of them are Morrison's favourite characters since they are symbolic of the good and the evil persistently present in the society. Morrison says: "Yet she [Sula] and Nel are very much alike. They compliment each other. They support each other. I suppose the two of them together could have made a wonderful single human being. They are like a Janus' head."[15] The height of intimacy and friendship between Sula and Nel makes explicit what can be called their interesting life-long bond:

> Their friendship was as intense as it was sudden. They found relief in each other's personality. Although both were unshaped, formless things, Nel seemed stronger and more consistent than Sula, who could hardly be counted on to sustain any emotion for more than three minutes. (53)

In both Sula and Nel there is a quest for social and gender identity to which bonds created between them bear testimony and relevance. Morrison describes how Sula "had clung to Nel as the closest thing to both an other and a self, only to discover that she and Nel were not only one and the same thing." (55) Nel and Sula are drawn towards each other out of their awareness that their lives, as black females, are restricted by their community and by the outer society.

Although Nel and Sula share these strong bonds, they are different from each other in several respects. Sula is emotional and adventurous and Nel is cautious and consistent. Whereas Nel becomes a slave to sexism and racism, Sula becomes a liberated woman. The standard of womanhood that Nel represents is not the pure image of the ideal southern lady, but one based on the status of working-class black men in the society. This role is seen by Nel's community as good, while Sula is seen as evil. For, Sula not only refuses the role, but steps outside the caste of woman, beyond any class definition within that caste, when she insists on making herself. She is interested neither in being beautiful nor becoming a mother. She keeps herself outside the sex, race, and class definitions of the society. Her becoming a pariah in her own community has much to do with her resistance to any clearly recognizable definition of a woman that the Bottom can tolerate.

Not only Nel and Sula but also their families contrast with each other. Nel's tense mother, Helene, barricades herself against racial humiliation. She rubs away all Nel's spontaneity negating her quest for identity. Conversely, Sula's mother, Hannah, is hardly aware of her only daughter's need for emotional nurturance. Nel's mother, who is class-conscious and precise about her manners, manipulates and turns her into an obedient daughter. Sula and Nel are, thus, isolated from their own mothers.

The relationship of Nel and Sula with men seems no stronger than their relationships with their families. Nel marries Jude out of sheer pity for his plight, but when she loses her husband to Sula's careless seduction, she knows that she will have no other men. As a grand daughter of a woman abandoned by her husband and a daughter of a woman exploited by men, Sula contemptuously uses black men and white men until she is deserted by the man she loves. Nel and Sula live in a world in which women must survive without men.

Nel and Sula also radically differ from each other in their attitudes to society. Whereas Nel listlessly observes the conventions of the society, Sula flouts them. She breaks all the rules that reflect the community's traditional values and becomes a pariah living outside the laws and mores of the community. She remains a social outsider as she defies the role she is supposed to play in society. Freeing herself from the narrow confines of traditional woman, she rebels against the set norms for woman's behaviour in the black community. She defies the traditional gender system that restricts female autonomy. What is more, by appropriating male prerogatives, she, in effect, abandons her sex and becomes a monstrous perversion of the passive nature that has been socially constructed for women. She summarily rejects the advice of settling down and having babies saying: "I don't want to make somebody else. I want to make myself." (92)

This rebellious spirit of Sula alienates her from her only friend, Nel. When the final, terrible test of Nel's friendship with Sula comes, she turns her back on love and affirmation and finds refuge, in that hardness and in isolation. Nel enjoys domestic bliss with Jude until Sula returns to destroy it. When Sula learns the pleasures of companionship, Ajax deserts her. Thus "both women are alone at the end—Nel in life and Sula in death—contemplating the futility of their search for wholeness in monogamy and domesticity."[16]

## III

Sula is an acutely sensitive, enigmatic, and defiant woman whose nonconformity is a "living criticism . . . of the dreadful lives of resignation other women live."[17] She is "the modern preternaturally sensitive but rudely thwarted black girl in today's society."[18] As a young girl she so startles the community with her extreme emotional impulses that her growth into a "strange, strong and independent woman" is all but predictable. She rejects "behavioral standards of all kinds" and attempts to "rely solely on herself." It is to herself, and only to herself that Sula wishes to be good. She is firmly of the view that "being good to somebody is just like being mean to somebody. Risky. You don't get nothing for it." (35) Thus, unlike Pecola, Sula lives out her own fantasies, creates her own realities, and sets her own personal objectives. In short, she is motivated by a firm sense of "Me-ness."

Sula openly challenges the limitations imposed on her individuality and, much to the consternation of the community, vengefully disregards time-honoured conventions and traditions. She categorically rejects the standards 'others' use to measure her life. The profundity of Sula's defiance is a reflection of the sharp contrast between who she is and what the Bottom decrees for its women. Thus, "Sula is a pariah whose values are often the polar opposites of those adopted by her provincial society. She becomes a pariah precisely because she rejects those values that aim at uniformity and stifle the self."[19] Her willingness to reject them "makes her evil" to those in the community who never express their own "freedom of the will." Sula is "evil" because she, unlike Nel does not live "totally by the law" nor surrender "completely to it without questioning anything sometimes" and is "perfectly willing to think the unthinkable."[20]

Sula's rebelliousness manifests itself in several ways. Unlike other Medallion women, she refuses to marry, settle down, and raise a family. She, moreover, attends their church functions underwearless. She feels no obligation to please any one. As she confesses to Nel: "I got my mind. And what goes on in it." (43) Her determination to achieve self-fulfilment allows her "to live in the world," (43) but not be caught up in the spiderweb-like life of the Bottom where she would be called upon to confirm, to "dangle in dry places suspended by (her) own spittle more terrified of the free fall than the snake's breath below." (103-4)

Though Morrison succeeds brilliantly in her treatment of Sula's rebelliousness, she is less convincing in her depiction of the impact that racism and sexism together have on Sula's defiance. She writes of Sula's discovery that being neither white nor male means denial of 'freedom and triumph.' But, a careful reading of the novel reveals that Morrison's emphasis is on sexual restrictions. It is sexism that counts most in Morrison's portrait of Sula.

To illustrate the point, when Sula speaks despairingly of black women's self-denial, she means their willing submission to black men. When she chafes at the notion of 'full surrender,' she means sexual surrender. When she demonstrates the 'self' she has created, she does so in a black environment in relationship with black men and black women. And when she reneges on her promise to create 'something else to be,' she does so in surrender to a black man. This surrender is the most conclusive argument against Barbara Smith's thesis of latent lesbianism. The sexist approach to women confers upon men the obligation to protect women because they are frail or to pamper them because they are like children in their inability to plan their own lives. In an interview Morrison explains that "the very thing that would attract a man to a woman in the first place might be the one thing she would give over once she falls in love."[21] In Sula's case, she gives up her independence, her toughness, and her wholeness to become Ajax's woman. Not realizing the dialectical relationships between the collective and individual interests, Sula ultimately betrays and alienates family, friends, and neighbours, thereby causing her own death.

Sula, thus represents unrestricted and multiple perspectives in the novel. Morrison endows her with a birthmark, startlingly appearing on the eyelid, that calls attention to Sula's original powers of perception. Sula, indeed, rejects traditional ordering principles as they relate to self and society. She rejects traditional notions of family, eschewing marriage, babies, and grandparental care. She rejects traditional sexual mores as well, ignoring the 'ownership' principle of marriage and operating on the principle that sex is non-competitive and non-threatening. Thus, her entire life represents a rejection of traditional notions of feminine 'responsibility.' Sula refuses to see women as only wives and mothers.

Though *Sula* thus breathes a new life into traditional Black stereotypes, Morrison is said to have fallen a victim to traditional stereotypes in her treatment of Sula and the blacks of the Bottom. Critics like Addison Gayle see her characters as "primitives"[22] Odette Martin associates Morrison's images such as Eva as "the folk woman," Hannah as the "primitive," Sabat as the "tragic mulatto" and Sula as the "exotic," with the romanticism of a Negritude tradition which Morrison herself tends to criticize. Martin says how it is "difficult to perceive that repeating images, even for critical purposes, is to provide them with certain legitimacy."[23] But, what these critics seem to have failed to understand is that Morrison is more interested in showing "the constriction and ultimate futility of any single ordering vision within the black community"[24] than in treating traditional stereotypes.

Morrison ultimately offers few answers to her carefully posed conflict between the new and old represented by Sula and Nel respectively. Here the figure of the circle, a frequently used image in the novel, becomes suggestive. Sula swings Chicken Little in circles before letting him fly to make circular ripples in the river. Hannah similarly makes elated circles in her cooking water before going to her death, and in the final line of the novel, Morrison leaves us with the ambivalence of circles: Nel's "was a fine cry—loud and long—but it had no bottom and it had no top, just circles and circles of sorrow." (174) Morrison, in Sula, thus "carefully refrains from offering a synthesis of her dialectic between the new and the old. She settles instead for a clear presentation of the limitations of both the traditional and the 'new' perspectual modes."[25] As we circle around the dialectical poles presented in Sula, Morrison suggests that the final synthesis is yet to be made.

IV

It is, however, to be noted that if the African people's struggle for individual freedom is the primary focus of *Sula*, their racial struggle for national freedom is a secondary focus. Morrison is concerned with issues of national importance that affect blacks as Americans, and with those of local importance that pertain to them as blacks. The culture in which the black man lives is American, but his status as a black prevents his full participation in white American culture. Racial issues are interwoven into the fabric of the novel throughout. The origin of the Bottom with its roots in Slavery and the lack of development of the Deweys are classic instances of racism. Each of the Deweys has physical characteristics completely distinct from others. Yet they appear to look alike, reminding the reader of the stereotype—'all niggers look alike.' And they never grow, suggesting that living in a racist society thwarts the natural development of African people.

The Bottom, situated high upon the hills, is ironically designated. Metaphysically, the Bottom is black America, whose ironic genesis is revealing of white society's failed promises. The naming of the Bottom denotes White man's lack of sympathy and concern for the survival of blacks. The white farmer's promise of a piece of land to the black man on the top of the hills for executing a difficult task becomes a 'nigger joke' as "the nigger got the hilly land, where planting was back-breaking, where the soil slid down and washed away the seeds and where the wind lingered all through the winter." (5) With its curious origin as a "nigger joke," the Bottom presents a version of reality that closely resembles a cyclic repetition of the historical injustices perpetrated upon blacks. The Bottom bears witness to the sociological, psychological and economic plight of the blacks in Medallion. It strikes a parallel to "the lower depths described by Maxim Gorky when discussing the poor and oppressed classes in the nineteenth century Russian society."[26]

Morrison proposes, however, that it is the pressures and false values forced upon blacks by white society that hamper the stability of the black family in general and woman in particular. She depicts in the novel the manner in which marriage, for instance, is regarded by male and female alike under the influence of white culture. Regardless of social or economic standing, all the residents of the Bottom share the common belief that a woman alone is an incomplete being and that she can find respectability and fulfilment only in the role of some man's mate. Tragically, the same women, who are the victims of this system help to perpetuate the system. For example, marriage for Nel constitutes embracing the very same repressive values that have left her bereft of imagination and a distinct sense of self. Because of her upbringing, Nel does not and cannot see anything singular about herself. She recognizes her individuality only when it is mirrored through someone other than herself. By marrying Jude, she dissolves the bond of interdependence she shares with Sula, only to substitute her husband in the place of her friend.

Morrison's characters discover that they escape the black community's socio-economic disorder only to face, later, the all-encompassing psychological chaos characteristic of life in a society polarized along racial lines. Constant racism forms a continuity in the cycle of frustration from which the townfolk cannot easily escape. The hostile environment that surrounds the blacks makes them 'helpless scapegoats of subservient acceptance of everything white.' *Sula*, thus, signifies the horrid inevitability of black culture facing cruel distortion against the backdrop of white man's oppression.

## V

In *Sula,* the issue of class, as has already been pointed out, is only incidental, playing third fiddle to sex and race. The few references to class that are present are made in connection with Helene Wright, who is said to be "the epitome of ideal womanhood."[27] Dignified, graceful, beautiful, religious and well-heeled, she has successfully assimilated white values, but only after being whisked from her mother who is clearly a subversive to the bourgeoisie and counselled "to be constantly on guard for any sign of her mother's wild blood." (20) Her success, however, is illusory. Despite her trappings of a lady, she finds that in going to her grandmother's funeral she is subhuman in the eyes of white society. When the train conductor humiliates her, she does not rebel but "smile(s) dazzlingly and coquettishly at the salmon-colored face of the conductor." (21) By this action Helene insures her own oppression and degradation.

However, like some sections of the novel about capitalism in *The Bluest Eye*, the passages relating to Helene's class interests are relatively insignificant in comparison to those on sex and race. Yet, they at least show that Morrison is aware of the role class-interests play in the lives of African people. In emphasizing to the community that her name is Helene rather than Helen, in severing her roots with her family, in stifling the imagination of her daughter, in making Nel pull her broad African nose in an effort to make it aquiline, in joining the most conservative church in Medallion, and, above all, in disassociating herself from the African masses and aligning herself with the white racist train conductor, Helene Wright exposes her class interests—wealth and status.

In accordance with the principles of dialectics, the consequences of Sula's thoughtless, often cruel, acts against her people, have both negative and positive effects. Although these acts anger and frighten the community, her people see in Sula someone against whom they can unite. But, at the same time, the community wrongly perceives Sula as the enemy. As Barbara Christian states: "Rather than focusing its attention on the pervasive evils of racism and poverty that continually threaten it, the community expends its energy on outlasting the evil, Sula."[28] The enemy is the capitalist society, not Sula, not men, not the Bottom community which "collapses under the weight of economic need and the encroachment of an ever-greedy white world."[29] Thus, with Sula, as with *The Bluest Eye*, gender, race, and class oppression are explored, the focus being on sexism.

## VI

To conclude, *Sula* picks up where *The Bluest Eye* ends. It reflects the evolutionary process that is the trademark of Morrison's canon. Of particular interest is Morrison's change in thematic emphasis from her first novel to her second. Whereas the emphasis is on racism in the first novel, it is on sexism in the second. Sula searches for self-identity, not group identity, a change that mirrors the developmental stages of the consciousness of the African masses. Hers is not a responsible individualism, but a "socially disintegrative version of individualism, that possessive individualism or sanctified rapacity which is extolled by capitalist societies."[30] This selfish quest for individual fulfilment only leads some Africans to see themselves in isolation from the community that has shaped, protected and nurtured them.

Although, at times, Morrison seems to doubt her own solution to the African female's exploitation, she ultimately avows that the African woman can obtain freedom from oppression by taking to an 'art form.' Morrison queries:

> Had she paints, or clays, or knew the discipline of dance or strings; had she anything to engage her tremendous curiosity and her gift for metaphor, she might have exchanged the restlessness and preoccupation with whim for an activity that provided her with all she yearned for. And like any artist with no art form, she became dangerous. (121)

Unfortunately, this solution does not take into account the roles of race oppression and class exploitation. It is an idealistic solution that reflects Morrison's own idealism, her own immature analysis of the role of capitalism. She does not seem to realize, at the moment, that individual fulfilment is dialectically related to group fulfilment and that the former is conditioned by the latter. As Sekou Toure observes: "The individual free will, freedom of action and thought and the full enjoyment of his/her personality should be led by a social consciousness which takes into consideration other people and society in absolute respect of common values, interests and duty."[31]

Thus, Morrison's weak class analysis, at the time she writes *Sula*, seems to have forced her to create a female character, who, because of gender oppression, makes individualism supreme over the collective, rather than a female character who struggles to change the oppressive nature of society in order to ensure the full development of each individual whether male or female. To put it in the words of Karen Stein, in *Sula* "the truest heroism lies not in external battle, as in the wars which destroy the novel's men, but in confrontation with the self."[32] Morrison's weak class analysis seems to have precluded her understanding of the symbiosis that exists between the individual and the group. Sula struggles to carve out a niche for herself as a woman, unmindful of the fact that the free development of each is conditioned by the free development of all. In other words, individuality is rewarding only if it is achieved within the context of the community well-being. This motif takes us to the world of *Song of Solomon*, Morrison's next novel, where she seems fully conscious of the relationship between the individual African and his community.

# NOTES

1. Calvin Hernton, *Sexism and Racism in America* (New York: Grove Press, 1965), 7.
2. Colette Dowling, "The Song of Toni Morrison," *New York Times Magazine* (20 May 1979), 58.
3. Luce Irigaray, *This Sex which is Not One* (Ithaca: Cornell University Press, 1985), 79.
4. Arunima Ray, "The Quest for "Home" and "Wholeness" in Sula and Meridian Afro-American identity in Toni Morrison and Alice Walker," *Indian Journal of American Studies,* 23, 2 (Summer 1993), 61.
5. *Ibid.*, 61.
6. *Ibid.*, 64.
7. Wilfred D. Samuels and Clenora Hudson-Weems, *Toni Morrison* (Boston: Twayne, 1990), 46.
8. Toni Morrison, *Sula* (London: Pan, 1973), 83.
9. Naana Banyiwa-Horne, "The Scary Face of the Self: An Analysis of the Character of Sula in Toni Morrison's *Sula*," *SAGE,* 2,1 (Spring 1985), 28.
10. Maxine Lavon Montgomery, "A Pilgrimage to the Origins: The Apocalypse as Structure and Theme in Toni Morrison's *Sula*," *Black American Literature Forum*, 23, 1 (Spring 1989), 132.
11. Diane Gillespie and Missy Dehn Kubitschek, "Women-centered Psychology in *Sula.*"
12. Barbara Christian, *Black Feminist Criticism: Perspectives on Black Women Writers* (New York: Pergamon Press, 1985), 27-28.
13. Barbara Smith, "Toward a Black Feminist Criticism," *All the Women are White, All the Blacks are Men But Some of us are Brave: Black Women Studies* (New York: Feminist Press, 1982), 168.
14. Naana Banyiwa-Horne, "The Scary Face of the Self: An Analysis of the Character of Sula in Toni Morrison's *Sula*," *SAGE*, 30.
15. Betty Parker, "Complexity, Toni Morrison's Women—An Interview Essay," *Study Black Bridges:Visions of Black Women in Literature* (Garden City: Doubleday, 1979), 253.
16. Denise Henize, *The Dilemma of "Double-Consciousness": Toni Morrison's Novels* (Athens and London: The University of Georgia Press, 1993), 82.
17. Barbara Smith, "Toward a Black Feminist Criticism," 168.
18. Joan Bischoff, "The Novels of Toni Morrison, Studies in Thwarted Sensitivity," *Studies in Black Literature,* 21.
19. Naana Banyiwa-Horne, "The Scary Face of the Self," *SAGE*, 31.
20. Robert Stepto, "Intimate Things in Place: A Conversation with Toni Morrison," *Chants of Saints* (Urbana: University of Illinois Press, 1979), 216-17.

21. Eric Bently, *The Life of Drama*.
22. Addison Gayle, "Blueprint for Black Criticism," *First World,* 1 (1977), 44.
23. Martin, "Sula," 36.
24. Grace Ann Hovet and Barbara Louns Berry, "Principles of Perception in Toni Morrison's *Sula," Black American Literature Forum,* 13 (1979), 126.
25. *Ibid.*, 129.
26. Bessie Jones, "Psychological Dis-Orientation in *Sula*," *The World of Toni Morrison* (Iowa: Kendall Press, 1983), 50.
27. Denise Heinze, *The Dilemma of "Double-Consciousness*," 80.
28. Barbara Christian, "Community and Nature: The Novels of Toni Morrison," *The Journal of Ethnic Studies,* 7 (1980), 67.
29. Denise Heinze, *The Dilemma of "Double-Consciousness,"* 81.
30. Gloria Wade-Gayles, *No Crystal Stair: Visions of Race and Sex in Black Women's Fiction* (New York: The Pilgrim Press, 1984), 1978.
31. Sekou Toure, "Africa on Walk: Revolution and Religion," International Ideological Symposium, Conakry, Guinea, November 13-16, 1978.
32. Karen F. Stein, "Toni Morrison's *Sula*: A Black Woman's Epic," *Black American Literature Forum* (Winter 1984), 149.

CHAPTER IV

# Class in Relation to Race and Gender: *Song of Solomon*

> Every summer my grandmother would have visitors come to our house. They would be older women of the family, her nieces, aunts and cousins, and every single evening . . . they would sit on the front porch in rocking chairs, and I would sit behind my grandmother's rocking chair and listen to them talking. They would tell about things that happened to the family . . . they went back and back and back.
>
> Alex Haley

> I had gone from being ignorant of being ignorant to being aware of being aware. And the worst part of my awareness was that I didn't know what I was aware of.
>
> Maya Angelou

After considering the dilemmas presented and the solutions posed in *The Bluest Eye* and *Sula*, Morrison seems to have become more aware of the dialectical relationship between capitalism, racism and sexism in her third novel, *Song of Solomon* (1977). She, therefore, subordinates sexism to both racism and capitalism, realising that the exploitation of the African woman by the African man is the result of his national and class oppression. Sexism is correctly viewed as the consequence of the African's lack of race and class consciousness.

As a result, class in relation to race and gender becomes more focal in *Song of Solomon*. The focus is not primarily on the concept of woman, as in *Sula*, for its protagonist is a man bearing a peculiar, but highly symbolic name—Milkman Dead. Though Milkman's quest for his identity is the dominant strand in the novel, the major obstacle he must overcome is the deadening effects of his father's need to own as much property as possible in order to protect himself against racism. This inordinate craze for ownership manifests itself in its worst forms, but is countered throughout the novel by the non-appropriative view of life, most often represented by the women. As Denise Heinze, a recent critic, says, in *Song of Solomon* "blacks are affected by a double-consciousness of racial values and gender."[1]

Written just after the publication of Alex Haley's *Roots, Song of Solomon* illustrates the importance of Africans' awareness and acceptance of their history, for without knowing where they have been, Africans do not know where they are going. Also, brought out after she had edited Chinweizu's *The West and the Rest of Us*, a work that condemns these petty bourgeois Africans who settle for individual handouts from their oppressors while the rest of their people wallow in poverty, *Song of Solomon* emphasizes that knowledge, acceptance, and commitment are needed to help liberate an oppressed people.

Thus, *Song of Solomon* provides an interesting instance of the manner in which equations of power and the levels of class, gender and race operate in a literary work. A character in Christina Stead's *Seven Poor Men of Sydney* remarks: "There are no women, there are only dependent and exploited classes in which women make one."[2] This reflects the belief that in economics lies the root cause of all oppressions. That patriarchy too has an equally responsible role to play in perpetuating systems of inequality has, of late, become increasingly self-evident. The complex and subtle interlocking of class and gender is evident in Engels' argument that "the first class-oppression coincides with that of female sex by the male,"[3] and in the by-now familiar equation of husbands with the bourgeoisie and wives with the proletariat. Class, race, colonization and slavery—all of which are dominant tropes of oppression—become, in a large sense, metaphorical of the oppression of women. To be black and woman, then, it is to be triply dispossessed as blacks in a white racist society, as women in a patriarchy and as the working class in a capitalist regime.

Of the first three novels of Morrison, only *Song of Solomon* has a male protagonist, and it alone is written from a supposedly male vantage point. Nevertheless, sexual exploitation of the female emerges as an issue of prominence in this work just as in the first two works—*The Bluest Eye* and *Sula*—with the exception that the focus of attention is more on the middle-class black woman. The only apparent difference between the third novel and its two predecessors is the lesser degree of physical abuse directed toward the black woman of the middle classes.

*Song of Solomon* presents the effects of middle-class values on black families as well as an exploration of African-American culture and myths that depict the conceptual notion of the ethnic experience. The author expounds the tribulations of black American life mentioned in *The Bluest Eye* and *Sula*, and investigates another vital dimension of the black experience—the effects of white middle-class values upon the interrelationship of blacks who adopt them. However, the work, as Bandler says, "bridges the information gap between the black experience mirrored in legends and century-old history and the contemporary black generation that knows little about the glory amidst the tribulations."[4]

Racism hovers in the background, but the actual presence of white America seldom intrudes upon the action in the novel. Most occurrences take place within the black community, and the characters' mental development progresses as a result of their inner growth, or lack of it.

## II

*Song of Solomon* narrates the saga of a black family—Macon Dead, his wife, Ruth Foster, and their children. Capitalist, racist, colonialist, even patriarchal, strategies display a marked interrelatedness in their attempts to culturally destabilize subordinated groups. Myths of superiority of the dominating groups over the dominated are created by promoting ideologies that have their basis in hierarchical distinctions of colour, class, sex, caste and religion. These ideologies work insidiously to systematically erode the marginalized group's cultural heritage and beliefs, while the marginalized receives in turn only a crippled culture. Guitar Baines' words to Milkman in the novel sum up the self-destructive nature of this part of black experience: "Listen, baby, people do funny things. Specially us. The cards are stacked against us and just trying to stay in the game, stay alive and in the game, makes us do funny things. Things we can't help. Things that make us hurt one another. We don't even know why."[5] This would, perhaps, approximate to the first phase of the evolution of native consciousness.

Macon Dead's household is certainly a model of black capitalism. Macon is the city's most affluent black property owner leading a life governed by greed and acquisitiveness. His obsessive need for money and power, his desire to further himself are totally in tune with the ethos of the technologically advanced capitalist culture that surrounds him. Fearing that Milkman may be influenced by Pilate's unhealthy, unmaterialistic ways, Macon advises his son: "let me tell you right now the one important thing you'll ever need to know. Own things." (55) Macon's wife, Ruth, is as elitist as he is. As the only daughter of the most important Negro in the city, Dr. Foster, she has become accustomed to luxury all her life. Her father is a classic example of the black bourgeoisie. He does little to help the plight of his fellow blacks, regarding himself as having risen above them. Macon later recounts to his son: "Negroes in this town worshipped him. He didn't give a damn about them though called them cannibals." (71)

*Song of Solomon* marks a qualitative leap in Morrison's consciousness as an African and as a writer in several other respects. She is now more aware of the importance of dialectical and historical materialism—the role that capitalism plays in the African's exploitation and oppression—and of the need to create a protagonist who develops during the course of the novel. She is also more aware of the importance of creating a text that allows theme to dictate structure. As regards the theme of *Song of Solomon*, Richard K. Barksdale astutely writes that Morrison "turns upside down many of the established social, moral and cultural beliefs that the western world has inherited from the Judaeo-Christian and Greco-Roman traditions."[6] Regarding the structure of the novel, Barbara Harris comments: "The textual richness of the novel derives from a present which spans three generations, with each narrative tied back into the development of the novel's hero. The digressions, explanations, and expansions which interrupt Milkman's own story suggest not a serial or chronological unfolding but an interlace, in which dominant narrative is embellished and enhanced through meticulously articulated subplots and images threading their way through Milkman's life."[7]

These two critical statements clearly indicate that in structure and in theme, *Song of Solomon* is a more advanced work of art than either *The Bluest Eye* or *Sula*. Thematically, Morrison understands that the African in the United States experiences national and class oppression. She is also aware that the African male's exploitation of the African female is related to this oppression. Such clearsightedness enables her, for the first time, to create a male as protagonist, one who must first become conscious of himself in relationship to his people and then, as a consequence, reject the individualistic, vulturistic class aspirations of his oppressor before experiencing a wholesome relationship with a woman. Cynthia Davies has a different interpretation of Morrison's use of a male protagonist. According to this critic, "Morrison is quite able to show black women as victims, as understanding narrator, or even as 'free' in the sense of disconnection. But when the time comes to fulfil the myth, to show a hero who goes beyond independence to engagement, she creates a male hero. Her own emphasis on the effect of particulars on meaning raises questions about at choice."[8] Structurally, Morrison's consciousness of the importance of discovering the cause of the African's oppression before proposing a solution empowers her to subordinate structure to meaning.

To fully appreciate the qualitative leap that Morrison makes in *Song of Solomon* in regard to the nature of the African's oppression in the United States and in regard to her artistic dexterity, her protagonist's growth can be viewed as having three distinct, yet interconnected developmental stages—the pre-liminal stage, the liminal stage, and the post-liminal stage—that lead to his increased race and class consciousness. There are general characteristics peculiar to each stage as well as particular characteristics associated with the protagonist's heightened consciousness.

III

Milkman's pre-liminal stage is marked by his low level of consciousness about his people's race and class oppression manifested in his very nickname—Milkman. As his nickname suggests, he milks women, pilfering their love and giving nothing in return. Even at the age of thirty one, he knows very little about women, an ignorance made evident by his inability to distinguish his sisters from his mother. Nor can he conceive of women as human beings, not even his mother. "Never had he thought of his mother as a person, a separate individual, with a life apart from allowing or interfering with his own." (75) All the women in the novel give primary importance to Milkman and do everything for him. His mother, Ruth, gives him undivided attention. His aunt, Pilate, treats him as her son she never had. To Hagar, his lover, he is the center of her life, her body and her affection. With all this attention, Milkman becomes the epitome of self-centredness, heartless and insensitive. He thinks of himself as a king who rightly deserves all this female homage.

For Milkman, women in general have value only as 'need providers.' The women in his house clean up his messes, cook for him, keep house for him, and generally 'shape their lives around his needs.' He takes all this for granted and never shows them any consideration, never bothers really to know them and their sufferings. As Magdalene says in a rage:

> You've been laughing at us all your life. . . . Using us, ordering us, and judging us: how we cook your food; how we keep your house. . . . Our girlhood was spent like a found nickel on you. When you slept, we were quiet; when you were hungry, we cooked; when you wanted to play, we entertained you; and when you got grown enough to know the difference between a woman and a two-toned Ford, everything in this house stopped for you. . . . And to this

> day, you never asked one of us if we were tired, or sad, or wanted a cup of coffee. (215)

Though Milkman's quest for his identity is dominant in the novel, the focus is on his mother, Ruth and his aunt, Pilate, who are brilliantly contrasted with each other. Ruth is a society-lady, whereas Pilate is totally outside the society as symbolized by her house outside the town. The distinction that Morrison makes between class and community and between autonomy and self-absorption is represented by the towering figure of Pilate who is totally beyond class distinctions and yet is the embodiment of the spirit of her community. In making Ruth and Pilate come together, Morrison seems to suggest that the effect of class distinctions and the fragmentation of community may be overcome by women in their over-riding concern for the living.

Although Morrison does not focus primarily on the relationship of gender to class in *Song of Solomon*, she does integrate that concern into her major theme. As the daughter of the only black doctor in the town, Ruth is bred to an upper middle-class existence. She is presented in the novel as the underside of the ideal southern lady image. She is totally cut off from life, benevolently imprisoned by her father who tries to make her into his girl-doll, spitefully contained by her husband who marries her because of her class position, then despised by him for her inherent weakness. Ruth's life is one of uneventful waste, interrupted only by the birth of her son, whom she tries to keep a baby as long as possible. Ruth is symbolic of the terror that awaits those women who become the emblem of a man's wealth and class position.

While Ruth is the quintessence of the ideal southern lady image, Pilate is a woman completely outside societal structures. She is the guide in the novel to essences beyond outward appearance or material things. Pilate is also the embodiment of the tradition of her family and is the Pilot for Milkman in his necessary journey to the past. Morrison compares and contrasts these two women in a marvellous passage:

> They were so different, these two women. One black, the other lemony. One corseted, the other buck naked under her dress. One well read but ill travelled. The other had read only a geography book, but had been from one end of the country to another. One wholly dependent on money for life, the other indifferent to it. But those were the meaningless things. Their similarities were profound. Both were vitally interested in Macon Dead's son and both had close and supportive posthumous communication with their fathers. (139)

They come together in the novel, the upper middle-class lady and the conjure woman to save Milkman who, in a sense, is the symbol of their continuity.

From Pilate, Milkman receives abundant love. Wallowing in it, Milkman feels for "the first time in his life that he remembered being completely happy."[12] Most important, it is because of Pilate that he steered in a conscious direction. Through her acknowledgment of dignity in and pride of her Africanness, despite her lack of material wealth, Milkman gets his first lesson in race and class consciousness: "While she looked as poor as everyone said she was, something was missing from her eyes that should have confirmed it." (38) Like Pilate, Milkman must learn to respect his African self and to realize that money does not ensure happiness. It is she who first forces him to confront his identity as the living dead who sucks the life force from his people and he learns from her the essence of life. What Milkman gives her in return for life is the murder of her daughter and the theft of her father.

However, it is Hagar who is most exploited by Milkman. While she genuinely loves Milkman, he loves her solely as a receptacle in which to empty his lust, considering her his 'private honey pot.' Milkman's treatment of Hagar makes him a heinous character in the reader's eyes. She gives him all her love, unconditionally and absolutely, telling herself that he would marry her some day. But Milkman treats her like a wad of chewing gum. This breaks Hagar's heart. She goes almost losing her mind and finally dies a wretched death. He sadly fails to see the tragedy and sacrifice implicit in Hagar's poignant death. All this happens because Milkman treats her as 'the third beer.' We learn that "After more than a dozen years, he was getting tired of her. Her eccentricities were no longer provocative. . . . There was no excitement, no galloping of blood in his neck or his heart at the thought of her." (29) It is excitement and passion that he looks for in Hagar, not steadfast love. On the other hand, Hagar recognizes in her relationship with Milkman a certain permanency and gives it all her devotion. She commits herself into his care, but Milkman avoids commitment and strong feelings.

In fact, the women of the novel become the gauge by which to measure Milkman's maturing race and class consciousness. Pilate's role in the novel is dialectically related to Milkman's developing consciousness. When Milkman first sees her, she is sitting with one foot pointing east and one west: east points to Africa and its culture and, thus, to Milkman's past; west points to the western world and its culture and, thus, to Milkman's present and future. Pilate symbolizes the bridge that connects the two. She is the source, the base from which Milkman must build his race and class consciousness.

Additional manifestations of Milkman's low level of consciousness are his overall state of confusion and his association with things behind him. Not knowing his past, he is unsure of the future: "Infinite possibilities and enormous responsibilities stretched out before him, but he was not prepared to take advantage of the former, or accept the burden of the latter." (68) Unconscious of the fact that responsibilities are an integral part of life, Milkman lives the limbo life of the living dead, always struggling to make up his mind whether to go forward or to turn back. His face reveals the confusion he feels. This confusion will last until he immerses himself in the life of his people. In spite of Milkman's lack of consciousness, he seems instinctively aware of the importance of the past, for he is obsessed with things behind him. However, he is not yet prepared to turn his instinctual awareness into a conscious search for his history.

Nevertheless, the general characteristics associated with Milkman in the beginning of the novel prove invaluable clues to his race and class consciousness. Milkman's race consciousness can be gauged by his relationship with the local community as well as his awareness of national events that affect African people. So isolated is he from his people that he is the last to know about the relationship between Henry Porter and his sister. Milkman is bored by all other events, revealing his complete estrangement from the community. When informed of the heinous murder of the fourteen year old Till, a murder which elicited the sympathy of both Europeans and Africans worldwide, Milkman replies: "Yeah, well fuck Till. I am the one in trouble." (87) The statement reflects Milkman's need to develop the race consciousness which allows him to see himself and other African people as one, having a common identity, a common history, and a common struggle.

Milkman's class consciousness is just as weak as his race awareness. Believing in his father's capitalist philosophy that to make wealth is the goal of life, Milkman has little regard for the masses in the community. Consequently the people have little regard for him. In order to establish close ties with the community, Milkman must rid himself of the Macon Dead mentality and what is more, he must begin to love his people more than his money like Pilate who "gave up, apparently, all interest in table manners or hygiene, but acquired a deep concern for and about human relationships." (280) But Milkman's associations till now are with the petty bourgeois St. Honore crowd, with the exception of Guitar.

## IV

Milkman enters the liminal stage of discovery and growth when he begins to question the people and events around him thereby developing his consciousness. He not only questions "everybody" but also discovers the answers to crucial questions of identity. What is more, he makes an attempt through his death wish to renounce all that he has learned so far inasmuch as such knowledge brings with it an acceptance of the responsibility of adulthood in general and Africanhood in particular.

> Above all he wanted to escape what he knew, escape the implications of what he had been told. And all he knew in the world about the world was what other people had told him. He felt like a garbage pail for the actions and hatreds of other people. He himself did nothing. Except for that one time he had hit his father, he had never acted independently, and that act, his only one, had brought unwanted knowledge, too, as well as some responsibility for that knowledge.[9]

Milkman's death wish, as Mbalia points out, is "a necessary phase in his development, for his confrontation with and subsequent defiance of death teach him both sensitivity and sympathy, allowing him to look beyond self."[10]

Milkman's liminal stage—a period of growth though not a full state of consciousness—can be documented by his increasing awareness of race and class. His awareness of race is made more poignant by his personal confrontation with the police. Stripped of his dignity, emasculated like millions of other African men throughout the world, Milkman is filled with shame: "Shame at being spread-eagled, fingered, and handcuffed. . . . But nothing was like the shame he felt as he watched and listened to Pilate. Not just her Aunt Jemica act, but the fact that she was both adept at it and willing to do it—for him." (210-11) While he feels ashamed of his father who buckles before the policemen, Milkman is proud of Pilate who sacrifices her dignity to free him from jail even when he was prepared to knock her down if she had come into the room while he was in the act of stealing from her. The fact that Milkman sees more dignity and life in poor Pilate than in rich Macon increases his class consciousness.

The incident with the police is the second that contributes to Milkman's developing class consciousness. The first results from the appearance of the white peacock, symbolizing both the race and the wealth of the ruling class in the United States. Ironically the peacock appears while Guitar and Milkman are planning to rob Pilate's gold. Significantly, it is Milkman who first sees it, "poised on the roof of a long low building that served as headquarters for Nelson Buick." (180) Equating both flight and money with freedom, Milkman asks Guitar why a peacock cannot fly. Although Milkman is not yet fully conscious of the connection between the diamond-like tail of the peacock and the gold he is planning to steal from Pilate it will only impede his search for identity. This incident contributes a good deal to Milkman's growing class consciousness.

## V

Milkman's post-liminal stage, which marks the height of his consciousness, is characterized by his initiation into a new society, the society of the Shalimar hunters. Like the pre-liminal and liminal stages, this stage is symbolized by linguistic, psychological and physical changes. According to Arnold Van Gennep, one must undergo several initiation rites prior to being incorporated into a new society. First, the initiate must be stripped of all that is psychologically and physically associated with his old society. Second, the initiate must be cognizant of the mores of the new society. Third, the initiate must put his newly learned humanistic theories into practice by participating in the rituals of the new society. In Milkman's case, he must learn that he cannot exploit the people. He can neither show nor receive gratitude with money, because humanism is a traditional African principle valued more than money and held in esteem more by African masses than by the African petty bourgeois. Small wonder, therefore, that the Shalimar community is offended by Milkman's capitalist behaviour: "They looked at his skin and saw it was as black as theirs, but they knew he had the heart of the whitemen who came to pick them up in the trucks when they needed anonymous, faceless laborers." (266)

As a result of his initiation into a new society, Milkman accepts the responsibility of adulthood and Africanhood for "he had stopped evading things, sliding through, over, and around difficulties." (271) Having learned to respect the natural world more than the material world and having gained the ability to laugh at himself, Milkman becomes a psychologically balanced individual:

> There was nothing here [on the Shalimar hunt] to help him—not his money, his car, his father's reputation, his suit, or his shoes. In fact they hampered him. . . . They [the hunters] hooted and laughed all the way back to the car, teasing Milkman, egging him

> on to tell more about how scared he was. And he told them. Laughing too, hard, loud and long. Really laughing. (277-80)

As regards race, Milkman's high level of consciousness is exemplified on two occasions—when he learns of his grandfather's murder and when he participates in the Shalimar hunt. Milkman first learns of his grandfather's murder from Pilate, at a time when his race consciousness is at its lowest level. When he hears of the murder for the second time he is infuriated. He asks, why the Danville Africans did not seek revenge: "And nobody did anything? Milkman wondered at his own anger, he hadn't felt angry when he first heard about it. Why now?"[11] His anger is aroused on this occasion because of his heightened awareness of himself and other African people. Eventually his consciousness manifests itself in a sincere love for his people. During the Shalimar hunt, Milkman's class consciousness also sharpens. Learning the insignificance of money and status when juxtaposed with a true communion with African people, Milkman commits class suicide. While it is true that the seeds of his decision to bond with the African masses instead of those having wealth and status are planted when he first meets Pilate, his conscious decision to do so germinates from his Shalimar experiences.

Regarding gender, it is only after Milkman has revolutionized his consciousness regarding race oppression and class exploitation that he sheds his sexist views of women. Prior to this increased awareness, Milkman has been milking the life out of women. Pissing on Lena, squealing on first corinthians, spying on Ruth, stealing from Pilate, and murdering Hagar are evidence of Milkman's low level of consciousness. At the time he commit these acts, he is not aware of that oneness which connects African people. As the prophetic Pilate explains to Hagar, all are acts of self-hatred: "How can he not love your hair? It's the same hair that grows out of his own armpits. The same hair that crawls up out his crotch on up his stomach." (318) Also, it is only after Milkman has stripped himself of the ruling class's views of race and class superiority that he is able to see women as his equals and understand the reciprocal nature of human relationships. For, trained by his father that money and all that it can buy is the only important lesson that needs to be learned. Milkman has never bothered before to cherish human relationships. Perhaps, the most significant evidence of Milkman's awareness of the principle of reciprocity as related to women is his commitment to guide Pilate to Shalimar to bury her father's bones, just as she had guided him to bury the Dead in him. With his revolutionized consciousness, Milkman becomes the Pilot, the source of life. Thus, the name 'Milkman' is transformed to signify that which is positive, not negative. The protagonist becomes the milkman who is capable of carrying the source of life for those in need. In sum, won, at first, by his father's command of business and dazzled by the quest for gold, Milkman eventually rejects Macon's materialism and embraces Pilate's aestheticism. He understands the importance of family and ancestral ties and the relative wasteland of an existence that commodifies every area of life.

## VI

Milkman's growth and initiation are firmly grounded in his journey to the South, a journey which conclusively opens his eyes and his mind. During this journey he realizes: "With two exceptions, everybody he was close to seemed to prefer him out of this life. And the two exceptions were both women, both black, both old. From the beginning, his mother and Pilate had fought for his life, and he had never so much as made either of a cup of tea." (331)

With this awakening, Milkman suddenly realizes that he has been a fool to have never valued what he has had. With self-awakening comes an epiphany. He begins to get an idea of what his womenfolk had gone through for him. He realizes how his growth as a man into mature adulthood has been made possible by Hagar's sacrificial death and Pilate's far-seeing wisdom. Once he becomes aware of his own weakness, Milkman is firmly set on the road towards recovery and wisdom. His knowledge liberates him and he begins to respect the poor blacks around him, as well as the sweet women who have continuously helped him.

In this respect, Morrison's *Song of Solomon* reminds us of Mariama Ba's recent novel, *So Long a Letter* which is a brilliant portrait of the existence of a woman, Ramatoulaye, within a male-dominated patriarchal society. When we make a comparative study of *Song of Solomon* and *So Long a Letter* what strikes us particularly relevant is Morrison's and Mariama Ba's analytical treatment of human growth towards maturity and self-knowledge. Milkman Dead, a young male, and Ramatoulaye, a middle-aged female, keep growing and maturing through the course of their stories. These two parables of growing maturity and wisdom, as Plakkoottam rightly observes, are "signifiers of a larger cultural, social and spiritual tradition which encourages such behaviour."[12]

Thus, it takes Milkman a long journey to understand the significance of life, its shallowness, artificiality and false values. He sees the emptiness of his past life stretch before him. Shalimar teaches him the stretch of human relationships and exposes him to a non-commodified way of life he has never seen before: "The women's hands were empty. No pocket book, no change purse, no wallet, no keys. . . . They carried nothing. Milkman had never in his life seen a woman without a purse slung over her shoulder, pressed under her arm or dangling from her clenched fingers." (258) Thus, Milkman passes through and learns about different phases of black American history, as his own family's history is embedded in it. Gradually he develops a historical consciousness and finally, as both the underlying and the main theme merge, the history of his family becomes his heritage. At the end we see a new Milkman—a man whose physical and geographical journey has enabled him to grow spiritually and emotionally. He is a changed man, a man who has faced up to his sins, his omissions, and his vast ignorance. Pilate is dead, but Milkman has inherited her mantle of honesty, wisdom and clearsightedness. Thus, he discovers that there is hope for the future, and that Pilate's prophecy comes true: "He don't know what he loves, but he'll come around one of these days." (55)

However, some critics argue that Milkman's discovery is not liberation. For instance, James Coleman argues that "While folk myth and primeval response keep Shalimar alive and active in a way that Danville is not, there is no indication that the people can use the myth, which they largely think of as superstition, to reach beyond their provinciality or to progress and make their lives better. There is no indication that Shalimar can move beyond the Neanderthal level where Milkman finds it."[13] Coleman feels that Milkman's flight is isolated, unrealistic, and futile. It may be liberating for him but it is useless to the community because "he is now outside the community and his act is incomprehensible to them." (153) Coleman further contends that Milkman's act is individual and thus the "situation for the black community is just as dismal as it was before Milkman left Michigan." (160-61) Thus, Coleman thinks that the novel would have been more effective if Morrison focused on the black community as a whole rather than the transcendence of one character.

But, we need not necessarily agree with Coleman's argument that Milkman's act is isolated and useless to the community. For it is the self, the individual who must first undergo realization. Otherwise change becomes as Denise Heinze says "the possession of fate and accident rather than intentionality."[14] What we have to realize is that what Milkman brings back to the community is the very essence of its meaning. As Susan Blake suggests, "community through community" is the key to understand Milkman's transcendence: "community . . . is closely related to individuality, for it depends on individual relationships, which in turn both produce and measure decency in individuals."[15]

Morrison's creation of a character who must develop both race and class awareness prior to developing an egalitarian and humanistic view of women reflects her own increased consciousness of the dialectical relationship between the African male's nation-class oppression and his exploitation of African women. Such a qualitative leap in her ability to analyse the nature of capitalism empowers her to structure *Song of Solomon* which is qualitatively better than the first two—*The Bluest Eye* and *Sula*. Evidently, Morrison's understanding that an awareness of the particular nature of the African's oppression must precede the development of a viable solution increases her awareness of the dialectical relationship between African men and women in white America.

Anyway, we may say that Milkman's awareness of the racial problem is very central to his quest. He consciously questions the dubious morality of the white race. He tells Guitar: "Whitemen want us dead or quiet—which is the same thing as dead. White women, same thing. They want us, you know, 'universal' human, no 'race consciousness.' Tame except in bed. They like a little racial loincloth in the bed. But outside the bed they want us to be individuals." (222) It is this alienation from the socio-logical environment that propels Milkman and his quest. His quest takes him with a knowledge, conscience and a sensitive understanding of the black psyche. He looks at the black mind and black life with a knowledgeable sympathy. His life passes through a conflict of living either like his father to become financially successful or like Pilate to create life of his own. There is an enlarged consciousness of the black problem as he understands the grim sufferings of the countless blacks in a white society.

## VII

Thus, realizing that to overcome his crisis he must first understand how he became crisis-ridden, thereby knowing his history, Milkman comes to understand how equations of power operate at the levels of class, race and gender and, what is more, learns to identify himself with the African masses and not, like Sula, to distinguish himself from them. However, it is important to remember that such a realization and identification are not enough. Milkman must understand that his awareness of the common oppression of African people as manifested in their history and in their present is relevant only if it used to struggle against the cause of that oppression. But, unfortunately Milkman sees himself as an African exploited by capitalism and oppressed by racism, but offers no solution to this dilemma. While his race and class consciousness develop sufficiently to allow him to recreate self, it never reaches the point where he moves beyond self-healing to other-healing.

To conclude, in spite of the growth her writing of *Song of Solomon* evidences, Morrison has not yet sufficiently matured to understand that while the African is exploited both racially and economically, his economic exploitation forms the basis for his national oppression. In the words of Kwane Nkrumah, while "capitalist exploitation and race oppression are complementary, the removal of the first ensures the removal of the other."[16] Without such an understanding, Morrison cannot propose a viable solution to the eradication of capitalism. And, proposing, with such an understanding, a viable solution to the problem seems to be Morrison's chief concern in her next novel, *Tar Baby*.

## NOTES

1. Denise Heinze, *The Dilemma of "Double-Consciousness": Toni Morrison's Novels* (Athens and London: University of Georgia Press, 1993), 132.
2. Christina Stead, *Seven Poor Men of Sydney* (London: Avon, 1965), 205.
3. Frederick Engels, *The Origin of the Family, Private Property and the State* (Moscow: Progress Publishers, 1973), 69.
4. Bandler J. Michael, "Novelist Toni Morrison: We Bear Witness," *African Woman* (September-October 1979), 28.
5. Toni Morrison, *Song of Solomon* (London: Pan, 1978), 34.
6. Richard K. Barksdale, "*Song of Solomon,*" *World Literature Today*, 52 (Summer, 1978), 465.
7. Barbara Harris, "Myth as Structure in Toni Morrison's *Song of Solomon*," *Melus* 7, 3, (Fall 1980), 71.
8. Cynthia Davis, "Self, Society and Myth in Toni Morrison's Fiction," *Contemporary Literature*, 23, 3 (Summer 1982), 337.
9. Dorcatha Drummond Mbalia, *Toni Morrison's Developing Class Consciousness* (Selingrove: Subsquehanna University Press, 1992), 55.
10. *Ibid.*, 56.
11. *Ibid.*, 59.
12. Alphy J. Plakkoottam, "The Dynamics of Man-Woman Relationships in Toni Morrison's *Song of Solomon* and Mariama Ba's *So Long a Letter*," *Indian Journal of American Studies*, 23, 3 (Summer 1993), 85.
13. James W. Coleman, "Beyond the Reach of Love and Caring: Black Life in Toni Morrison's *Song of Solomon*," *Obsidian*, 2 (Winter 1986), 158.
14. Denise Heinze, *The Dilemma of "Double Consciousness*," 142.
15. Susan Blake, "Toni Morrison," *Dictionary of Literary Biography*, Vol. 33, *Afro-American Fiction Writers after 1955*, ed. Thadious Davis and Trudier Harris (Detroit: Gale Research, 1984).
16. Kwame Nkrumah, *Class Struggle in Africa* (New York: International Publishers, 1970), 27.

## CHAPTER V

# Individual Class Struggle against Capitalism: *Tar Baby*

> I love white women and hate black women. I'd jump over ten nigger bitches just to get one white woman. . . . A white woman is beautiful even if she is bald-headed and only has one tooth. . . . There is softness about white woman, something delicate and soft inside. But a nigger bitch seems to be full of steel granite hard and resisting, not soft and submissive like a white woman.
>
> Eldrige Cleaver

> The obligation of anyone who thinks of himself as responsible is to examine society and try to change it and to fight it—at no matter what risk. This is the only hope society has. This the only way societies change.
>
> James Baldwin, "The Negro Child—His Self-Image"

In her first three novels—*The Bluest Eye*, *Sula* and *Song of Solomon*—Morrison confronts the notion of ideal family to which the black community aspires and, what is more, exposes the surface respectability and security represented by the husband, wife and children. The focal point of her criticism, as Susan Willis explains, "is not necessarily the nuclear family per se, but the capitalistic patriarchy that reifies the nuclear family."[1] She uses insanity and death as a way to bring the reader back to the reality of the corrupting and destructive forces of race, gender and class in an oppressive society.

However, after her first three novels Morrison shifts from polarizing feminine households and nuclear families to exposing the decadence of the white family, and finally to historicizing the emotional and psychological obstacles to familial bliss incurred by blacks. She thus expands her vision of the family beyond the constraints of time, place and dimension in an endeavour to reconstruct the origins and significance of family. She no longer focuses exclusively on the black family and community, using them mainly as a referent for showing how far blacks have strayed from their "ancient properties."

*Tar Baby* is an assimilation and advancement of the primary theme of Morrison's three earlier works. For the first time, she frees her work from the narrow geographical boundaries of American society. Unlike *Song of Solomon* which depicts Milkman's emergence and recuperation from 'cultural illness' through his journey of immersion into the South, *Tar Baby* is set on a Caribbean island, Isle des Chevaliers, owned by a retired Euro-American candy magnate—Valerian Street. It focuses on a variety of relationships, within Valerian's household between the butler/maid couple—Sydney and Ondine Childes—and Valerian and his wife, Margaret, and between the indoor house servants and the outdoor field servants, Gideon and Therese. The central focus, however, is on the relationship between the European-educated African-American woman, Jadine Childes and a Florida-born African man, Son. The most striking aspect of the relationship between Jadine and Son is that "each, viewing the other's world as impoverished and/or unsafe, sees it as an occasion to 'rescue' the other."[2]

Recognizing that people of African descent, no matter where they live, share a common identity, a common history, and a common oppression, Morrison uses the Caribbean island as an island that presents conflicting myths. As Morrison herself states: "Black culture survives everywhere pretty much the same, and that, Black people take their culture wherever they go."[3] The respective myths of the white and black inhabitants determine their relationship to the island. For the whites, the French horsemen with their steel sabres poised represent aggressive and brutal action, a necessary evil for development. As a result of their ideology, the Isle des Chevaliers, once a subtropical paradise, is now "the end of the world," an expression suggesting apocalypse and revelations, but also the last victim of exploitation. The French have so defiled the island that even the river, the source of life, has become a "witch's tit . . . a shriveled fogbound oval sleeping with a thick black substance that even mosquitoes could not live near." (8)

By setting her novel in the Caribbean, Morrison is able to incorporate several different cultures, including the island natives, Philadelphian Negroes, and Western imperialists, who are mutually dependent on one another based on economic need, but, at the same time, alienated from any sense of community. The place which the characters inhabit, the land of the community, plays an important role in Morrison's novels inasmuch as land and communities are part of black American heritage.

This is endorsed by Barbara Christian when she says: "As in the ancestral African tradition place is as important as the human actors. For the land is a participant in the maintenance of folk tradition. It is one of the necessary constants through which the folk dramatize the meaning of life, as it is passed on from one generation to the next. Setting then is organic to the characters' view of themselves. And a change in place drastically alters the traditional values that give their life coherence."[4]

The setting of the novel outside the borders of the United States reveals both Morrison's awareness of the innate viciousness of capitalism and her understanding that all people of African descent have a common oppression and need a common solution. Furthermore, it reflects Morrison's own maturing consciousness of the fact that African people must struggle and seek a common solution to their plight. However, in *Tar Baby* the class struggle against capitalism does not go beyond an individual—Son, the revolutionary protagonist, who fails to realise that there are some Africans like Jadine who would refuse to struggle against capitalism even though they are conscious of the fact that it is the primary enemy of African people.

Anyway, Morrison's heightened class awareness creates qualitative changes in both the thematic and structural development of the novel. The qualitative leap evidenced in Morrison's theme is her use of European-Americans as major characters. In earlier works they serve as minor characters, usually as invisible foes who are just referred to or ignored altogether. In *Tar Baby* their rise to prominence parallels Morrison's rise in consciousness, for she now understands the dialectical role they play as the ruling class in the African's oppression. Significant, therefore, is the fact that she does not choose Europeans of the lower or middle classes, but those of the ruling class.

As with her previous novels, the structure of *Tar Baby* is dialectically related to the thematic development of her canon. It is testimony to Morrison's increased class consciousness. Certainly, it is not by accident that the narrative form in this work is more socialist in nature since in the work she reveals her awareness of the selfish individualism promoted by capitalism and its devastating effects on African people. So, just as Morrison searches thematically for a viable solution to the problem of having a system whereby a few exploit the majority, she searches structurally for an artistic form, a framework that will allow her characters to participate equally in the telling of the story. There is not one single narrative voice in the novel but many, each belonging to a major character and each contributing to the universal truth of the work.

From this it is clear that Morrison's emphasis in *Tar Baby* is on class struggle—the struggle between the ruling class and the subject class. Racism, the primary focus of *The Bluest Eye*, is discussed in this novel as a coequal but consequential cause of the African's oppression. The struggle between the sexes, having been explored in *Sula* and resolved in *Song of Solomon*, gets little of the author's attention, for Morrison has sufficiently matured to understand that the fundamental cause of the African's oppression is the exploitive economic system of capitalism. Thus, racism and sexism, although equally oppressive, are treated as by-products of capitalism in *Tar Baby*. The idea now developed is that the eradication of the latter ensures the eradication of the former two. Morrison's increased consciousness is reflected in her ability and commitment to explore the relationship between class, race and sex.

As class struggle is the dominant theme of the novel, it is useful to analyse the novel first by employing a structural framework that examines two major forces in contention—the ruling class and the subject class.

Unlike Pecola, who struggles with the question of racial approbation, Sula, who struggles against the traditional role of African women, and Milkman, who individually struggles with the issues of race and class, the two protagonists in *Tar Baby*—Son and Jadine—must struggle together to resolve their opposing class interests in order to unite. Though in love with each other they are sharply divided in their attitudes to the dominant ruling class as well as to their own traditional culture. Symbolically they reflect the schism that exists within the African community—the class conflict that African people must resolve in order to form an effective, unified force against their primary enemy, capitalism.

## II

Valerian Street, a white man, is a symbol of American capitalism and imperialism. He is a typical capitalist who has made his fortune by exploiting the labour of the African masses and by stealing their land. And it is quite significant that "his wealth emanates from the production of candy, the main ingredients of which—sugar and cocoa—come from the Caribbean, once the sugar capital of the Western world."[5] This economic factor becomes even more poignant after Valerian fires Gideon and Therese for stealing just a couple of apples. From Son's, Morrison's and the reader's perspective, Valerian, "had been able to dismiss with a flutter of the fingers the people whose sugar and cocoa had allowed him to grow old in regal comfort."[6] Quite aptly, he is named after a plant, the dried roots of which have small clusters of white or pinkish flowers used medicinally as a sedative. And as his name suggests, Valerian is asleep throughout most of his adult life, unconscious of or unconcerned by the exploitive means by which he has amassed his wealth. Responding to Valerian's inhumanity, Ondine shouts: "I may be a cook, Mr. Street, but I am a person too." (178) For Valerian, however, one's worth as a human being is measured only by non-human values—wealth and status.

Since his desire is to control life, not live in it, Valerian uses his money to impress upon others. He buys for Margaret expensive clothes and pays Jadine's college tuition. In fact, it is not until he is discourteously treated and abused by his son that he exhibits some genuine feeling. But, even this emotional display reeks more of self-pity for his ignorance of the abuse than sorrow for the psychological well-being of his wife and child.

It is true that the ruling class in the United States consists largely of whites who own and control the means of production. But, at the same time, it is also true that there are some blacks who so ardently wish to belong to this class that they exhibit the same behavioral patterns, dress in the same manner, use the same language patterns, and most unfortunately share the same ideology as those of their oppressors. Often referred to as petty bourgeois, this group of people exists between the two worlds, as they are denied entry into the ruling class owing to their lack of wealth or their skin colour and as they refuse to identify themselves with African masses to whom they owe allegiance. Sydney, his wife, Ondine, the black servants in the white Street family, and Jadine, their orphan child, represent the African petty bourgeois.

Sydney, Ondine and Jadine take pride in the qualities that make them valuable to Valerian. As they define themselves almost exclusively to him, they become appendages rather than autonomous human beings. Ondine, and particularly Sydney, justify their servant status by virtue of being personal attendants to such a rich and important man as Valerian. Jadine is a beautiful and successful model accomplished in the arts and highly educated—"the epitome of ideal white womanhood,"[7] as Denise Heize suggests. As Valerian's dependents, Sydney, Ondine and Jadine, exist only as manifestations of a culture they have not created.

Sydney and Ondine symbolize those unconscious servants who identify themselves more with their employers' culture than they do with their own people and their own culture. Sydney, in the light of day, proudly refers to himself as one of those industrious Philadelphia Negroes, the proudest people in the race. Ondine, painfully reminiscent of Mrs. Breedlove in *The Bluest Eye*, calls the Streets' kitchen "my kitchen" and does not want it violated by the African masses. Perhaps, most significant is that they are surnamed Childes, for they are, indeed, the children of Valerian who do as they are told. Yet, despite the humiliation and degradation of being adults treated as children, they both share the racist, capitalist ideology of their employers.

Not only do they embrace the same racist stereotypes as do their exploiters, but the Childes use the same negative jargon to refer to people who look just like them: "The poor African masses are niggers who steal; in contrast, the Childeses are Negroes, respectable Africans." (32) It is a craze for responsibility that prevents them from seeing themselves as a part of the African masses. For instance, in seeking to disassociate himself from Son, Sidney proudly reveals his ignorance of African culture: "I am a Phil-a-delphia Negro mentioned in the book of the very same name. My people owned drugstores and taught school while yours were still cutting their faces open so as to be able to tell one of you from the other." (40) Indeed, it is only by understanding Sydney's petty bourgeois mentality that we can account for his reaction to Son's humane and friendly greeting that at once establishes a bond and an equality between the two men.

Morrison's most intricate exploration of the African petty bourgeois is, however, expressed through Jadine, not Sydney and Ondine. Significantly called Copper Venus, Jadine is a brown white woman, a Europeanized African, and an art history graduate. Though Jadine is a black woman, she is, as James Coleman puts it, "an antithesis of the black folk and community values."[8] She loses her identity as a black woman and internalizes white values. She is a tar baby—a creation of capitalist America. Her behavioral patterns, dress, language, associations and ideology are all those of the ruling class and demonstrate her hatred of Africa and all that is associated with it. Her fiance is a wealthy European Parisian who will bring her wealth and unquestioned status. Not surprisingly, her allegiance is more to the Streets, whom she regards 'like family, almost,' than to Ondine and Sydney, who slave for her. In fact, except for her aunt and uncle whom she visits only in troubled times, her acquaintances are all Europeans or Europhiliacs like her. Ideologically, she thinks like the European.

Not only does Jadine think like a European, but she feels that she is a European. When Son's presence at L'Arbe de la Croix is discovered, she questions his reason for stealing as if she too owned the house: "It depends on what you want from us." Surprised by her irrational and suicidal association with the Streets, Son replies: "Us? you call yourself us?" (101) Once this association is made clear, it does not surprise us that Jadine often assumes the position of an adoring daughter to the Streets. At dinner time, she "poured [Valerian's] wine, offered him a helping of this, a dab of that and smiled when she did not have to."

(175) And thinking that Valerian's and Margaret's way of life is normal, she belittles African art and ridicules it. Michael attempts to politicize her Africanness: "Actually we didn't talk; we quarreled. About why I was studying art history at that snotty school instead of—I don't know what. Organizing or something. He said I was abandoning my history. My people." (61-62)

It is this attempt to be other than herself that causes Jadine's insecurity throughout the novel. As a Europhiliac, she feels threatened by African women who are not only unashamed of their identity, culture, and beauty but also proud of dignity and heritage. The African woman in yellow is an example of one such woman. What so mesmerizes Jadine and the others, who appear to be Europeans, is the natural beauty of the African woman in yellow—a beauty based on the African's own unique features, but not on those of another race.

Evidence of Jadine's obsession with European looks and culture and her own repugnance of all African things is apparent in her responses to Son. Her recognition of Son's beauty comes only after he has cut off his dreadlocks and shaved his beard. With them, Son is too African, too unlike the European for Jardine: "In a white shirt unbuttoned at the cuffs and throat, and with a gentle homemade hair cut, he was gorgeous. He had preserved his moustache but the kinky beard was gone along with the chain-gang hair." (134) In fact, the pervasive image of tar, associated with Jadine throughout the novel, illuminates her lack of self-esteem and, more importantly, serves as a measure of Jadine's consciousness of herself as an African.

In fact, Jadine has so absorbed the capitalist values of making money and acquiring status that she is ignorant of the traditional African principles that have ensured the survival of African people despite their dehumanized conditions. Unequipped with a sense of humanism, collectivism, and egalitarianism to inform and guide her, she allows her aunt and uncle to wait on her, plays daughter to them instead of being daughter to them, and abandons them to the caprices of Valerian, not knowing what their fate might be. And she ignores Ondine's wise words that "a girl has to be a daughter first. She have to learn that. And if she never learns how to be a daughter, she can never learn how to be a woman. I mean a real woman; a woman good enough for a child; good enough for a man—good enough even for the respect of other women." (242) But we cannot expect Jadine, one who shuns all association with the poor and struggling African masses, to stoop to being a real daughter to a cook.

## III

Unlike Jadine, who internalizes capitalist white values, Son reflects a people-class mentality. He possesses socialist, not capitalist, tendencies. He continues to be "a human being capable of spiritual, emotional and intellectual growth."[9] He is at once aggressive and passive, logical and intuitive, carnal and spiritual. He becomes the Christ-like figure on the L'Arbe des la Croix who saves his people, the revolutionary who politically educates his people, the son, everyone's son devoid of selfish individualism and conscious of himself as an African Son who has a sincere love for living things in general, African people in particular, and the African poor especially. He feels at home in natural environments and, as a consequence, is attuned to nature. For the African masses, he has a special love, despite his feeling of "disappointment nudging contempt for the outrage Jade and Sydney and Ondine exhibited in defending property and personnel that did not belong to them from a black man who was one of their own." (124) Unlike Jadine, Sydney, and Ondine, who harbour no love for the struggling African masses, who, in fact see them as nebulous entities struggling and suffering while they themselves receive only the leftovers of capitalism, Son looks at Gideon and compares this yardman with himself:

> [Yardman] was kneeling, chopping at the trunk of a small tree—while he himself was so spanking clean, clean from the roots of his hair to the crevices between his toes . . . now he was as near to crying as he'd been since he'd fled from home. . . . "Thanks," whispered Son. (120)

So conscious is Son of the plight of the African masses that on two occasions the overwhelming oppressiveness of their existence brings him close to fainting. The first occasion occurs when he hears the story of the slaves struck blind when they saw Dominique. The second occurs when he realizes the magnitude of the African's self-hatred caused by race and class oppression. Examples of Son's sincere love for African people are present throughout the novel, revealing his sensitivity to his people's oppression.

Son is not only race-conscious, but also class-conscious. He sees himself as a member of the exploited class, although he himself is not directly exploited: "He saw the things he imagined to be his, including his own reflection, mocked. Appropriated, marketed and trivialized into decor. He could not give up the last thing left to him—fraternity." (144) Clearly, he understands that if African people in general are exploited, then he too is exploited, that if African people are not free, then he too is not free.

With his unobscured race and class consciousness, Son understands that the primary enemy of African people, that is, the primary cause of the African's plight, is capitalism:

> Son's mouth went dry as he watched Valerian chewing a piece of ham, his head-of-a-coin profile content, approving even the flavor in his mouth although he had been able to dismiss with a flutter of his fingers the people whose sugar and cocoa had allowed him to grow old in regal comfort; . . . he turned it into candy, . . . and sold it to other children and made a fortune . . . and buil[t] a palace with more of their labor and then hire[d] them to do more of the work he was not capable of and pay them again according to some scale of value that would outrage Satan himself. (175)

This passage substantiates Son's class-consciousness. He understands that it is the African's land and labour, not his skin colour, that primarily results in his exploitation.

Conscious of both the plight of the African and the cause of his plight, Son attempts to launch a political education campaign, his primary target being Jadine, and his indirect target being the entire Street household. Valerian Street reveals his true capitalist nature during Christmas dinner by firing at Gideon and Therese for stealing a few apples while he himself has stolen both their land and their labour, and by responding to Sydney and Ondine as mere servants despite the fact that they have lived with him, and for him, for thirty years. It is also during this occasion that Jadine reveals her unequivocal ruling-class aspirations, her petty bourgeois tendencies. While Valerian abuses all present at the dinner including her aunt and uncle, she "had defended him. Poured his wine, offered him a helping of this, a dab of that and smiled when she did not have to as if he were Christ Himself at the Last Supper." (191)

It is because Jadine so blindly accepts the capitalist lifestyle and, more importantly, because Son so ardently loves her that she becomes Son's main target for political education. He attempts to kill Jadine's old capitalist ideology. Son does help Jadine become more conscious of herself as an African by exuding a pride and dignity in his Africanness.

No doubt, we find changes in Jadine but they all are little, convenient ones for her. They do not demand her to commit 'class suicide' by giving up her capitalist lifestyle. Jadine resists any efforts on Son's part to sensitize her to a more mass way of life. Any hope that Jadine is undergoing an ideological renaissance is rendered infructious in the light of her response to being back in New York. "This is home, she thought with an orphan delight; not Paris, not Baltimore, not Philadelphia. This is home." (107) It is a reaction just the opposite of Son's, for whereas he is in tune with the devastating plight of the African people there, she responds to its material convenience and personal benefits: "If ever there was a black woman's town, New York was it." (191) Of course, she is referring to petty bourgeois African women like herself, because for common African woman like Nommo, New York is hell. It is the place where all the negativisms and capitalism converge and blossom. It is, in fact, symbolic of the capitalist world, reflecting the two extremes of capitalism—the poor, struggling African masses and the rich European finance bankers and corporate magnates.

Since Jadine loves New York, it is not surprising that she hates Son's Eden, Eloe. It is just the opposite of New York. In Eloe, Jadine's capitalist lifestyle is crystallized. She acts like a typical European tourist, taking the people's pictures and insulting them. Moreover, because she has longer association with Europeans than with Africans, her ways are, in fact, more European than African. Figuratively and literally, Eloe is the blackest thing she has ever seen: "She might as well have been in a cave, a grave, the dark womb of earth, suffocating." (217) It is, indeed too black, too much like Africa and its culture for Jadine. Thus, her willingness to share her life with Son, an African man attuned to his culture, becomes contingent upon his willingness to embrace the capitalist ideology that she holds so dear.

## IV

In her characterization of Jadine and Son, Morrison accentuates initially the extreme differences in their cultures. Jadine and Son can be said to be a sociological study of two divergent cultures—the sophisticated, accomplished Jadine epitomizing the best of white culture, and the primitive, sensual Son representing the best of black culture. As a pair, they represent the schizophrenia inherent in being black in a white America. The hostility that is generated in their confrontation is an ironical racial tension. As Denise Heinze points out: "Jadine and Son could be no further apart culturally and ideologically had they been of different races."[10] As they cannot resolve their differences, their relationship becomes violent which is a manifestation of the psychic fragmentation of the culture as a whole. Jadine can never go back to the non-material, simple life of black folk inasmuch as she has become addicted to the white world. Similarly, Son can never become a middle-class black accepting western definitions of value and meaning.

While the conflict of genders may originate in 'cultural illness,' the depiction of that illness in *Tar Baby* is both sexualized and gender inflected. The references in the text to Son's attempts to "insert" a culturally conscious dream into Jadine, and to Jadine's attempt to "press" her capitalist dreams into Son, reveal the gendered aspects of this conflict. This sexualised and gendered liaison between Jadine and Son dominate the cast of contentious relationships. In the words of J.S. Ryan, "Son's and Jadine's competing agendas for rescue and conflicting perceptions of the threat facing them underscore the central thematic axis in the novel."[11]

From the moment that Jadine and Son meet, we are aware that the relationship between them is antagonistic for Jadine struggles on behalf of the interests of the ruling class whereas Son struggles on behalf of those of the poor class. Since these interests are diametrically opposed, their relationship can only survive if one of them is prepared to change. Son hopes that he can make Jadine so conscious of the plight of her people that she will see the vicious nature of capitalism and, thus commit 'class suicide.' But, unfortunately, what happens is the other way round. Son is so mesmerised by Jadine and so surrounded by ruling class interests that he is corrupted by the capitalist lifestyle: "He had it straight before: the pie ladies the six-string banjo and then he was seduced, corrupted by cloisonne and raw silk and the color of honey and he was willing to change, to love the cloisonne, to abandon the pie ladies and the nickel nickelodeon and Eloe itself." (257) Son becomes the rabbit entrapped by the tar baby—Jadine who repudiates African people, in general, and Son, in particular, by her blind acceptance of capitalist values. In persuading her of the negative and baneful effects of these values, Son gets trapped.

From the beginning of the novel there are clues that it is Son, not Jadine, who would commit 'class suicide.' First, Jadine is nurtured by the lifestyle, the values, the food, the clothes, the language and the behavioral patterns of the Streets to such an extent that it becomes almost impossible for Son to take her to a new state of awareness in regard to African people. Second, and consequently, Son gradually changes his dress habits to resemble these of his oppressor. Third, and the most important, Son's solution to the capitalist way of life—a return to African traditionalism as represented by Eloe is utopian. Not until Jadine leaves him, opting for cloisonne rather than himself, does he begin to realise the utopian nature of his solution: "Out came the photos [Jadine] had taken in the middle of the road in Eloe Beatrice, pretty Beatrice, Soldier's daughter. She looked stupid. Ellen, sweet cookie-faced Ellen, that he always thought so pretty. She looked stupid. They all looked stupid, backwoodsy, dumb, dead. (234-35)

Eloe is a backward community, largely illiterate and economically underdeveloped. After experiencing the exploitative system of slavery, colonialism, neocolonialism, and domestic colonialism, and after being exposed to the ideologies associated with the teachings of Islam and Christianity, neither Son, Jadine, nor African people in general can return to this past, highly romanticized way of life. In the words of Aime Cesarie, "If the African . . . were merely to copy his past, failure would be the inevitable result."[12] Instead of a return to woebegone days, Son and Jadine, in particular, and all the African people, in general, must extract the positive from traditional Africa and the modern capitalism, with Africa as the centre in order to forge a new society. Eloe, with all its positive elements, has its negative features in its being a poor, underdeveloped, uneducated community.

Thus, in the love story of Jadine and Son, Morrison develops her most compelling relationship between class and race. Jadine is presented in the novel as essentially class-bound. Her desire to "make it" in the world binds her not just to whites, but to upper-class whites. Her values are not so much that of the ideal southern lady as they are of the white male world. She does not wish to be the lady dependent on husband's wealth and status. She wants parity, but it must be parity in a world of material gain. In no way is she a nurturer, not even to her aunt and uncle, who made her access to wealth possible by becoming lifelong servants to the rich Valerian. To Jadine independence for a woman means looking out for herself. She is not concerned with any community or with justice for anyone. She is feminist in appearance without any concern for social justice that the concept should embody.

In contrast to Jadine, Son is presented as essentially race-bound, taking pride in being African. Like Pilate in *Song of Solomon*, he resists the materialism of the society. However, he has no future like Pilate, for he really lives in Eloe, a community of the past. More importantly, he refuses to contend with the social forces that deprive him of fulfilment. His solution to the African problem, is to retreat, run and opt out. Although he displays an intense racial identity, he does not join with others, bringing about any change. Alienated from his own society he finally moves into the realm of myth.

Both Jadine and Son are at a dead end since things do not resolve themselves in either's favour. Jadine goes back to her former lifestyle in Paris and Son is urged back to his roots. In going to Paris Jadine will probably marry a wealthy Parisian, repeating the pattern of some of her foremothers, except that they were forced by circumstances to become part of the more dominant race and class through the use of their sexuality. Though Jadine appears to be quite independent, her need for material well-being makes her dependent on the wealthy and powerful class. Son, on the other hand, returns to the Isle des Chevaliers, futilely looking for Jadine. He is advised by Therese to leave Jadine to her inauthentic existence and look to his own people who are awaiting his return. He, finally retreats to the horsemen of the island and is thought to have joined them in their never-ending roaming of the forest like the rabbit thrown back into the briar patch.

Thus, Morrison explores the passionate love-affair of Jadine and Son to examine the conflict between the life and humanism of black culture and the deadness and materialism of white culture. Jadine, the beautiful black woman, finds herself torn between the rich white culture of Paris and the world of her black lover. On the other hand, Son finds himself torn between the poor black culture and the world of his petty bourgeois lover. Jadine emerges as a hard-driving, selfish, materialistic black woman with no strong affiliation to other people and to the folk past, and Son as an aggressive black man with great fraternal feeling and strong connections with black folk culture, but who is left unfulfilled, lonely and unstable because of a tenuous connection with a materialistic future. Together, "each was pulling the other away from the maw of hell—its very ridge top. Each knew the world as it was meant or ought to be. One had a past, the other a future and each one bore the culture to save the race in his hands." (269) Yet, each retreats to an old citadel of safety and security. Perched fixedly in extremities of their positions, unwilling to temper them, the two now only pose ultimate to each other. However, we see clearly that Son needs Jadine to direct him toward material achievement in life, and Jadine needs Son to give her a feeling of security and belonging. Morrison in the end shows clearly what the possibilities are for Son, a twentieth-century black man burdened with black cultural tradition and Jadine, a twentieth-century black woman who has reverted to negative white Western values.

In sum, Jadine's inability to resolve the obstacles in her life prevents her from becoming whole. She fails to resolve the cultural conflict and personal fragmentation. Son, on the other hand, does emerge as one who gets back to his roots so as to be in touch with himself. Hence he becomes close to achieving wholeness in the end in spite of a contradiction of his cultural life-style. Morrison, thus, successfully meshes opposites rather than pit them against each other in an effort to communicate the intertwining nature of things in the universe. In other words, "In merging the legends with modern-day phenomena and the living with the living-dead in articulating the quest for wholeness, Morrison has succeeded in creating yet another work that can be read and reread for insights into human nature in general and into the human condition as it relates to race, class and gender in particular."[13]

V

*Tar Baby* is, thus, a black novel deeply perceptive of the black's desire to create a mythology, of his or her own to replace the stereotypes and myths the white man has constructed for him. It is also a book about a woman's act and her denial of her need for an impossible man, and in this regard it is a woman's novel too. Yet Morrison's greatest accomplishment is that she has raised her novel above the kind of social realism explored by many black novels and women's novels. She has succeeded in writing about race and women symbolically. Morrison has made herself into the D.H. Lawrence of the black psyche, transforming individuals into forces, and idiosyncrasy into inevitability. Along the way, the novel has yielded up some of the irreducible mystery, the fluidity of Morrison's best work.

Thus, of Morrison's first four novels, *Tar Baby* is the most problematic. It might appear that this is so because Morrison attempts two innovative narrative strategies, situating the central plot within an insular setting beyond the geographical boundaries of the United States mainland and juxtaposing black and white characters to dramatize the racial complexities that determine the American cultural landscape. While dislocation and cross-cultural relationships figure strongly in the novel, the characterization of the protagonist, Jadine, draws attention to a more fundamental narrative problem than either of these strategies might suggest. On the one hand, Morrison wants to affirm the self-reliance and freedom of a black woman who makes choices for her own life on her own terms. On the other hand, she also seeks "to point out the dangers . . . that can happen to the totally self-reliant if there is no historical connection."[14] More specifically, Morrison's dilemma in *Tar Baby* is how to narrate the quest of the contemporary black female protagonist who happens to be a cultural orphan, and whose sense of self is based upon a denial of her own cultural heritage and an identification with one that is not her own.

While at one level, *Tar Baby* appears to be simply the story of unsuccessful love-affair between a man and a woman with diametrically opposed values and lifestyles, at a deeper level, the novel is about the disparity Morrison sees between the women of her remembered past and the women of the present epitomized in the character of Jadine. Indeed, the text reveals the dilemma Morrison has faced in trying to depict the potential consequences of success predicated upon disconnection from one's racial identity and cultural heritage.

Ironically, while Morrison was still in the process of writing *Tar Baby*, she delivered the 1979 commencement address at Barnard college, which expresses the precise thematic concerns of the novel:

> I am suggesting that we pay as much attention to our nurturing sensibilities as to our ambition. You are moving in the direction of freedom and the function of freedom is to free somebody else. You are moving towards self-fulfilment and the consequences of that fulfilment should be to discover that there is something just as important as you are. In your rainbow journey toward the realization of personal goals, don't make choices based only on your security and your safety. . . . Let your might and power emanate from the place in you that is nurturing and caring.[15]

The double-voiced nature of this speech foreshadows the dilemma Morrison faced in writing *Tar Baby*. The novel gives voice to both perspectives in varying degrees of success. But, more importantly, it deconstructs the difference that Jadine finds between these perspectives by employing mothering as a metaphor for nurturing. By doing so, Morrison affirms the recent and historical nourishment that indigenous black culture could provide. The novel serves, then, both as a remembrance of cultural tradition of nurturing and as a cautionary tale for those like Jadine, who define themselves against themselves and their cultural past in the interest of self-fulfilment.

Thus, *Tar Baby* can be interpreted as a modern cautionary tale in which Morrison draws on the African-American oral narrative tradition to expose the pitfalls of white middle-class aspirations for the black woman and to illustrate the consequences of her social and cultural misbehaviour. Although the text illustrates these consequences by examining the tensions inherent in the binary oppositions of black and white, poor and rich, female and male, African and European, the central reasons for Jadine's divided consciousness have to do with her rejection of the cultural constructions of race and mothering that are part of her African-American heritage.

Jadine's quest is for psychic wholeness, but because she does not heed the cautions that come to her in various forms, she experiences a failed initiation or an aborted quest. Indeed, her quest for wholeness is unsuccessful because she accepts values and mores of white middle-class culture without question and she rejects the very cultural constructions of race and mothering that could heal and transform her consciousness. Jadine's failure to embrace a maternal role detracts seriously from her integrity. Calling Jadine a cultural exile, Susan Willis remarks: "As the individual whose cultural exile is the most profound, Jadine is haunted by waking visions, born out of guilt and fear. In her most terrifying vision, a mob of black women—some familiar, some only known by their names—crowds into her room. Revealing, then waving their breasts at her, they condemn Jadine for having abandoned the traditional, maternal role of black women."[16] But if Jadine's rejection of traditional cultural roles cannot be disputed, she still merits the label Morrison gives her "culture-bearing black woman." (232)

The case of the other protagonist, Son, is not much different. Having discovered first the importance of knowing one's history and one's relationship to his people, Son commits himself to sharing this knowledge with other Africans. Thus, by struggling to politically educate Therese, Gideon, Sydney and Ondine in general, and Jadine in particular, Son becomes a disciple for African people, 'a modern-day revolutionary.'

Unfortunately, although his goal is a noble one, Son's solution of a return to a traditional African lifestyle is based on idealism. Such a solution as the novel documents is just as impossible as it is undesirable. For, the idea of returning to a pre-colonial, pre-slavery existence is tantamount to asking the African to erase the experiences and consciousness of five hundred years, in essence to metamorphose into one of the blind horsemen of the Isle des Chevaliers. Although Son realizes the inadequacy of his solution, he does not try to replace it with a more realistic one. Instead, he willingly forsakes his role as revolutionary and chases Jadine to share her role as reactionary. Once again, Morrison's protagonist escapes reality, this time by binding himself to the role he must play in liberating African people: " Looking neither to the left nor to the right Lickety-split Lickety-split. Lickety Lickety-Lickety-split." (309)

## VI

Thus, the individualistic, materialistic Jadine and the roots-bound Son do not mesh. For, Son moves to another world that has little impact on this one, and Jadine cops out to a world of values that eventually must be a dead end most decidedly for her own. Finally, both their solutions are individual and not at all applicable to the concrete realities that their brethren must face every day. As Barbara Christian points out, "at no point does either Son or Jadine act with others to dissolve the group dilemma."[17] Resultantly, *Tar Baby* projects only individual class struggle against capitalism which is rendered infructious to solve the nagging problem of Africans in America.

To conclude, *Tar Baby* reveals Morrison's own clarity in regard to the irreconcilability of the interests of the ruling and subject classes. While she clearly rejects vulturistic capitalism, she just as clearly rejects the naive prescription of Kenneth Kaunda, President of Zambia, for an African communal socialism, a way of life that seeks to return to a glorified past without the benefit of modern technology, modern sciences or modern consciousness. Unfortunately, however, Morrison does not provide a viable alternative existence for African people, despite her new awareness that the primary cause of the plight of African people is capitalism and despite her knowledge that a return to a past way of life is impractical.

Furthermore, *Tar Baby* reflects Morrison's heightened class consciousness both thematically and structurally, projecting as it does the positive principles of traditional African society—humanism, collectivism and egalitarianism. But, unfortunately this increased awareness does not enable her, even at this stage of her literary career, to propose a viable solution for the age-old oppression of the African people in America. Eradication of the plight of African people demands, not individual, but collective class struggle against capitalism—a unified African people who control their own destiny, extracting and utilizing only the positive from their past such as unity in struggle in order to build a better future. Such a viable solution to the oppression of Africans takes us to Morrison's masterpiece, *Beloved*.

## NOTES

1. Susan Willis, "Eruptions of Funk: Historicizing Toni Morrison," *Black American Literature Forum*, 16 (1982), 36.
2. Judylyn S. Ryan, "Contested Visions/Double Vision in *Tar Baby*," *Modern Fiction Studies*, 39, 3-4 (Fall/Winter 1993), 601.
3. Judith Wilson, "A Conversation with Toni Morrison," *Essence*, 12 (July 1981), 86.
4. Barbara Christian, "Community and Nature: The Novels of Toni Morrison," *Journal of Ethnic Studies*, 7 (Winter 1980), 65.
5. Eric Williams, *Capitalism and Slavery* (New York: G.P. Putnam's, 1944), 28.
6. Toni Morrison, *Tar Baby* (London: Pan, 1981), 174.
7. Denise Heinze, *The Dilemma of "Double-Consciousness" in Toni Morrison's Novels* (Athens and London: The University of Georgia Press, 1993), 87.
8. James Coleman, "The Quest for Wholeness in Toni Morrison's *Tar*

*Baby,*" *Black American Literature Forum*, 20, 1-2 (Spring/Summer, 1986), 64.

9. Denise Heinze, *The Dilemma of* "*Double-Consciousness*," 90.
10. *Ibid*., 37.
11. Ryan, "Contested Visions/Double Vision in *Tar Baby*," 602.
12. Chinweizu, *The West and the Rest of Us*: *White Predators, Black Slaves and the African Elite* (New York: Random House, 1975), 303.
13. Wilfred D. Samuels and Clenora Hudson-Weems, *Toni Morrison* (Boston: Twayne, 1990), 92.
14. Toni Morrison's, "Interview," *The Soho News*, 11 March 1981, 2.
15. Toni Morrison, "Rootedness," an interview published in *Black Women Writers (1950-1980)*: *A Critical Evaluation*, 344.
16. Susan Willis, "Eruptions of Funk: Historicizing Toni Morrison," *Black American Literature Forum*, 16 (1982), 37.
17. Barbara Christian, "Testing the Strength of the Black Cultural Bond: Review of Toni Morrison's *Tar Baby*," *Black Feminist Criticism*: *Perspectives on Black Women Writers* (New York: Pergamon Press, 1985), 68.

## CHAPTER VI

# Collective Class Struggle against Capitalism: *Beloved*

A slave is enslaved
Can be enslaved by unwisdom
Can be enslaved by black unwisdom. . .
Speak the truth to the people
To identify the enemy is to free the mind
Speaks truth.

Mari Evans

The big bee flies high,
The little bee makes the honey;
The black folk makes the cotton,
And the white folk gets the money.

William Wells Brown, Clotel

In her four earlier novels, Morrison demonstrates a keen awareness of, concern for, and dedication to African people in America. As Mbalia puts it, almost "like a scientist, she uses each work as a laboratory in which to research a hypothesis as to the nature of oppression experienced by African people and to posit a solution to it"[1] in terms of fictional art. Starting with the issue of race as the primary form of oppression in *The Bluest Eye*, demonstrating that sexism is as oppressive as racism in *Sula*, adding the problem of class exploitation to that of race in *Song of Solomon*, and then recognizing capitalism as the primary target against which the blacks must struggle in *Tar Baby*, Morrison proposes in *Beloved* (1987) collective class struggle against capitalism as the only viable solution possible for the African people in the white-dominated American society.

To show the historical truth that collective struggle is the only practical solution for African people, Morrison writes a historical novel, *Beloved,* which explores the most oppressed period of slavery in the history of African people. The novel is based on a newspaper clipping about a fugitive slave in Ohio who killed her own infant rather than see her return to bondage in the South. Morrison found the newsclipping in *The Black Book* which chronicles the life of the African people in the United States from slavery through the civil rights movement. Morrison gets the kernel of her novel from the news article entitled "A Visit to the Slave Mother Who Killed Her Child":

> I found her with an infant in her arms only a few months old, and observed that it had a large bunch on its forehead. I inquired the cause of the injury. She then proceeded to give a detailed account of her attempt to kill her children.
>
> She said, that when the officers and slave-hunters came to the house in which they were concealed, she caught a shovel and struck two of her children on the head, and then took a knife and cut the throat of the third, and tried to kill the other,—that if they had given her time, she would have killed them all—that with regard to herself, she cared but little, but she was unwilling to have her children suffer as she had done.
>
> I inquired if she was not excited almost to madness when she committed the act. No, she replied, I was as cool as I am now; and would much rather kill them at once, and thus end their sufferings, than have them taken back to slavery, and be murdered by the piece-meal. She then told the story of her wrongs. She spoke of her days of suffering, of her nights of unmitigated toil, while the bitter tears coursed their way down her cheeks and fell in the face of the innocent child as it looked smiling up, little conscious of the danger and probable suffering that awaited it. . . .
>
> The two men and the two other children were in another apartment but her mother-in-law was in the same room. She says she is the mother of eight children, most of whom have been separated from her; that her husband was once separated from her twenty-five years, during which time she did not see him; that could she have prevented it, she would never have permitted him to return, as she did not wish him to witness her sufferings, or be exposed to the brutal treatment that he would receive.
>
> She states that she has been a faithful servant, and in her old age she would not have attempted to obtain her liberty; but as she became feeble, and less capable of performing labor, her master became more and more exacting and brutal in his treatment, until

> she could stand it no longer; that the effort could result only in death, at most—she therefore made the attempt.
>
> She witnessed the killing of the child, but said she neither encouraged nor discouraged her daughter-in-law,—for under similar circumstances she should probably have done the same. The old woman is from sixty to seventy years of age, has been a professor of religion about twenty years, and speaks with much feeling of the time when she shall be delivered from the power of the oppressor, and dwell with the Savior, "where the wicked cease from troubling, and the weary are at rest."
>
> These slaves (as far as I am informed) have resided all their lives within sixteen miles of Cincinnati. We are frequently told that Kentucky slavery is very innocent. If these are its fruits, where it exists in a mild form, will some one tell as what we may expect from its more objectionable features? But comments are unnecessary.[2]

With the essence of this newsclipping, Morrison concocts the story of *Beloved*. She, however, expands, refines, and shapes it so that *Beloved* picks up where *Tar Baby* leaves off. While mulling over this news article what evidently clicked in Morrison's mind was the fact that conditions of oppression then and now as well as our reactions to them have not qualitatively changed.

Because Africans are faced with circumstances almost equally oppressive as those in slavery, Morrison shows them the need to unite as one to confront a common enemy—capitalism, the same enemy they struggled against more than one hundred years ago. Certainly Morrison has come to understand that "capitalism is but the gentleman's form of slavery."[3]

Morrison's conscious focus on collective rather than individual struggle is clarified through her repeated assertions that *Beloved* is the story of a people rather than a person. She says: "The book was not about the institution—Slavery with a capital S. It was about those anonymous people called slaves. What they do to keep on, how they make a life, what they are willing to risk, however long it lasts, in order to relate to one another—that was incredible to me."[4]

Although the novel begins as Sethe's story, it evolves into a story about "these people who don't know they are in an era of historical interest. They just know they have to get through the day . . . and they are trying desperately to be parents, husbands and a mother with children."[5] Morrison's conscious focus on the collective rather than Sethe's personal history is further clarified when she says that the novel "has to be the interior life of some people, a small group of people and everything they do is impacted on by the horror of slavery, but they are also people."[6] The impact of slavery on a people, thus, involves the way internalization of oppressors' values can distort all intimate human relationships and even subvert the self.

*Beloved* deals with not only 'reconstructed memory,' but also deconstructed history. Set in post-civil war Ohio, this haunting narrative of slavery and its aftermath, traces the life of a young woman, Sethe, who has kept a terrible memory at bay only by shutting down part of her mind. The novel deals with Seth's former life as a slave on Sweet Home Farm, her escape with her children to what seems a safe haven, and the tragic events that follow. Although Sethe physically survives, she remains emotionally subjugated, and her desire to give and receive love becomes a destructive force. Morrison also addresses the difficulties faced by former slaves in keeping the horrors of their pasts submerged within the subconscious. In the words of Ann Snitow, Morrison "twists and tortures and fractures events until they are little slivers that cut. She moves the lurid material of melodrama into the minds of her people, where it gets sifted and sorted, lived and relived, until it aquires the enlarging outlines of myth and trauma, dream and obsession."[7] Thus, Morrison recreates a past, however painful, to undercut the ideological basis upon which it has largely been constructed by whites, employing not only available accounts in slave narratives, but also disengaging the materials from historical documents in order to revitalize them as lived experience.

The novel hinges on the death of Sethe's infant daughter, Beloved, who mysteriously reappears as a sensuous young woman. Beloved's spirit comes back to claim Sethe's love. Sethe struggles to make Beloved gain full possession of her present and throw off the long, dark legacy of her past. Sethe's experience is treated with many ironic overtones that point to certain paradoxes and many fundamental complexities of her quest for freedom.

On a socio-psychological level, *Beloved* is the story of Sethe Suggs' quest for social freedom and psychological wholeness. She struggles with the haunting memory of her slave-past and the retribution of *Beloved*, the ghost of the infant daughter whom she has killed in order to save her from the living death of slavery. On a legendary and mythic level, *Beloved* is a ghost story that frames embedded narratives of the impact of class, race and sex on the capacity for love, faith and community of black families, especially of black women, during the Reconstruction period. Set in post-civil war Cincinnati, Beloved is a womanist neo-slave narrative of double consciousness, a post-modern romance that speaks in many compelling voices and on several time levels of the historical rape of black American women and of the resilient spirit of blacks in surviving as a people.

*Beloved* contains Morrison's most extraordinary and spellbinding womanist remembrances of things past. As Alice Walker's epigraphs to *In Search of Our Mother's Gardens* suggest, womanist connotes a black feminist, "a woman who, among other things, is audaciously committed to [the] survival and wholeness of entire people, male and female."[8] And it is "because of the silences in the slave narratives due to authorial compromises to white audiences and to self-masking from a painful past, Morrison sees her role as a writer as bearing witness to the interior life of people who didn't write their history and to filling in the blanks that the slave narrative left."[9] Unlike James Baldwin, who also defines the role of slave as bearing witness, Morrison privileges the authority and epistemology of black and Third World women in America.

As in her previous novels, the need for women to re-establish connections with one another is powerfully rendered in Morrison's *Beloved.* It was all the more important in that era of slavery because there was a profound and real need for physical as well as psychological survival. Commenting on her effort to explore a relationship between two women, Morrison says: "We read about Ajax and Achilles willing to die for each other but very little about the friendship of women, and them having respect for each other, like it's something new. But black women had always had that, they have always been emotional life supports for each other."[10] When Sethe arrives with her new-born daughter tied to her chest, Baby Suggs welcomes her. Sethe has a powerful culture mentor in Baby Suggs who kindles a desire in her to know her past and to love herself as a person.

Sethe, like Morrison's other female protagonists, is a victim of both sexist and racist oppression. She is a runaway slave woman, a slave mother, who is brutally treated by white men, the school teacher and his nephews. Morrison explores a black woman's self-conscious protest to the dual oppression. It is not only the sexual exploitation that Sethe feels most oppressed by, but the humiliation of her nurturing abilities as a mother—the stealing of her milk.

One of the most damaging effects of the dual oppression of black women, against which Morrison writes, is murder of one's own child. Murder becomes Sethe's act of mother love, which she explains saying, "I took and put my babies where they'd be safe."[11] She prefers to murder her daughter, Beloved, rather than see her in bondage. According to Deborah Gray White, infanticide represents one of the avenues of resistance on the part of a slave woman. Although Sethe's murder might be viewed by contemporary standards as limiting the context in which she committed it, it does not diminish her stature. If it was possible for a black slave woman like Sethe to live with her family with dignity and self-respect in the America of the 1850s, she would not have committed this hideous crime which was the mutilation of her vibrant mother love.

Balancing the polemics—racial and sexual—that is at the back of every personal outrage suffered by Sethe, is the brilliant "poetics . . . of the long black song of many thousands gone."[12] Sethe's back is so hardened that she cannot feel Paul D. pressing against it, "but could not feel, that his cheek was pressing into the branches of her chockecherry tree." (21) Similarly, through another powerful image, that of the truckless quiet forest abruptly appearing after the first dialogue of Sethe and Paul D. the implied author brings out the metaphysical ambivalences of Sethe, the slave mother. As observed by Bernard W. Bell: "This metaphorical silence is an ingenious, ironic use of the technique of call and response that invites the implied reader in Wolfgang Iser's words, that network of response inviting structures, which impel the reader to grasp the text."[13]

By choosing to narrate the real life and actual experiences of a runaway slave woman, Morrison proves the power of art to demolish stereotype. Sethe's experience is treated with many ironic overtones that point to certain paradoxes and many fundamental intricacies of her quest for freedom. Other novels like *Song of Solomon* and *Invisible Man* have done this through numerous adventures of the hero examining the intricate legacy of the past and of history. Yet, *Beloved* strikes a different and perplexing note because it deliberately avoids chronological development of the narrative and linear structure. Beloved's mother, Sethe, is caught in the ambiguities of a quest that presents itself as a succession of rememories. Each recorded incident, act or word further unfolds her story. Sethe's story is presented piece by piece through the act of rememory, a pattern of revelation of her past, of recognition of the history.

Sethe's black awareness and rejection of white perceptions and inscriptions of herself, her children, and other slaves as non-human are synthesized with her black feminist sense of self-sufficiency. Sethe reconciles gender differences first with her husband, Halle Suggs, and later with Paul D., in heterosexual, endogamous relationship. Although by implication the author blends racial and sexual consciousness, the structure and style of the text foregrounds the ambivalence of slave women about motherhood that violates their personal integrity and that of their family.

The feminist qualities that Morrison advocates through Sethe's portrayal are the traditional beauty, strength, resistance and integrity of black women. She is sensitive to feminist concerns and includes all those elements of black female experience in her text which are of compelling significance to a woman. In her interview with Rosemarie K. Lester, Morrison expresses her views on an extremely painful and unattractive history of black women in the States where black women have always been both mother and labourer, mother and worker, and have worked in the fields along with men: "They were required to do physical labour in competition with them, so that their relations with each other turned out to be more comradeship than male dominance/female subordination. . . . Black women are both ship and safe harbor."[14] Morrison, thus, uses a beautiful metaphor to emphasize that black women are much more suited to aggressiveness in the mode that feminists are recommending.

III

As in her previous works Morrison's thematic astuteness is reflected in her artistic narrative structure, thereby integrating her social and political concerns into the norms of fictional art. In *Beloved*, on the one hand she creates a text unencumbered by symbols indicating divisions and defiant of the linear tradition of the western world in order to create in form what she does in substance—the qualitatively unchanged status of African people. On the other hand, she creates such a text in order to point to solution which is collectivism.

To crystallize the dire necessity of collective action for the survival of African people, Morrison juxtaposes isolated struggle with collective struggle and selfish individualism with individualism conditioned by social responsibility. In *Beloved* most forms of isolation are genocidal for the race. For instance, when Baby Suggs labours alone to feed the community, she insults it: "Too much, they thought. Where does she get it all. Baby Suggs, holy? . . . And loving everybody like it was her job and hers alone. . . . Loaves of bread and fishes were His powers." (136) Since it is usually best for all that individual needs and desires be conditioned by those of the collective, Baby Suggs' self-oriented behaviour is tantamount to heresy. Indeed, the repercussions of this God-like action—the attempt to do alone which should be done together—is felt for two generations. For the community, in spite, refuses to warn Baby Suggs that slave trappers are approaching, setting in motion the conditions under which Sethe murders Beloved:

> The good news . . . was that Halle got married and had a baby coming [Baby Suggs] fixed on that and her own brand of preach-

ing, having made up her mind about what to do with the heart that started beating the minute she crossed the Ohio River. (147)

Interestingly enough, Beloved becomes the symbol by which African people are to measure the devastating effect of isolation. Isolation literally tears apart the family. The personification of isolation and all things inherent in it, including selfish individualism, greed and destruction, Beloved succeeds in dividing 124 from the rest of the African community. Denver's isolation in life, 124's isolation in the community, and Beloved's isolation in death all serve to further divide the African community and, as a consequence, leave it vulnerable to the oppression and exploitation of the slave society. It is she who drives Howard and Burglar from home and separates Paul D., Sethe, and Denver just when their three shadows hold hands and just when they erect bonds with the African community: "Paul D. made a few acquaintances; spoke to them about what work he might find. Sethe returned the smiles she got Denver was swaying with delight. And on the way home, although leading them now, the shadows of three people still held hands." (49)

Not until the cause of the separation is clarified, struggled with and struggled against, can African people come together again. Beloved must materialize into a visible, tangible entity of which the community is aware, instead of an amorphous apparition, an oppression of which the community is unconscious. Paul D. gives this apparition substance. He is the son who does not give up but returns to struggle again and again, the Malcolm who teaches his people the value of struggle. His presence sets in motion the necessary purgative confrontation between Sethe, and the Cincinnati African community. Significantly when he comes, things become what they are, not what Sethe and African community have imagined. Once the enemy is identified, the community struggles collectively against that which divides them.

Thus, the stress on shared relationships, community and race responsibility—the traditional African principle of collectivism—is the dominant theme of the novel. As we go through the novel, we find that life is hell, but togetherness, shared experience and brotherly love help the characters to survive, if not to forge better lives for themselves. This emphasis on social responsibility, the unselfish devotion of Africans helping other Africans, makes Beloved Morrison's most conscious novel.

IV

In the spirit of the flying African of the Virginia Hamilton myth, Hi Man takes the responsibility for the collective. One, more experienced with the hardships of slave existence, teaches other Africans that a man could risk his own life, but not his brother's. And, most important, he teaches that all must be freed from oppression or none. This lesson, which has its beginning in *Song of Solomon*, is learnt in *Tar Baby* and acted out in *Beloved*. Focusing on the post slavery convict lease system, Morrison uses the chain as a literal symbol of the spiritual link necessary between African people: "They trusted the rain and the dark, yes, but mostly Hi Man and each other." (110)

Crucial in her exploration of the collective solution to the African's oppression is the slave setting, for it serves to enhance the theme of *Beloved* by painting up the dialectical relationship between problem and solution. The solution to the problem arises from the conditions that create it. Simultaneously, Morrison's setting has to be one in which the strategy for solving the problem is not only clearly evident but also inevitable. For she understands that the solution then is the solution now. The most skilful method of unveiling this truth is by choosing a historical period in which the African's primary enemy, capitalism, is unobscured by its secondary and consequential effects—race and gender oppression.

In *Beloved* gender oppression is not a visible problem that exists between African men and women, but is one that exists within the context of the economic relationship between master and slave and race is only a later justification for the oppression of the African people. Clearly, then, Morrison's choice of setting is germane in crystallizing the nature of the African's oppression, for the economic source of both race and gender oppression is unobscured in slavery.

Refreshingly, the relationship between African men and women is generally positive. Paul D. is the Son of *Tar Baby* who returns to the struggle, wiser and more committed. In regard to women, he is characterized as a man who has never mistreated a woman in his life and as a man who is grateful to women for his life. He is described as Christ-like on occasion, at least in his manner toward women: "There was something blessed in his manner. Women saw him and wanted to weep—to tell him that their chest hurt and their knees did too." (17) Not long after he sees Sethe for the first time in many years, "He rubbed his cheek on her back and learned that way her sorrow, the roots of it; its wide trunk and intricate branches." (17) It is his presence at 124 Bluestone that forces the necessary purgative confrontation between Sethe, the community, and Beloved. Paul D. is, in fact, the only major male protagonist in the Morrisonian canon who has a positive relationship with a female and, furthermore, who struggles with a female to forge this positive relationship. He believes that "only this woman Sethe could have left him his manhood like that. He wants to put his story next to hers." (273)

It is a mark of Toni Morrison's heightened consciousness that she depicts the life that Paul D. struggles to build with Sethe as one based on a common history and a common struggle. It is not based on sex like the Milkman-Sweet affair in *Song of Solomon*, nor on physical appearance like the Son-Jadine affair in *Tar Baby*. Sethe is a typical African woman who is satisfied with the real happiness love brings, not with the artificial contentment bought by status and wealth:

> Perhaps, it was the smile, or may be the ever-ready love she saw in his eyes—easy and upfront, the way colts, evangelists and children look at you; with love you don't have to deserve—that made her go ahead and tell him what she had not told Baby Suggs, the only person she felt obliged to explain anything to. (161)

Unlike Son and Jadine, Paul D. and Sethe struggle together to forge a positive life under the most oppressing conditions.

Like gender oppression, race oppression is examined as a consequence of the economic exploitation of African people. The thesis of Eric Williams's *Capitalism and Slavery* is threefold. According to him the economic demands of the budding capitalist nations led to the slave trade and slavery. And out of the need to justify the enslavement of human beings, these nations institutionalized racism. He rightly feels: "Slavery was not born of racism: rather, racism was the consequence of slavery."[15] Morrison seems in agreement with Williams's thesis. The very fact that African people today are oppressed equally because of the colour of their skin and their poverty clearly proves that race is a later justification for the enslavement of African people.

To accomplish her goal of clarifying the dialectical relationship between race oppression and class exploitation, Morrison documents history by showing that the European and the Native American Indian were enslaved before the African. The European slave is represented by Miss Amy Denver of Boston. Denver says: "My mama worked for these here people to pay for her passage. But then she had me and since she died right after, well, they said I had to work for 'em to pay it off." (34) The parallels between her experiences and those of Africans are similar. She shared the same work experience and punishment as those of Africans. She too is denied education, making her English vernacular almost indistinguishable from that of the African slave.

Also, the novel precisely speaks of the bond forged between the African and the Indian based on their common oppression. Morrison shows the Indian's willingness to make a home for run away African slaves, allowing them to become a part of the tribe or to leave as they pleased:

> Buffalo men, they [the Indians] called them [the runaway slaves] . . . Nobody from a box in Alfred, Georgia, cared about the illness the Cherokee warned them about, so they stayed, all forty-six, resting, planning their next move. Paul D. had no idea of what to do and knew less than anybody it seemed. (112)

The primary enemy of all the three groups—the exploited European indentured servant, the Native American Indian, and the African—has been capitalism. First the theft of raw materials for developing industrial countries and then the theft of a labour force to work within these countries have created the notions of inferiority and superiority leading to race and gender oppression. According to Walter Rodney, "The simple fact is that no people can enslave another for centuries without coming out with a notion of superiority, and when the colour and other physical traits of those peoples were quite different it was inevitable that the prejudice should take a racist form."[16]

Morrison seems to be at her best in documenting slavery and its aftermath. The treatment of slaves as beasts of burden and the sexual exploitation of African women by European men are driven home to the reader. Perhaps, more important than Morrison's skilful way of bringing to life the facts about slavery is her adeptness at correcting myths about slavery. One such myth is that slave life for some was good. Morrison shows how slavery was slavery, on Sweet Home or any other plantation. The conditions of slavery were qualitatively indistinguishable whether the slave had a 'good' master or a 'bad' master. For instance, Baby Suggs reveals that life for her has been one continuous cycle of oppression. Her past has been intolerable like her present. Also for a 'free' African living in a slave society, life is not qualitatively different either. Morrison, therefore, demonstrates that the African's plight can be potentially extirpated only through a collective struggle: "Days of company: knowing the names of forty, fifty other Negroes, their views, habits; where they had been and what done: of feeling their fun and sorrow along with her own, . . . at 124 and in the Clearing, along with others she [Sethe] had claimed herself." (95)

Unity is the only way by which African people can survive. It is only when the African, through self or forced isolation, exists outside the collective that the struggle appears endless and the burden unbearable. In *Beloved*, Morrison reinforces her theme of one people, one struggle, and one solution in several ways. First, she begins each chapter in the novel in the present, and then returns to the past in order to bridge the gap between occurrences of the past and those of the present. Second, the beginnings are often structured in such a way that they seem more like middles thereby emphasizing the fact that oppression for the African exists as one uninterrupted continuum. Another skilful structural device that Morrison uses to reflect the unchanging status of African people is the repetition of key words, phrases or sentences.

Morrison further shows that Africans all over the world are one people having the same history and sharing the same plight since they are seen as one by those outside the African nation, no matter what their class status might be. Clearly she wants African people to see themselves as one people, undivided by their class status. The novel reiterates its theme of solidarity by implicitly reminding the reader chapter after chapter that collective struggle is the only practical way to alleviate the oppression African people have been experiencing.

V

Thus, in *Beloved* Morrison comes to terms with both the dilemma confronting African people and a part of the solution that must be espoused by them. The novel makes it clear that the plight of Africans in America stems from their nation-class oppression, that their primary enemy is capitalism in all its disguises, and that the solution to this problem lies in collective, not individual, class struggle against capitalism. Furthermore, Morrison crystallizes the strategy which ushers in the solution of collective struggle.

Morrison's greatness as a novelist, however, lies in her extraordinary power of achieving a harmonious fusion of her social concerns and the demands of novel as an art form. The ultimate solution of collective struggle to the problem of economic exploitation of the blacks in white America is offered invariably in terms of fictional art. What Morrison has worked out in *Beloved* is an extraordinarily effective Gothic blend of post-modern realism and romance as well as of racial and sexual politics. For the characters of the novel as well as the implied author, the scars of racial, sexual, and class oppression are more horrible on the soul than those on the body.

Thus, Morrison has brilliantly succeeded in her attempt to make *Beloved* "unquestionably political and irrevocably beautiful." It is a beautiful narrative about the survival of the heritage of slavery, on the power of rememory, and the collective memories kept alive through oral tradition. It is also a story of the genesis of a culture and of a people who, living on the edge of life and death, have managed to create that culture and to keep their history alive. Morrison's self-conscious interest in the celebration of black women's strength, their values and beliefs, stems from a desire to correct the wrongs that have been historically levelled against black women. She seeks to celebrate the legends of black women like Baby Suggs and Sethe, and weave their dreams into myths that allow us to recover their past.

By using the kind of narrative pattern in which each character becomes part of his or her own history and must be put together in quilt fashion, Morrison reminds us that the oral tradition is so strong in black culture that it is still alive. The stories of different characters bear witness to the past, to the struggle of black slaves to survive and escape to freedom. The reality and fantasy of their lives create history. Thus, in form and content, *Beloved* is about gaps which must be imaginatively filled in and intelligently interpreted by the reader.

Thus, *Beloved* is as artistically appealing as it is socially and politically gratifying. It is full of beautiful prose, dialogue as rhythmically satisfying as music, living characters and scenes so clearly etched. Morrison tries to do what Dickens did—"create wild, flamboyant, abstractly symbolic characters who are, at the same time, not grotesques but sweetly alive, full of deep feeling."[17] Usually in contemporary fiction, the grotesque is mixed with irony, not with passion and romance. Morrison rejects irony, a choice that immediately sets her apart. Instead, like Alice Walker, she wants to tend the imagination, search for an expansion of the possible and nurture a spiritual richness in the black tradition even after three hundred years in the white desert.

## NOTES

1. Doreatha Drummond Mbalia, *Toni Morrison's Developing Class Consciousness* (Selingrove: Subsquehanna University Press, 1992), 87.
2. P.S, Bassett, Fairmount Theological Seminary, Cincinnati (Ohio), Feb. 12, 1856.
3. Kwane Nkrumah, *Conscienism: Philosophy and Ideology for De- Colonization* (New York: Modern Reader, 1964), 72.
4. Angelo Bonnie, "The Pain of Being Black: An Interview," *Time*, 22 May 1989, 48.
5. Mirriam Horn, "Five Years of Terror," *US News and World Report*, 19 October 1987, 75.
6 "Toni Morrison's *Beloved* Inspired by a slave who chose to kill Her Child," *Atlanta Journal and Constitution* (29 August 1987), 33.

7. Ann Snitow, "Death Duties: Toni Morrison Looks Back in Sorrow," *VLS*, No. 58, September, 25.
8. Alice Walker, *In Search of Our Mother's Gardens* (New York: Harcourt, 1983), xi.
9. Wilfred D. Samuels and Clenora Hudson-Weems, *Toni Morrison* (Boston: Twayne, 1990), 97.
10. Mary Helen Washington, *Midnight Birds: Stories by Contemporary Black Women Writers* (New York: Anchor Press, 1980), xvi.
11. Toni Morrison, *Beloved* (London: Pan, 1987), 163.
12. Bernard Bell, "*Beloved*: A Womanist Neo-Slave Narrative, or Multivocal Remembrances of Things Past," *African-American Review*, 26, 1 (1992), 11.
13. *Ibid.*, 9.
14. Rosemarie Lester, "An Interview with Toni Morrison," Hessian Radio Net Work, West Germany. In Mckay, 1988, 48-49.
15. Eric Williams, *Capitalism and Slavery* (New York: G.P. Putnam's, 1944), 7.
16. Walter Rodney, *How Europe Underdeveloped Africa* (Dar es Salaam: Tanzania Publishing House, 1972), 100.
17. Mbalia, *Toni Morrison's Developing Class Consciousness*, 89.

## CHAPTER VII

# Gender Solidarity through Women Bonding: *Jazz*

> when racism prevented black people from attaining social equality with whites, black men responded as if they were the sole representatives of the black race and therefore, the sole victims of racist oppression. They saw themselves as the people who were being denied their freedom and not black women.
>
> Bell Hooks

> I am the name of the sound
>     and the sound of the name.
> I am the sign of the letter
>     and the designation of the division.
>
> "Thunder, Perfect Mind," *The Nag Hammadi*

All art, as Walter Pater avers, aspires to the condition of music. Perhaps, nowhere is this maxim truer than in the African-American tradition, whose music is often thought of as its greatest achievement. It is a commonplace that the achievement of black literature does not rival the range and depth of its musical counterpart. As Henry Louis Gates points out, "few musical traditions . . . have had more modern masters than has the African-American tradition, from the blues to rhythm-and-blues, from soul to rap, from ragtime to jazz."[1] While many black writers have used musicians and music as theme and metaphor for their writing, none has attempted to draw upon jazz as the structuring principle for an entire work of art until Toni Morrison's new novel, *Jazz* (1992), set in Harlem in 1926, so near to the black literary movement known as the New Negro, or Harlem Renaissance.[2]

Just as Morrison's *Beloved* was sparked by an actual historical event, so too is *Jazz*. Morrison first came across the story of star-crossed lovers when she read Camille Billops' manuscript, *The Harlem Book of the Dead*, which contains photographs and commentary by the great African-American photographer, James Van Der Zee, and poems by Owen Dodson. Van Der Zee described to Camille Billops the curious origins of his photograph of a young woman's corpse:

> She was the one I think was shot by her sweetheart at a party with a noiseless gun. She complained of being sick at the party and friends said, "Well, why don't you lay down?" And they taken her in the room and laid her down. After they undressed her and loosened her clothes, they saw the blood on her dress. They asked her about it and she said, "I'll tell you tomorrow, yes, I'll tell you tomorrow, yes, I'll tell you tomorrow." She was just trying to give him a chance to get away.[3]

As she lay dying, the young woman refused to identify the person who shot her. Morrison protected the seedling of this story line nurturing it for over a decade, until it assumed the shape it has in *Jazz*. The novel is meant to follow *Beloved* as the second volume of a trilogy. However, it does not extend the story told in *Beloved* in a conventional way. The characters as well as the location are new. Even the narrative approach is entirely different. All the same, in terms of chronology, *Jazz* does pick up roughly where *Beloved* left off and continues the greater story Morrison wishes to tell in her trilogy in progress—the story of her people passing through their American experience from the days of slavery up to the present.

Morrison addresses all her novels to the need for black people to see themselves within a culture. The very title of the novel, *Jazz*, reiterates the black folk nature of Morrison's inspiration. As we go through the novel, we are with youth versus old age, sterility versus sex, and the swamps versus the gaudy hubub of city. The novel tells the pathetic story of Violet and Joe Trace who were married over twenty years. The narrative glides between the present and the past, to the rural Virginia of the 1880s where Joe and Violet met and from which they eventually migrated to the magical place they call the city. As the story unfolds, we come to understand what happened. Like many jazz pieces, the novel has a fast opening, establishing a dominant note and theme and then breaks into different parts—various stories (passages) and voices (instruments), various motifs, images and relative themes. As the novel-jazz piece goes on it comes back again and again to the dominant issue of human passion.

Known to have adopted various fictional modes like the Gothic, the supernatural, the detective, or the historical, or even "poetic realism," Toni Morrison mainly writes from the perspective of Black consciousness, covering the whole gamut of black experience. In her latest novel, *Jazz*, she uses the mode of jazz to depict the experience of black community in the city of New York during the 1920s, a decade itself known as the Jazz Age. We find that Morrison's approach in interpreting black experience is quite innovative. No doubt, John A. Williams has already given a fictional interpretation to a real-life jazz artist, Charlie Parker, in his novel, *Night Song*, using musical literary devices in narrating the story of 'Birdie.' Ralph Ellison has also successfully employed the Blues elements in his masterpiece, *Invisible Man*. But, Toni Morrison carries the tradition still further, giving a refreshing interpretation to black experience in her novel, *Jazz*. The energizing, life-giving force of jazz originates from mystery, continues with surprises and end in a sense of renewal. This is how the novel *Jazz* works too. It is inspired by the whole range of human feelings. As the complicated story moves along, it modulates back and forth in sometimes very unexpected ways. In the end human passion is urged on as a creative force, with the narrator telling us that we are "free" to "remake."

Through a meticulous use of the jazz idiom, Morrison relates the story of Joe Trace, a 50-year-old sample-case beauty products salesman, and his wife, Violet, a hairdresser, both of whom had in 1906 train-danced to the New York city, leaving behind all the traumas of their childhood. The backdrop of the action is New York of 1926 "when all the wars are over and there never will be another."[4] Amidst this post-war euphoria, the black community receives a jolt when Joe Trace kills his paramour, an eighteen-year-old creamy-complexioned girl, named Dorcas. Joe shoots Dorcas dead at a dance party because she has left him for another boy, Acton. And then, his crazy wife crashes the funeral of Dorcas and disfigures with a knife the dead girl's face. To find out why any of this happened, all of it on the first page of *Jazz*, we will have to listen to the end of Morrison's song—"as if Sidney Bechet had met the Archduke Trio; as if Ellington had gone Baroque."[5]

Like William Faulkner, whose finest work comes to our mind again and again as we read through *Jazz*, Morrison's new novel serves to redefine the very possibilities of narrative point of view. Like Duke Ellington, Morrison has found a way to create an ensemble of improvised sound out of a composed music. *Jazz* is made up of rhythmic paragraphs, subsections, and sections that together compose a musical score. The novel has a loose fluid non-Aristotelian experimental form—not the tight climactic, Freytag-pyramid structure of conventional fiction, but the form of a jazz piece. What precisely Morrison seeks to do is to oralize print. She also uses her language instrument to try out some daring modes and techniques of play and to create the informal, improvisatory patterning of jazz. Elements of blues, march, rag, spirituals or hymns get fused into the matrix of jazz. The music produced is a combination of melody, rhythm, and harmony with a basic theme or composition which provides for a large scope of improvisation.

What is, however, compelling in *Jazz* is not the novel's plot, but how the story is told. In the telling of the story of *Jazz*, Morrison has adopted a unique narrative method in which the omniscient narrator addresses the reader, but at times allows other characters to relate their stories from their own point of view. Like Faulkner's *As I Lay Dying*, *Jazz* has several narrators, or points of view, whose arias or speaking consciousness bring forth harmony and contrapuntal texture to the novel. Morrison gives us a multi-faceted view of Joe, Violet, and Dorcas as well as of the rest—Malvonne, Joe's neighbour, Rose Dear, Violet's mother, True Belle, her grandmother, Alice Manfred, Dorcas' aunt, Acton, her boy friend and Felice, her girl friend—by the seemingly simple device of letting different voices tell the story or related episodes of the same story. The vision of Morrison's nameless narrator frames the love story, and this anonymous voice slowly draws readers into the rhythm of the city, especially Harlem, where jazz casts bewitching spells on people's psyches. A disembodied narrator slips easily and guilelessly from third-person all-knowningness to first-person lyricism, without ever relaxing its grip upon our imagination. As Henry Louis Gates puts it: "It is a sensitive, poetic narrator, in love with the language of fiction, enraptured with the finest and rarest of arts, the art of telling a good tale, reflecting, as it goes along, upon its responsibilities as a composer, and its obligation to the individual characters whose sole destiny is to make this composition came alive, to sing."[6]

Thus, "*Jazz* becomes a multi-perspective novel in which the main narrator and the characters are like the performers in Jazz ban, each, by turn, improvizing upon his respective past, and then merging into basic theme or composition."[7] Just as the musical mode of jazz uses familiar material to express various sentiments, uniting performer and the audience, the fictional mode of *Jazz* establishes an instant contact between the characters and the reader. In this way, Morrison avoids what Robert Roth calls "authorial dominance." Instead of trying to deduce the writer's intentions, "readers are engaged in a productive dialogue in which their own purposes and practices come into play, often taking the foreground."[8] This leads to a sharing of control as well as to a breaking down of the adversarial writer-reader relationship. Thus, *Jazz* represents "the culmination of Morrison's fictional attempts to connect with her readers, to move them beyond sympathy, empathy, and even understanding of what it means to be black in a white America."[9]

## II

As Toni Morrison is deeply concerned with and committed to African people in America, she uses each of her novels as a framework for investigating various solutions to the African's race and gender oppression and class exploitation, of course, in terms of fictional art. After proposing collective class struggle against capitalism, as a viable solution to African's problem in America, in *Beloved*, Morrison adds a new dimension to the solution arrived at, in her next novel, *Jazz* (1992),[10] with its thematic emphasis on the unity of women as a solution to gender oppression. Since the African people are connected by their history and culture, the solution to the problem of exploitation and oppression that women in particular face is unity. And the promotion of gender solidarity to the major theme in *Jazz* suggests how acute the problem of gender oppression is in the African community. Separated from her man, who was either sold during slavery, or who left the black woman when he went to seek jobs in the North during Reconstruction, the black woman had to depend on other women in the community who became "a source of survival, information and psychic and emotional support."[11]

No doubt, the idea that African-Americans are one people bound by history and culture, in general, and by race, gender, and class oppression, in particular, pervades all of Morrison's work. In *The Bluest Eye*, Claudia recognizes that Maureen Peal is not her enemy inasmuch as both of them are products of the same society in that they are taught that beauty has to be measured by the standard of the ruling class: "And all the time we knew that Maureen Peal was not the enemy and not worthy of such intense hatred. The Thing to fear was the Thing that made her beautiful, and not us." (62) In *Sula*, Nel comes to realize the truth of Eva's words: "You, *Sula*, what's the difference?" (168) that she and Sula, though from drastically different social backgrounds, are bound by factors much stronger than those which tend to separate them. In *Song of Solomon* Milkman sees himself as a part of community in Michigan and in Shalimar as a prerequisite to becoming a part of his living. In *Tar Baby* Jadine's isolation from her people, including Sydney and Ondine, makes her more a tanned European ("Copper Venus") than an African. In *Beloved* Sethe relies on the African community in order to purge the ghost from 124: "unloaded, 124 is just another weathered house needing repair." (264)

While the unification of all African people is not new, gender solidarity and women bonding as the only viable solution to gender oppression, as exemplified in *Jazz*, is altogether new. The idea of women coming together as a result of gender oppression may not be a new idea in the Morrison's canon, but as Mbalia rightly suggests, "it is a jazz melody plucked anew and given prominence by the musician who is Morrison."[12] In *Jazz* Morrison transposes music into another medium—novel—the music that sprang out of her people and expressed their joys and sorrows, their beliefs and their psyche. As this music—spirituals, blues, ragtime, and jazz—has spread throughout the world in our time, and is no longer uniquely or exclusively African-American, Morrison feels that there is a need now to make fiction do what the music used to do, and tell the whole, wide world the ongoing story of her people. So, her novels are not just to narrate, but to sing those origin myths and archetypes of blacks in America. This is what Zora Neale Hurston does in her novels like *Their Eyes Were Watching God*. This is also what other great writers like Paule Marshall, Gwendolyn Brooks, James Baldwin, Richard Wright, Ralph Ellison, and particularly William Faulkner have done in their brilliant literature. As a critic, John Leonard, has recently pointed out, Morrison "ate Faulkner for a snack."[13]

For that matter, we may say that Toni Morrison has always been a jazz musician, "not only because she signifies, assimilates, and advances the themes and structures of great African works, but also and primarily because she signifies, assimilates, and advances the themes and structures of her own canon."[14] *Jazz* continues this tradition of signifying, assimilating and advancing the mutuality of theme and structure. Just as in jazz, the story and the telling of the story are one, so in *Jazz*, theme and structure blend together to suggest the unity that must exist among African women. We are first made aware of this unifying process in the novel's inscription:

> I am the name of the sound
> and the sound of the name.
> I am the sign of the letter
> and the designation of the division.[15]

From this it is implicit that nothing is separate and distinct and that theme is structure and structure is theme. Morrison gives us yet another clue to the unifying process in the first word of the novel—"Sth." This word, rather sound, like buzz, is both the name of the sound and the sound of the name as suggested in the inscription of the novel. Thus, the message of gender solidarity through women bonding cannot be conveyed in a better way than in jazz, a music form in which songster, song, and song telling are one and the same. As the great Charlie "Bird" Parker does for music, Morrison assimilates the best of African literature and, what is more, moves the tradition forward by testing its limb. We may justifiably say that James Lincoln Collier's description of a great jazz musician is applicable to Morrison as well: "The truly great jazz musician is great for the same reasons that a great writer or painter is great: He can make a unified whole out of fascinating parts which join in surprising ways. And we can only explain how he does it by saying that he is a genius."[16] Like any great jazz musician's, Morrison's genius in *Jazz* lies in erasing the seams between theme and structure. Just as with jazz the storyteller is not distinct from the story he is telling, so in *Jazz* the narrator is not distinct from the story she is telling.

III

It is the story of African women that Morrison is most anxious to present in *Jazz*, because it is only they who experience the triple oppression of gender, race, and class. She takes a current problem facing African people, relates it to a problem African women confronted in the 1920s, and shows that the solution then and now remains the same. All African people were in danger of exploitive conditions caused by the changing U.S economy in the 1920s—an economy that moved rapidly from slavocracy to industrialism, and the racism that this economy spawned. The results were the worst race riots in the history of America. If conditions for all African people were barbaric and wild, then conditions for African women were downright warlike. For, unlike African men, African women were also in danger from the sexism that, like racism, is spawned by capitalism.

Conditions of African women were no better in the South than in the North. The main reason parents gave for sending their daughters north was fear of molestation. As Jacqueline Jones points out: "significantly black men mentioned the degraded status of their womenfolk as one of the prime incentives to migrate, along with low wages and poor educational opportunities for their children. Husband told of sexual harassment of wives and daughters by whitemen and of other forms of indignities woven into the fabric of southern society."[17] Northern cities like Harlem are not much different from the South especially for women: "Every week since Dorcas' death, during the whole of January and February, a paper laid bare the bones of some broken women. Man kills wife. Eight accused of rape dismissed. Women and girl victims of. Woman commits suicide. White attackers indicted. . . . In jealous rage man." (74) So, while migrating, the African's thought that they were coming to a tame place, free of exploitation and oppression, they were actually coming to a wild place, perhaps, even wilder than the South since racism and sexism were alive as much in the North.

Hence the dire need for gender solidarity through women bonding. Morrison's dedication for *Tar Baby*:

For
Mrs. Caroline Smith
Mrs. Millie MacTeer
Mrs. Ardelia Willis
Mrs. Lois Brooks
—and each of their sisters,
all of who knew
their true and ancient
properties.

seems to have been realized in *Jazz*. The epithet, "their sisters" contains within itself two of Morrison's concerns—the need for a black person to delve into her own culture and understand its "ancient properties," and the need for one black woman to relate to another in order to seek the "true" self. It is interesting to note that Morrison's dedication voices Zora Neale Hurston's vision in her *Dust Tracks on a Road*: "When I had to come to these women, then I would be at the end of my pilgrimage, but not the end of my life. Then I would know peace and love, and what goes with those things, and not before."[18] Black women's identification and solidarity, as Lorraine Bethel puts it, "is most simply the idea of Black women seeking their own identity and defining themselves through bonding on various levels—psychic, intellectual and emotional as well as physical—with other Black women."[19]

While dealing with various racist and sexist issues, Morrison looks at the concepts of women bonding as a means of coming to an understanding of the self in *Jazz* more than in any of her earlier novels. Her novels are replete with such women-women relationships. To cite but a few examples, in *The Bluest Eye*, Claudia dreams of "security and warmth of big Mommas kitchen." (21) In *Sula*, Nel has been to Sula "the closest thing to both and other and a self." (103) In *Song of Solomon*, Pilate becomes a source of strength for Ruth to stand off Macon Dead. In *Tar Baby*, Jadine's identification with the black women at Eloe as the "other" leads to a discovery of the self. In *Beloved*, Sethe finds a culture mentor in Baby Suggs who kindles a desire in her to know her past and to love herself as a person.

In *Jazz* Violet too finds herself through her relationship with Dorcas, Alice Manfred, and Felice. It is the identification of self with the black women that leads Violet to discover the real "me," as she goes out in search of Dorcas' past, and encounters Alice Manfred, Dorcas' aunt. Unlike Jadine in *Tar Baby* who rejects her culture and solidarity with those black women who help her confront reality, Violet accepts the influence of various black women on her life. Dorcas, Alice, and Felice not only lead Violet to self-discovery but also help her work on her relationship with Joe Trace.

Violet, the wronged wife, is a many-faceted creature and, like Hermann Hesse's Steppenwolf, admits to many selves within herself, occasionally stumbling into a psychotic limbo. Like Joe's mother, Violet is described as being black and skinny. Felice describes her vividly when she says: "herself is very very dark, bootblack, the girls at school would say. And I didn't expect her to be pretty but she is. . . . She is what my grandmother calls pick thin." (206) Once in the New York city Violet experiences exploitive work conditions. Because she does not have the necessary licence to set up a hairdresser shop, she must be at the beck and call of women who want their hair done and accept lower wages as a result. Also, once in the city, Violet becomes more concerned with possessions than with love and communication. For instance, the parrot who squawks "love you" is the one she calls my parrot, just as Joe is "my Joe Trace, Mine." She says: "I picked him out from all the others. . . . My Joe Trace, my Virginia Joe Trace." (96) But as with the parrot, she thinks of Joe as hers without bothering to communicate with him. Like Wild, Violet is silent with Joe: "Over time her silences annoy her husband, then puzzle him and finally depress him." (24) Ultimately these silences cause Joe to act crazy, twice shooting off a gun without meaning to do so. And like Wild, Violet is mistakenly thought to be "violent": "Violent they call her now." (75) The novel traces the path to the understanding of the self Violet comes to in her relationships which are not quite apparent with other black women. Morrison adopts a new technique of telescoping the "philosopher's double" into a "split personality." She attempts to show how Violet turns "violent" and how she recovers her lost self by destroying the violent in her self.

When Violet tries to disfigure Dorcas' face at the latter's funeral, this "violent" act stuns the entire community, but it is women who empathize with her just as it is the women in the community who understand Sethe in *Beloved* and come out to save her. Even a woman like Malvonne, Joe's neighbour, who admits that she hates Violet, cannot turn her back on another black woman. She tells Joe: "Okay, there's no love lost between Violet and me, but I take her part not yours." (46) For, Violet has never ever met Dorcas, nor seen her when alive. Her "memory is a sickness in the house—everywhere and nowhere." (28) Having to live with her memory, Violet realizes that she is falling in love with Dorcas: "When she isn't trying to humiliate Joe, she is admiring the dead girl's hair; when she isn't cursing Joe . . . she is having whispered conversations wit the corpse in her head." (15) Violet reminds us of Sethe in *Beloved*. Though Sethe kills her daughter with the idea of saving her from slavery, she, later on feels guilty of murder, till the dead daughter returns to her in flesh to redeem her mother from the torment. The photograph of Dorcas serves the same purpose in *Jazz*. It becomes a symbol of her guilt. Her sense of guilt is based on the notion that an induced miscarriage is also an infanticide. In Violet's perverted thinking, Dorcas becomes the child she miscarried. Violet finds herself both loving and hating the girl.

## IV

As Joe mourns for Dorcas, Violet wants to know more about the girl she hates so much. She goes out in search of Dorcas' past. As Violet starts her journey into the past, as she learns more and more about Dorcas, she also learns to associate herself with her. She recognizes that Dorcas could have been the daughter she never had, or rather miscarried, a daughter whose hair she, as a hairdresser, would have liked to dress. Violet starts to wonder if Dorcas was "the woman who took the man, or the daughter who fled the womb." (109) Thus, Dorcas, the woman who used to "wear" Violet down, becomes a woman Violet learns to admire and love. As Yamini K. Murthy observes, "Violet's relationship with Dorcas becomes an affirmation of love of one woman for another, although Violet starts out with hatred in her heart."[20] Violet's identification of self with the black women like Dorcas gradually leads her to discover the real "me."

This affirmation of love and, more importantly, identification with the "other" develops into an understanding of the self in Violet's relationship with Alice Manfred. As Violet had tried to disrupt her niece's funeral, Alice Manfred recognizes Violet as "violent" and hence refuses to see her, in spite of the latter's repeated attempts to see her. Alice assumes that Violet wants to see her to seek forgiveness. But, when Violet finally meets her to seek forgiveness, she is willing to sit with her and talk to her. She says that "she had to sit down somewhere. I thought I could do it here." (82) Thus, Alice becomes the person Violet can sit with, and talk to someone who will try to understand her. Alice does understand Violet and Violet soon becomes the only visitor she ever "looked forward to." Though both are initially apprehensive of each other, Alice and Violet come to an understanding of each other, and of the self. Alice begins to speak to Violet in a way she never did with other people. Soon "the women . . . . become so easy with each other, talk wasn't always necessary." (112) More importantly, Alice and Violet learn to laugh and learn that "laughter is serious . . . more complicated, more serious than tears." (113)

Finally, Violet convinces Alice as to why she had to disfigure the face of dead Dorcas. She makes Alice realize that she, a woman who had never held a knife to harm others, would definitely fight and kill for her man. This realization leads Alice to an understanding of Violet's "violent" act at Dorcas' funeral. Thus, Alice's friendship helps Violet to look into herself and view the real "me" inside her. It is Alice who helps Violet define herself and become self-confident. Besides, Violet learns from Alice the true meaning of life. She understands that she has been denying herself all along and that she has to make the most of it. Alice teaches Violet to love. She tells her: "You got anything left to you to love, anything at all, do it." (112) Small wonder, if Violet identifies herself with Alice almost totally. And through her identification with Alice, Violet establishes her own identity and becomes a person even Joe learns to love and admire. What is, however, important to note is that Alice needs the company of Violet just as Violet needs the company of Alice. What Violet helps Alice to understand is that there is no significant class difference between African women inasmuch as all face a triple oppression based on gender, race, and class. The only two classes that exist are the owner class—capitalists—and the ownerless class—workers. This is revealed in the following conversation between Violet and Alice:

> "They're just women, you know. Like us. . . . "
>
> "Don't they fight all the time? when you do their hair, you're not afraid they might start fighting?"
>
> "Only when they sober." Violet smiled.
>
> "Oh, well."
>
> "They share men, fight them and fight over them, too."
>
> "No woman should live like that."
>
> "No. No woman should have to." (84)

From this conversation it is clear that both poor, uneducated African women and educated middle-class African women are victims of triple oppression.

Alice learns not only from Violet's teaching but also from her own voice. Alice speaks her mind to Violet. She develops a wild tongue and 'lets the wild come up and out.' And through this cathartic process, she learns about herself. This bonding and sisterhood between Violet and

Alice allow them not only to talk but also to cry and to laugh—all three signs of healing. What Alice helps Violet to do is to laugh, especially at herself:

> Crumpled over, shoulder shaking, Violet thought about how she must have looked at the funeral, at what her mission was the sight of herself trying to do something bluesy, something hep, fumbling the knife, too late anyway. . . . She laughed till she coughed and Alice had to make them a cup of settling tea. (14)

It is only after this act of seeing herself objectively as others may see her that Violet becomes one whole again instead of two halves of a whole. Morrison has already investigated the idea of two halves of one whole in *Sula*. Nel and Sula make one good whole. In *Jazz*, however, Violet experiences a "double-consciousness" based on her triple oppression.

Violet not only helps Alice, but also Felice, Dorcas' girlfriend, to re-view her life. Felice arrives at the Trace household only to retrieve her lost ring, but stays back not only to discover her own self, but also understand her relationship with her mother. Violet makes her feel perfectly at home. For the first time in her life she confesses and reveals her past to Violet. Just as Denver and other black women in the community help Beloved in *Beloved* to realize that her mother's act of killing was necessitated by love, by not wanting her daughter to be a slave, Violet makes Felice realize that her mother stole a ring from the shop only "out of spite." (203) As in the case of Alice Manfred, Violet's relationship with Felice also helps her understand her mother, Rose, and her grandmother, True Belle, better. Above all, Felice's arrival re-establishes harmony in the Trace household. Violet's understanding of the self leads her to a more harmonious relationship with her husband by sharing and talking personal things again in their chequered life. Thus, "as Violet, Alice, and Felice come together as black women, and discover their own selves through bonding with other black women, they come to an end of a pilgrimage to know and be their own true selves."[21] When each one comes to this end, each of them not only knows how to live, but also how to dream. Particularly, Violet reaches an end of her pilgrimage in discovering her self that only puts her on the threshold of a more meaningful life.

## V

Thus, through bonding, African women become more than close friends. Actually in nurturing each other, as the previous paragraphs have shown, each becomes a 'mama' for the other. As Mbalia rightly points out, "what Violet, Alice, Dorcas, and Felice have in common is the need for 'mamas.'"[22] Violet's mother commits suicide, Dorcas' mother is killed and Felice's mother is absent. That is why, in times of crises, Violet, Alice, and Dorcas each utters the word 'mama.' As regards Alice and Violet: "'Oh, Mama.' Alice blurted it out and then covered her mouth. Violet had the same thought. Mama. Mama?" (110) When Dorcas is asked, on her deathbed, the name of her killer she says: "I know his name but Mama won't tell." (193) Fortunately, Felice gets in Violet a 'mama' just in time: "I can see why Mrs. Manfred let [Violet] visit. She doesn't lie, Mrs. Trace. Nothing she says is a lie the way it is with most older people." (205)

Furthermore, Morrison in *Jazz* shows how, through bonding, all the African women benefit from each other's companionship. To illustrate the point, by the end of the novel Violet, whose cultivated silences caused her husband to act crazy, communicates with Joe: "A lot of the time, though they stay home figuring things out, telling each other those little personal stories they like to hear again and again, or fussing with the bird Violet bought." (223) Similarly, Alice Manfred, having now discovered a taste for brightly coloured dresses, moves back to Springfield and is no longer afraid of men: "The cheerful company may be of someone who can provide the necessary things for the night." (222) Almost in a similar manner, Felice, learning from the experiences and communication of other black women, including Dorcas, grows into a strong woman not to be used, abused, or played with as before: "She's nobody's alibi or hammer or toy." (222) Other black women—Rose and True Belle—too learn and benefit from this sisterhood.

To conclude, Toni Morrison once again proves in *Jazz* that she is not only a committed novelist but also a superb artist. She reveals herself as a virtuoso artist by merging form and content in such a way that one enhances the other. *Jazz* marks another development in her canon because form not only reinforces theme, it is theme. Morrison makes herself an admirable fictional artist in *Jazz* mainly because of the crucial nature of her subject matter. As Mbalia aptly describes:

> Conditions make people Wild, bring out the Wild in people, make women run Wild. What other topic more appropriately expresses the conditions that African people confront today. With over 60% of African families headed by women and nearly 70% of these families living in poverty; with the alarming and increasing rate of teenage pregnancy; with crack and new, deadlier chemical drugs being introduced in the African community every day; with in-

creasing numbers of middle school youth dropping out; with inadequate health care, poor nutrition, and increasing numbers of Africans in their thirties dying from AIDS, cancer, and heart attacks—is it any wonder there are Wilds in the African community?[23]

Thus, Morrison succeeds brilliantly in her latest novel, *Jazz*, in arriving at the solution of gender solidarity, in terms of fictional art, for the dilemma of African women. As a committed fictional artist, she drives home to us the need for sisterhood in the African community through which communication, not silence, will forge the way toward a healthy, wholesome future for all people of African descent, especially women. To conclude, even before Morrison finishes her ambitious trilogy about the historical odyssey of African-Americans, we may already recognize her as one of our most important international novelists.

# NOTES

1. Henry Louis Gates, Jr., *Black Literature Literary Theory* (New York: Methuen, 1984), 52.
2. In 1926 a renaissance in the arts created by a group of writers called "New Negroes," and centered in and about Harlem, was at its zenith. Wealthy white patrons and mainstream New York publishers were sponsoring young black writers as never before. Civil rights and political leaders had come to believe that it would be through the arts that full social, political, and economic liberation for the black elite would come. For the first time black writers were feted as literary lions. To cite but a few classic instances, Langston Hughes published his jazz and blues poems in a volume entitled *The Weary Blues*, as well as his manifesto of black criticism—*The Negro Artist and the Racial Mountain*. Zora Neale Hurston, Hughes, and Countee Cullen launched their boldly experimental magazine, *Fire*!! Carl Van Vechten published his controversial novel, *Nigger Heaven*, and Paul Green won a Pulitzer Prize for his novel, *In His Abraham's Bosom*.
3. Henry Louis Gates, and K.A. Appiah, ed., *Toni Morrison*: *Critical Perspectives Past and Present* (New York: Amistad, 1993), 53.
4. Toni Morrison, *Jazz* (London: Pan, 1992).
5. John Leonard, "*Jazz*," *The Nation,* May 25, 1992.
6. Gates and Appiah, *Toni Morrison*, 54.
7. Usha Shourie, "The Morrison Music: Narrative Style in *Jazz*," *Indian Journal of American Studies*, 23, 2 (Summer 1993), 68.
8. Robert Roth, "Deconstructing Audience: A Post-Structuralist

Rereading," *A Sense of Audience in Written Communication*, ed. Gesa Krisch and Duane H. Roen (London: SAGE, 1990), 181.

9. Denise Heinze, *The Dilemma of "Double-Consciousness": Toni Morrison's Novels* (London: The University of Georgia Press, 1993), 195.
10. Toni Morrison has made *Jazz* from a photograph in James Van Der Zee's *Harlem Book of the Dead* of the body of a young girl, shot at a party by a jealous boyfriend, who died refusing to identify her assailant.
11. Lorraine Bethel, "'The Infinity of Conscious Pain': Zora Neale Hurston and the Black Female Literary Tradition," *But Some of Us Are Brave* (New York: The Feminist Press, 1982), 179.
12. Doreatha Drummond Mbalia, "Women Who Run With Wild: The Need for Sisterhood in *Jazz*," *Modern Fiction Studies*, 39, 3 and 4 (Fall/Winter, 1993), 635.
13. John Leonard, "*Jazz*," *The Nation*, May 25, 1992.
14. Mbalia, "Women Who Run With Wild," 623.
15. Epithet to the novel, *Jazz*.
16. James Lincoln Coiller, *Inside Jazz* (New York: Four Winds P, 1973), 31.
17. Jacqueline Jones, *Labour of Love, Labour of Sorrow*: *Black Women, Work, and the Family, From Slavery to the Present* (New York: Vintage, 1985), 157.
18. Zora Neale Hurston, *Dust Tracks on a Road* (Philadelphia: J.B. Lippincott, 1971), 58.
19. Yamini K. Murthy, "Gender Solidarity and Discovery of Self in Morrison's *Tar Baby* and *Jazz*," *Indian Journal of American Studies,* 23, 2 (Summer 1993), 82.
20. *Ibid.*, 83.
21. *Ibid.*
22. Mbalia, "Women Who Run With Wild," 634.
23. For additional information on the current oppression of African women, see the following works—*The World's Women—1970-1990, Trends and Statistics* (New York: United Nations, 1991) and Jaynes Gerald D. and Robin M. Williams Jr., *A Common Destiny*: *Blacks and American Society* (Washington, D.C.: National Academy P, 1989).

# CHAPTER VIII

# Conclusion

Toni Morrison is not only a leading African-American woman novelist, but also one of the most significant and relevant writers on the literary scene today. Her genius was apparent from the publication of her very first novel, *The Bluest Eye* (1970), so much so that it was clear in 1970 what she would come to mean to us by 1997. In the course of her twenty-six year career as an author, Morrison has become the American and African-American woman writer to reckon with. She has been amply recognized for her combined greatness as a voice for black people and as a master craftsperson of the dominant literary artistic form. In fact, as Trudier Harris puts it, Morrison has entered superstardom: "By any standard of literary evaluation, Toni Morrison is a phenomenon, in the classic sense of once-in-a-lifetime rarity, the literary equivalent of Paul Robeson, Michael Jordon, Wayne Gretzky, Chris Evert, or Martina Navratilova, the super star whose touch upon her profession makes us wonder if we shall ever see her like again."[1] Such spectacular praise represents not just a hallmark in Toni Morrison's career, but quite possibly in the literary history of African-American writers in American literature.

Toni Morrison belongs to a group of writers in America—Maya Angelou, Toni Cade Bambara, Paule Marshall, Alice Walker, and Gloria Naylor—for whom writing is a liberating tool, a subversive strategy and an artistic mode for self-expression. Combining the aims of the Black Freedom Movement and Women's Liberation, Morrison seeks to produce literature which is irrevocably and indisputably black. Like Edward Said who exposed orientalism as a western style for dominating, restructuring and having authority over the Orient, she explores the distortion of black reality by the dominant group for its vested interest. She refutes the hierarchical order shaped by the concepts of centre and periphery and questions the ideology on which the order is based. She is simultaneously engaged in the project of constructing an Afrocentric perspective, and evolving an African-American poetics.

Exploring the complexity of black female experience in white America, Morrison attempts to resolve the contradiction inherent in her African-American identity. Conscious of her own marginalisation within the context of the mainstream, she starts valuing her peripheral existence. Titled as a 'Black Woman Writer,' Morrison claims to be concerned, above all, with the idea of 'a black community'—what such a community once meant, how it has changed, and how, despite those changes, it is and should be maintained. In an interview with Salman Rushdie, she says:

> I am not sure what the word 'negro' means, which is why I write books. What is a black child/woman/friend/mother? What is a black person? It seems to me that there are so many that inform blackness. One of the modern qualities of being an African-American is the flux, is the fluidity, the contradictions.[2]

Naturally, her novels are an exploration of the meaning of blackness—what it means to be black in white America, to be a black woman in a white male hegemonic society, to believe in an indigenous African culture in a world that endorses only Eurocentric culture, and to strive for visibility in a society in which blackness signifies invisibility. They record the triumphs and complexities of black life from the painful past of slavery to the frustrating, racist present.

Moreover, Morrison talks of her writing as 'archaeological explorations,' one of her major concerns being the rewriting of African-American history from a black female perspective. Until the 1940s, black women in both Anglo- and African-American literature have been usually assigned stereotyped roles. Throughout the novels of slavery and reconstruction periods, the Southern white literature fashioned an image of the black woman intended to further create submission and a dumping ground for those female functions which a basically Puritan society could not confront. Following the advice Shirley Chisholm gave in the sixties on the need to speak truthfully and courageously about their plight as women, Morrison girds up her loins and speaks out:

> I write for black women. We are not addressing the men, as some white female writers do. We are not attacking each other, as both black and white men do. Black women writers look at things in an unforgiving, loving way. They are writing to repossess, rename, reown.[3]

Resultantly, we have in her novels a woman-to-woman, rather than a woman-to-man, approach. If Alice Walker explores the oppression, the insanities, the loyalties, and the triumphs of black women, Morrison illuminates, in the lives of imaginary black women, the presence of beauty, love or, more often, the absence of love. Thus, by focusing on the pertinent issues, Morrison lays the cornerstone for a sound, thorough articulation of the black feminist aesthetic.

## II

The lives of African-American women have been critically affected by racism, sexism, and classism which are systems of societal and psychological restrictions. The racist, sexist, and classist structure of the American society compartmentalizes its various ethnic groups, denigrates the coloured as inferior and characterizes males and females as centre and margin respectively. Just as blacks as a group are relegated to an underclass by virtue of their race, women are relegated to a separate caste by virtue of their sex. Black women have been victimized not only by racist and sexist assumptions but also by class exploitation which is, perhaps, the greatest source of oppression of blacks in America. The basic myth of racism is that the white are more intelligent and more virtuous than the black by the mere fact of being white. Furthermore, whiteness is automatically equated with beauty and culture, and blackness with ugliness and slavery. Sexism mutilated the backs and minds of African-American women and, what was worse, defiled their sexual beings and scarred them psychologically. Thus, to be black and female is to suffer from the twin disadvantages of racial discrimination and gender bias. The double whammy of blatant white racism and black male sexism have hurled black women headlong into the dismal abyss of 'geometric oppression.' If the dominant racist group has condemned them through an abusive ideology, black men, by virtue of their phallic superiority, have held black women as their scapegoats, victimizing them in every conceivable way. Black women suffer not only because they are black and female but also because they are economically poor. The ideal concept of woman in American society is not just racist and sexist but essentially classist. And poor, black women, who could hardly approximate the norm, are discriminated against and dehumanized.

Race, gender, and class—the three main sources of oppression of blacks in white America—are not separate entities, but are closely linked with each other. They are so organically connected that one must understand their interrelationship in spite of their ever-shifting appearance. Racism and sexism can be understood as by-products of capitalism. The economic system of slavery, an early form of capitalism, is the cause of racism and sexism rather than the result of it, as ably demonstrated by Eric Williams, Nkrumah, and Rodney.[4] In other words, racism and sexism stem from class exploitation. Thus, as sources of oppression of blacks, racism, sexism, and classism are mutually interdependent, and arise from the same set of circumstances.[5] In sum, being black the African women suffer from racial discrimination, being females they are the victims of sexual atrocities at the hands of the white patriarchs as well as the blacks, and being former slaves they are compelled to remain poor. In this manner, the black women in America are made victims of triple jeopardy—racism, sexism, and classism. In the contemporary period, black women novelists like Frances Harper, Jessie Fauset, Nella Larsen, Zora Neale Hurston, Ann Petry, Paule Marshall, and Alice Walker have continued to analyse the relationship between race, gender, and class. Significantly, Toni Morrison has illuminated in her novels, more than others, the definition of woman in relation to race and class assumptions.

## III

Toni Morrison's novels artistically document the author's awareness of and concern for the historical conditions of oppression of African people in America, thereby revealing her heightened consciousness of the interrelationship of race, gender, and class. Although all the three elements are present in all her novels, the emphasis on them varies from novel to novel. Morrison examines the problems of race and gender oppression before exploring class contradictions within the race. At the beginning of her writing career, she thinks that racism is the main source of oppression of blacks in white America because of her low level of gender and class consciousness. Then, becoming aware of the indispensability of the sexuality of American racism, she finds that sexism is equally oppressive. Finally, she realizes that racism and sexism are by-products of capitalism—the economic systems of slavery.

In Morrison's first novel, *The Bluest Eye*, the emphasis is on racism. Specifically, she investigates the effects of beauty standards of the dominant culture on the self-image of the African female adolescent. Although the novel is basically concerned with the contradictions fostered by racism, sexism, and class distinctions affecting the black girls in white America, Morrison, at this stage of her literary career, considers racism the African's primary obstacle. *The Bluest Eye* attempts to show terrible consequences for blacks internalizing the values of a white culture that both directly and indirectly rejects them. Eleven-year-old Pecola is a poor, ugly, black girl who longs to have blue eyes in the poignant, wistful hope that this will bring her the love she longs for and also somehow alleviate the multiple miseries of her hate-filled, quarrelsome, violent family, ironically named Breedlove. Pecola becomes the victim of one after another in a chain of black people including her own mother and father who have been twisted and perverted by the false and often vicious standards of the white world. Pecola suffers not only as a black, but also as a female. If, as a racial being, she is forced to relinquish her individual, cultural ways, as a gender being she is made to subordinate her femininity and remain subsumed in the orbit of patriarchy. Although her class analysis is immature in this novel, Morrison is at least conscious of a limited role that economics plays in the exploitation of African people.

In Morrison's second novel, *Sula*, the thrust is on gender. It is the intriguing story of Sula Mae Peace, an acutely sensitive and defiant woman whose nonconformity is a "living criticism of the dreadful lives of resignation other women live."[6] As a young girl, she startles the community with her extreme emotional impulses and grows into a "strange, strong, and independent woman." She rejects "behavioral standards of all kinds" and attempts to "rely solely on herself."[7] Even though the focus of the novel is on gender bias, the racial issues—the origin of the Bottom with its roots in slavery and the lack of development of Deweys—are interwoven into the fabric of the novel throughout. The concerns of class, whether of the capitalists or the masses rank third after gender and race. The issue of class is only incidental, the thrust being on sexism. The switch in the thematic emphasis suggests that Morrison, at this stage of her literary career, considers the lack of individual rights on the part of black women in America as the primary cause of the African's oppression.

Morrison's third novel, *Song of Solomon*, does not primarily focus on the concept of woman, for its protagonists are men. Nevertheless, class, in relation to race and gender, becomes more focal in this novel than in *The Bluest Eye* and *Sula*. Morrison subordinates sexism to both racism and capitalism, realizing that the exploitation of the African woman by the African man is the result of his national and class oppression. Closer to Ralph Ellison's *Invisible Man* than to Morrison's earlier works, *Song of Solomon* "combines the epic quest with bildungsroman motif and the search for the Grail of identity theme."[8] Like Alex Haley's *Roots*, it illustrates the importance of African's awareness and acceptance of their history in order to liberate themselves from race and class oppression. Though Milkman's quest for his identity is the dominant thread of the novel, the major obstacle he has to overcome is the deadening effects of capitalism. Milkman is accidently propelled on his search for himself as a result of his desire for gold. The long journey leads him back through his personal past to a racial history that had been vehemently opposed to materialism and greed. His knowledge liberates him and he begins to respect the poor blacks around him as well as the sweet women—Pilate and Hagar—who have continuously helped him. *Song of Solomon*, thus, marks a qualitative leap in Morrison's consciousness as an African-American woman writer. She is now more aware of the dialectical relationship between capitalism, racism, and sexism.

Morrison's increased class consciousness is reflected in her ability and commitment to explore the cause-and-effect relationship between class, race, and gender as evidenced in her fourth novel, *Tar Baby*. Morrison has sufficiently matured by now to understand that the fundamental cause of the African oppression is the exploitative economic systems of capitalism. The two protagonists in *Tar Baby*—Son and Jadine—are sharply divided in their attitudes to the dominant ruling class as well as to their own traditional culture. They must struggle together to resolve their own class interests in order to unite. Morrison's emphasis in the novel is, therefore, on class struggle against capitalism. Racism and sexism, although equally oppressive, are treated as by-products of capitalism. The idea now developed is that eradication of capitalism ensures eradication of racism and sexism. Eradication of the plight of African people demands not individual but collective class struggle. But, the materialistic Jadine and roots-bound Son do not struggle together. Jadine's quest for psychic wholeness is unsuccessful because of her acceptance of the values and mores of white culture without question, rejecting her own African-American heritage. A conscious, socialist-oriented Son tries unsuccessfully to politically educate the selfish, capitalist-oriented Jadine. His failure to do so is in part due to his own seduction by the capitalist way of life. Their solutions to the common problem they face are individual and not applicable to the concrete realities of everyday life. Thus, *Tar Baby* projects only individual class struggle against capitalism which is finally rendered fruitless.

Recognizing by now that capitalism is the primary target against which the blacks must struggle, and, what is more, understanding that capitalism is but the gentleman's form of slavery, Morrison proposes in her widely acclaimed and most conscious novel, *Beloved*, collective class struggle against capitalism as the only viable solution possible for the African people in America. Gender oppression in the novel is not a visible problem that exists between African men and women, but one that exists within the context of the economic relationship between master and slave. Like gender oppression, race oppression is examined as a consequence of the economic exploitation of African people. Based on the most oppressed period of slavery in the history of African people, *Beloved* dramatizes a haunting amalgam of the past and present experiences of an escaped female slave, Sethe, tracing the heroine's quest for meaning and wholeness in slavery and in freedom. Through flashbacks to past tragedies and deeply symbolic delineations of continued emotional and psychological suffering, the novel explores the hardships endured by former slave woman, Sethe, and her family during the Reconstruction era. It is Morrison's goal in this work to demonstrate that collectivism is the first step in eradicating the national oppression and class exploitation of African people. To drive home the dire need for collective action for the survival of African people, she juxtaposes isolated struggle with collective struggle and selfish individualism with individualism conditioned by social responsibility. Toni Morrison uses Beloved as a vehicle to propose solidarity as the solution for African people. The message conveyed in terms of fictional art in *Beloved* is as follows:

> No longer should African people be physically intimidated by Europeans as in *The Bluest Eye*; no longer should African people indulge in the selfish individualism of *Sula*; no longer should African people ignore their duty to pass on the knowledge of their history as in *Song of Solomon*; and no longer should African people attempt to wage struggle alone and, thus, unsuccessfully as in *Tar Baby*. Solidarity, the theme of *Beloved*, is the solution for African people.[9]

After affirming collective class struggle against capitalism in *Beloved*, Morrison seems to have realized that the problem of gender oppression, peculiar to women, can be solved only through gender solidarity. Hence the thematic emphasis on the unity of women in her latest novel, *Jazz*, which adds a new dimension to the solution for the African dilemma. Just as African people as a whole must bond together to survive and to progress, so also must African women—the most exploited adult sector in the African community—help one another in order to live healthy and wholesome lives. Morrison's purpose in the novel is to make fiction do what the music does whereby she exploits the mode of jazz to depict the experience of black community during 1920s known as the Jazz Age. Just as the musical mode of jazz is known to have used familiar material to express various sentiments, uniting performer and audience, the fictional mode of jazz, used in the novel, establishes quick contact between the characters and the reader. The novel traces the path to the understanding of the self. Violet, a wronged woman, comes to in her relationships with other black women—Dorcas, Alice, and Felice. Although it begins with Violet's inability to understand Dorcas, she finally does through her interaction with Dorcas' aunt, Alice, and her friend, Felice. Defining themselves through bonding on various levels—physical, intellectual, emotional, and psychic—with other black women, these black women seek their own identity. In nurturing each other, teaching and learning from each other, each black woman in the novel becomes a 'mama' for the other.

## IV

A close study of the interrelationship of race, gender, and class in the novels of Toni Morrison reveals the emergence of an evolutionary pattern. One can perceive a progressive, thematic and structural development in her works. She uses each novel as a framework for investigating various problems of and solution to the African's dilemmas. In each of her novels Morrison explores some aspect of oppression afflicting African people. Each successive novel reflects her growing understanding of the nature of the African's oppression. As her narrative structure develops, she learns to shape her theme artistically so as to provide accurate presentation. One can perceive the thread that runs through and connects novel after novel as one picks up where the other leaves off thematically and structurally.

Starting with the issue of race as the primary form of oppression of the African people (*The Bluest Eye*), next demonstrating that woman's individuality is rewarding only if it is achieved within the context of the community well-being (*Sula*), adding the problem of class exploitation to that of race (*Song of Solomon*), and then recognizing capitalism as the primary target against which African people must struggle (*Tar Baby*), Morrison proposes solidarity—collective class struggle against capitalism—as the only viable solution possible for African people (*Beloved*), and gender solidarity—women bonding—as the solution for gender oppression (*Jazz*). Thus, the evolution from *The Bluest Eye* to *Jazz* is really one of maturation and clarification rather than revolution.

From this it becomes clear that Morrison is gaining knowledge as she experiences life, reads about it, writes about it and, what is more, thinks as she writes. As her knowledge of the dialectical way in which the laws of nature apply to society increases, she moves from a weak to a strong class analysis, always recognizing the role of race and gender in the African's oppression. And, as she continues to think about, write about, and experience the ongoing oppression of the African people in racist America, Morrison becomes conscious of the fact that gender is as much the African's enemy as race, and finally she becomes more conscious of the fact that class, not race and gender, is the African's greatest enemy.

While each of the earlier novels concentrates on a different but related factor in the oppression of African people, all are symbiotically related. In fact, each serves as a stepping stone that enables Morrison to move to the next level of discovery. In Morrison's novels each character is a development of the preceding one. The twelve-year-old Pecola becomes the twelve-year-old Sula, the thirty-year-old Sula becomes the thirty-one-year-old Milkman, the conscious Milkman, who flies away unburdened by the material objects of the capitalist world, becomes the Son who single-handedly tries to politically educate the people in vain. The unsuccessful Son becomes the Paul D., who defies defeat, a part of the struggling collective, by returning again and again to struggle for the people.

The ambivalent, noncommital endings of the first four novels and the clear, confident endings of *Beloved* and *Jazz* can be used as examples to gauge the author's own developing consciousness regarding both the nature of African oppression and the solution. *The Bluest Eye* ends with the demise of the main character, Pecola Breedlove, who becomes mentally unstable at twelve years and miscarries her child. In *Sula*, the selfish individualism of the protagonist brings death. In *Song of Solomon*, Milkman, having gained consciousness about himself and his people, flies away instead of passing on his political consciousness. In *Tar Baby*, a conscious, socialist-oriented Son tries unsuccessfully to politically educate the selfish, capitalist-oriented Jadine because of his own seduction by the capitalist way of life. But, *Beloved* ends on a note of unity by reiterating that collective struggle is the only way out for the survival of African people in America. Similarly, *Jazz* ends on a note of gender solidarity as the viable solution for gender oppression.

In this way, after six novels—*The Bluest Eye*, *Sula*, *Song of Solomon*, *Tar Baby*, *Beloved*, and *Jazz*—most carefully and consciously written in the course of twenty-two years, Toni Morrison comes to terms with both the dilemma confronting African people in America and a part of the solution that must be embraced by them. The novels make clear the facts that blacks in America suffer from a crisis of the African personality stemming from a three-pronged oppression of race, gender, and class. Each successive novel reflects her growing understanding of the nature of solution to the African dilemma. The novels also make clear that the primary enemy of the Africans in America is not so much racism or sexism as capitalism in all its disguises. It is further made clear that the solution to the African's plight lies not in individual, but in collective class struggle against capitalism and in gender solidarity. Furthermore, Morrison crystallizes the strategy of political education through communication which ushers in the solution—collective struggle. Thus, Morrison's novels reflect a thematic and a structural evolution that coincide with her own growing class consciousness.

In sum, a close look at the Morrison canon reveals that there is an evolutionary pattern in her novels. One can perceive a thematic and structural unity not only in her individual novels, but in her very canon as a whole. Each novel moves forward to a new concern, but without having completely left behind the previous ones. Thus, the movement is both linear and circular, "a Yeatsian gyre that spins back on itself but inevitably leads upward to new ways of seeing old systems of belief."[10] In this respect Morrison's novels can be considered, as Robert Stepto suggests, "an intratextural call and response, a progressive troping of her own works." In other words, each Morrison novel in progression is an increasingly bold and original revoicing of her previous concerns.

V

A study of the interrelationship of race, gender, and class in the novels of Toni Morrison lays bare her intention of being a cultural affirmationist. As a black woman writer, she seeks to affirm what Alice Walker calls the "accumulated collective reality"—the "dreams, imaginings, rituals, and legends that make up the subconscious of a people."[12] Like Zora Neale Hurston's, Morrison's fiction challenges not only black people to "unearth the values that could restore the balance . . . and give men and women the words to speak . . . to set their spirits free,"[13] but also her readers to be transformed by reaffirming the very values and material which the larger white culture minimized or devalued. She consciously reclaims the rural and small-town experience that was being pushed aside or forgotten. In resisting change by affirming the value of black cultural artifacts—the customs, manners, language, and stories of commonplace people in commonplace locales—Morrison becomes a cultural archivist. But, at the same time, she is more than a mere archivist moving as she does beyond what Hazel Carby calls "a romantic evocation of the folk," and engaging in a vigorous critique of the relationship between "the folk and American culture."[14] By so doing, she implicitly and explicitly proposes a revision of received notions of race, gender, and class. Furthermore, her novels reveal that she seeks to challenge "the culture's assumptions inscribed in the binary oppositions of rural versus urban people, of old versus young, of the values and traditions of the past versus those of the present, and of male versus female roles and experience."[15] From this it is clear that the goal of her fictional art is not to deny the importance of progress altogether but to challenge those who, in its name, would negate the values embodied in their folk aesthetic. In other words, the goal of her art is to redeem or transform the black culture through narrative fiction.

Toni Morrison finally comes to us as an ethnic, cultural feminist celebrating the strengths of black women against the heavy odds of racism, sexism, and classism. Morrison's development of the women characters in her novels parallels the way in which most black women writers like Zora Neale Hurston, Gwendlyn Brooks, and Paule Marshall combine their concern for feminism and ethnicity. Though her women characters like Mrs. MacTeer, Ėva Peace, Pilate and Ondine do not have a societal support system that pays them well or appreciates their beauty and the dual role as housemaker and provider they assume in their families, they keep their vision and their energies focused on that which is worthwhile and sustaining. Morrison's emphasis on their selflessness and their strength is not to romanticize their limited opportunity for adventure or fulfilment outside the boundaries of their own communities. Instead, it is to show the value and the difficulty of the role that they play. Morrison believes that the ability of these women is too often ridiculed in negative matriarchal jargon. Morrison exposes the damage that sexist oppression both inside and outside of the ethnic group, has had on black women. But, at the same time, she does not advocate, as a solution to their oppression, an existential political feminism that alienates black women from their ethnic group. Morrison is more concerned with celebrating the unique feminine cultural values that black women have developed in spite of and often because of their oppression. For, as an ethnic, cultural feminist it is a feminism that encourages allegiance to rather than an alienation from the ethnic group that she ultimately wants to achieve.

In short, Morrison has not proclaimed herself to be a black feminist as vehemently as writers like Alice Walker, Gloria Naylor, Ntozake Shange, June Jordon, Gayle Jones, Barbara Smith, and Deborah McDowell. However, in her novels she goes much deeper into the very roots of racism, sexism, and classism, and in a subtle way, she exposes the ideological basis of these pernicious social evils. And, to bring them out effectively she digs out the legends, myths, folk stories and folk songs of African-Americans. Thus, Morrison's role, as ethnic, cultural feminist, has been to alleviate the prejudices and misconceptions and to seek ways to reinforce the values that racism, sexism, and classism would take away from the beauty, the work, and the cultural values of black women.

## VI

A study of Toni Morrison's treatment of the interrelationship of race, gender, and class makes it clear that she is not only a deeply committed novelist, but also a highly conscious artist. The award of the 1993 Nobel Prize for literature for Toni Morrison marks not only the validity of the black woman's voice, but also the recognition of her artistry of African-American fiction. As Lubiano observes, Morrison's work "remaps the terrain of African-American cultural and social history and allows for a community of the imagination" and, what is more, it "interprets the ideology that produces the kind of world we inhabit."[16] Unlike other black artists—Gwendolyn Brooks, Clarence Major and Albert Yound—who use fictional art for purely political purposes, Morrison subordinates the political in order to establish a positive black identity, realizing that strict adherence to political dogma would be insufficient to promote the aesthetic qualities of art. While firmly believing that "the best art is political," she is able to make it "unquestionably political and irrevocably beautiful at the same time."[17]

Combining political consciousness with aesthetic sensibility, Morrison achieves a delicate balance between her political commitment to her people and her aesthetic responsibility to her art of fiction. While exploring the dynamics of racism, sexism, and classism, Morrison does not limit herself to an indictment of the dominant white class only. She turns her gaze to the problems within the black community as she relentlessly exposes intra-racism, black male brutalities, female sexual abuse, and incest. Thus, without directly denouncing white society, she valorizes the black community. By indirection Morrison avoids the polarization of black and white humanity—one as inherently good and the other as irrevocably corrupt—thereby allowing all people to vicariously experience a rebirth. Thus, Morrison brilliantly succeeds in her attempt to elevate through fictional art the reclaimable and beautiful in the human condition.

Though a product of her times, Morrison is a visionary "capable of shelving her personal accomplishments to uncover the ashes behind the glitter."[18] Morrison's multi-layered vision has been shaped by her complex relationship to literary traditions. As a black woman writer Morrison is a double outsider in the patriarchal white culture—a position which allows her to criticize both the white and the black worlds. But, whatever may be the source of her unique vision, it results in the complex, literary and moral texture of her novels. And, as Karen Stein suggests, "as we are drawn into Morrison stories, we must shed our misconceptions and question our judgements until we arrive at the core of truth."[19] Morrison's richly textured fiction also reflects her special and unique vision—a vision which is neither white nor male. It is, in fact, a black woman writer's distinctive feminine vision. Her vision, as Jung has defined in "Psychology and Literature," is "a real experience. It is not something derived or secondary—. It is true symbolic expression—this is, the expression of something existent in its own right."[20] It is this "real experience" which has been defined by the Nobel Prize Swedish Academy as 'an essential aspect of American reality' in Morrison's fiction.

Toni Morrison is essentially a fictional artist, and not a historian or a sociologist. She writes fiction thereby acting as a mediator of the real world rather than its mimic. She presents an ideological representation of the African-American social reality. As an artist, Morrison negotiates a very complex matrix of reality in which she is both despised and revered. This results in her double-visionary canon—a symbiosis of novel writing in which Morrison has complete mastery over the fictive reality she creates. Her creative mediation between the real and fictive worlds generates possibilities rather than merely recording continued frustration and oppression. As Heinze observes: "Morrison may not write from a stance of art as life, but she may be a psychological and spiritual wizard of Oz for life as art."[21]

As a committed novelist and a conscious artist, Morrison validates black culture and reaffirms its adaptive survival power—"its creativity amidst oppression, its life-affirming qualities as well as its ancient wisdom and humanity and its capacity for survival."[22] In denouncing the dominant culture she presents, to an aging America, alternatives that have always existed and are now emerging, but which have long been suppressed by the rhetoric of an entrenched ideology.

## VII

As a highly matured fictional artist, Morrison stands an apt comparison with novelists of other countries and climes, as she plays with a variety of viewpoints, as whites and blacks, husbands and wives, parents and children, observe and misunderstand each other. As in the fiction of great novelists like Jane Austen, Salman Rushdie, and R.K. Narayan, in Morrison's novels of black American life, appearance and reality, the magical and the real, the comic and the tragic are continually juxtaposed. Irony operates, as in Jane Austen, on many levels, as the hopes and plans of Morrison's characters are frustrated by their white neighbours. She frames her tales within mythic narrative structures thereby creating a heroic context for her themes and characters. At the same time, she develops a rich irony by juxtaposing heroic expectation with mundane reality. Furthermore, by pitting contrasting figures against one another, Morrison repeatedly reverses the reader's expectations. Through the craft of writing and art of storytelling she seeks to discover the consequences of choices and the actions of her characters. Her readers are not handed over ready answers but rather must become part of a tale's resolution.

Like Salman Rushdie, Morrison uses the mode of magic realism with great success to critique historiography. Magic realism, which is a post-modern device, takes an unexpected turn in the hands of Morrison to emerge as a component of African-American poetics, since it becomes the means of creating an African world view. African cultural traditions are thus integrated into contemporary western literary tradition in the fiction of Toni Morrison. Her novels transport us into a world in which there are flying black men (*Song of Solomon*), blind horsemen (*Tar Baby*), swamp women, spirits and even a wild woman living naked in the forest. The fabulous world she presents in her novels postulates a belief in an alternate reality in which spirits can co-habit with human beings. For instance, in *Beloved* no one questions the idea of the ghost co-habiting with Sethe and Denver, because her appearance is not a violation of African religion and philosophy. The mode of magic realism, thus, facilitates the presentation of an alternate reality.

As a superb fictional artist Toni Morrison invariably reminds us of Virginia Woolf, an early twentieth century British woman writer. Like Virginia Woolf's works, Morrison's novels are bracketed by war. Although from different cultures and times, both of them faced problems as women writers. While Virginia Woolf had to "kill the angel in the house,"[23] Toni Morrison had to "kill the mammy in the big house."[24] Although Virginia Woolf's and Morrison's views might seem to be different, both of their writings are riveted on the relationship between the inner life of their characters and the world within which they find themselves. As in Virginia Woolf's, in Morrison's work inner time is always transforming outer time through memory. Since memory is not only individual but merges with others to create a communal memory, outer time also transforms inner time as in Woolf's *Mrs. Dalloway* and *The Waves* and Morrison's *Song of Solomon* and *Beloved.* Both the novelists clearly acknowledge that imagination is central to their temperment and they have used some similar narrative strategies like 'interior monologue' and 'stream-of-consciousness.'

As a novelist artistically dealing with racism and sexism as sources of oppression of black women in white America, Toni Morrison reminds us of Anita Desai, a distinguished contemporary Indian woman novelist in English, who sensitively presents female alienation and oppression in the post-colonial Indian society. Like Toni Morrison, Anita Desai deals with the world of lonesome and sensitive heroines—Maya, Monisha, Sita and Nanda Kaul—who are pitted against the dehumanizing forces abroad in Indian society. When these heroines seek a higher communion of free spirits, they are compelled to conform and yet are denied even the ordinary comforts in marriage and motherhood. The compulsion to succeed in conformity leads them to despise themselves as in the case of Toni Morrison's heroines like Pecola, Sula, and Jadine. Anita Desai's heroines are a study of female psyche alienated owing to a lack of compassionate companionship. Their predicament is all the more touching as these female protagonists long for the human touch, sensitivity and companionship of their husbands. Maya of *Cry, the Peacock* is haunted by the Albino's reading of her horoscope and prophesizing an early death of one of the partners. She reflects on her husband's non-attachment when she fervently longs for his affection. Right from the beginning she intuitively feels that her husband "knew nothing that concerned me."[25] Monisha in *Voices in the City* is a sensitive young woman who falls a prey to her monitoring in-laws. Her sister, Amala, is a painter who learns the survival techniques like Claudia and Frieda, the MacTeer sisters in Morrison's *The Bluest Eye*. Sita in *Where Shall We Go This Summer?* is a charismatic personality who suffers at the hands of her businessman-like husband, Raman. She does not want her child to be born into the chaotic, insensitive world where new life will be jeopardized. Sita invariably reminds us of Sethe in Morrison's *Beloved*. Nanda Kaul in *Fire on the Mountain* suffers lifelong negligence at the hands of her Vice-Chancellor husband. Thus, in the fiction of both Morrison and Anita Desai, the crucial issues of female alienation and oppression are authentically mirrored and artistically expressed.

As a highly conscious fictional artist, Toni Morrison also reminds us of James Joyce and William Faulkner, two other most distinguished novelists of the twentieth century. A comparison of Morrison with Joyce and Faulkner seems to be rather irresistible in regard to an exhaustive, mythical exploration of place, and search for the nexus of past and present. What Morrison is to the Black milieu of Lorain, are Joyce and Faulkner to Dublin and Oxford respectively. Like Morrison's, the stories of Joyce and Faulkner translate a multiplicity of places, often superficially tawdry, into a rich cultural matrix. Like Morrison, they make the legendary altogether new and discover in colloquial habit and naming, the altogether legendary. As in the novels of Morrison, in Joyce's and

Faulkner's fiction legend includes not only folktales but also the myths of world literature. If Morrison has excluded caucasians from her fiction, Joyce and Faulkner have excluded ethnic 'others' from theirs. Like Joyce's and Faulkner's, Morrison's focus on human personality and character is indisputably universal.

## VIII

Though concentrating exclusively on the articulation of African-American experience in her fiction, happily enough, Morrison reaches out to the entire world, but more specifically to the third world countries like India. Emerging as it does from a specific political, economic, social and cultural experience, Morrison's work has considerable interest for the Indian people. The African-American experience and the post-colonial Indian experience have many similarities. The tendency of the colonized to imitate the colonizers' viewpoint seems to last much after attaining freedom. The inclination on the part of Indians to validate their thoughts and ideas with reference to western ideology reveals a need to reassess themselves and to reclaim their own heritage and culture as precisely is the case of African-Americans.

Besides the commonality of the third world consciousness, there is another factor that brings Morrison's writing close to Indian experience—the issue of double oppression raised by the 'dalit' women. The problem of double marginalization caused by the systems of caste and gender oppression in India is almost the same as the race and gender oppression in America. Like the African-Americans, the Indian 'dalits'—the scheduled caste, the scheduled tribe as well as the other socially and economically oppressed sections of Indian society, including women, irrespective of their caste and economic status—are a marginalized group, the 'other' of the dominant group and hence the women the 'other' of the 'other.'

Furthermore, the slavery experience in the United States has some relevance to the system of bonded labour in India, more particularly in Andhra rural areas, as Lakshmi Narasaiah observes.[26] Hence the possibility of looking for a comparison between American literature based on slavery and Telugu literature based on bonded labour. To cite but one instance, Kalipatnam Rama Rao's magnum opus, *Yajnam*, bears an apt comparison with Morrison's masterpiece, *Beloved*. Just as *Beloved* deals with psychic consequences of slavery, Rama Rao's *Yajnam* treats the mental agitation created by bonded labour, "Kambaritanam." Both Morrison and Rama Rao seem to be dealing with socio-psychic interaction with reference to their specific problems of social situation. The fact that 'dalits' are treated in India as sub-human beings and are given the most humiliating jobs coincides with the black predicament in America to a considerable degree. One can discern that the system of untouchability and low social status given to 'dalits' impose a double burden on them as on the Africans in America. The protagonists of the two novels—Sethe of *Beloved* and Seetaravudu of *Yajnam*—are placed almost in the same predicament. Both of them escape from the cauldron of slavery almost in similar situations. Sethe murders her daughter, Beloved, preferring death to bonded labour. Showing the headless body of his son to his father, Seetaravudu says why he preferred death to "kambaritanam" (bonded labour) for his son: "I have great love for my son. He should not live like a slave. My son is not a 'kambari.'"[27] Thus, both Morrison's Sethe and Rama Rao's Seetaravudu are held up in an inescapable psychic state which is the outcome of their socio-economic oppression.

Although Morrison takes great pride in her black identity, values her ethnic heritage, and, more importantly, inscribes her community, her artistic genius enables her to reach out to the entire world. Just as James Joyce's fictional work can never be reduced to anthropological treatises about the Irish, or Wole Soyinka's drama into treatises about Yoruba, Morrison's work is always symbolic of the shared human condition, both engaging with and transcending lines of race, gender, and class. The novels of Morrison do more than inform us of what kind of life or lives black people in America lead. What they seek to do is to make us see experiences from the black perspective. In her novels plot, character, action and language convey, through a circular development, not only the way black folk live, but a way for anyone to live. Her novels are critiques of being and as such suggest strategies for survival in a world where the individual confronts tangible, immediate threats as well as impersonal and abstract hazards. Toni Morrison has done perhaps more than any other novelist to foster the authentic, inclusive national literature she has called for. Her six novels that mirror the triple perspective of black American woman, bring much of the American experience out of the marginal shadows and help give American literature as a whole a more complete and finer dimension.

Morrison's rigorous and unsparing intellect, displayed as much in her fiction as in the sophisticated literary analysis of her *Playing in the Dark*, is surely inseparable from her considerable achievement as a narrative lyricist. Morrison's greatest capacities as a writer are her ability to create a densely lyrical narrative texture that is instantly recognizable as her own, and to make the particularity of the African-American experience the basis for a representation of humanity as a whole.

It is only through an analysis of Morrison's language that we can reconstruct an idea of the political and artistic revolution constituted in her work. Hers is the language of black and feminine discourse—semiotic and maternal, informed as much by silence as by dialogue, as much by absence as by presence. Morrison seems to conjure her language, to invent a form of discourse that is always at once both metaphysical and metafictional. One of the freedoms Morrison claims in her novels is to move beyond the denotation of words, to render experience and emotion as musicians do. Like the blues-singing women who populate her fiction, like the prostitute Poland in her 'sweet strawberry voice' or like Claudia's mother who can "make pain sweet," so Morrison also sings her novels. And as some critics observe, anyone who has heard Morrison read from her work would know that this is literally as well as metaphorically true. Images of music pervade her work, but so also does a musical quality of language, a sound and rhythm that permeate and radiate in every novel.

One of the prominent messages of Toni Morrison's Nobel Lecture is her utmost concern for language. She suggests that language ought to be "a device for grappling with meaning, providing guidance, or expressing love."[28] As she has expressed in various interviews, part of Morrison's project as a writer has been "to clean the language up and give words back their original meaning, not the one that's sabotaged by constant use."[29] She reflects on the loss of oral traditions and values that her novels seek to redress. She succeeds exceedingly well in her attempt "to restore the language that black people spoke to its original power."[30] Small wonder if some critics have approached her novels, in general, and *Jazz*, in particular, as if they were musical scores. Eusebio L. Rodrigues, for instance, argues that *Jazz* must be "ear-read and eye-read."[31] Comparing Morrison to Louis Armstrong, Rodrigues eloquently celebrates her ability to turn language into a musical instrument that trumpets the desires, disappointments, and triumphs of African-Americans.

The result, in all events, is to vouchsafe Morrison's unique stature in American as well as in world literature. It is an important feature of today's literary culture that Toni Morrison is more widely read by a broader cross section of the American reading public than any other black writer. Morrison's devoted readers are found not only in America but on every continent, representing both sexes and all colours, ages and creeds. With memory and experience, which is essentially African-American, Morrison breathes life into "what is not the self" in order to "familiarize the strange and mystify the familiar."[32] This is really the test of the power of a great writer. Today Morrison stands as a powerful figure on the international literary scene. Her place in American letters leaves her standing next to such eminent writers as Thoreau, Sherwood Anderson, Sinclair Lewis, and William Faulkner. She ranks worldwide with great masters—Dostoevsky and Gabriel Garcia Marquez. Like these writers "Morrison's ultimate message is that each person should and must respect the reality of the human landscape of the world, with its unlimited possibilities and interpretations, if mankind is to achieve wholeness and if the global community is to once again be whole."[33] It is not just in the field of literature that Morrison has become the touchstone, as the winning of the Nobel Prize suggests. She has, indeed, become the symbol of African-America, of human struggle against various kinds of oppression, and, above all, of the global longing for liberation.

## NOTES

1. Harris, "Toni Morrison: Solo Flight through Literature into History," *World Literature Today,* 68 (1994), 9.
2. Salman Rushdie, "An Interview with Toni Morrison," *Brick*, 44 (Summer 1992), 39.
3. Nellie Mckay, *Critical Essays on Toni Morrison* (Boston: Massachusetts, 1988), 46.
4. Eric Williams, *Capitalism and Slavery* (New York: G.P. Putnam's, 1944), 18-19.
   Walter Rodney, *How Europe Underdeveloped Africa* (Dar es salaam: Tanzania Publishing house, 1972), 16, 100.
   Kwame Nkrumah, *Class Struggle in Africa* (New York: International Publishers, 1970), 29.
5. See Gloria Wade-Gayles, *No Crystal Stair: Visions of Race and Sex in Black Women's Fiction* (New York: The Pilgrim Press, 1984), 3-4.
6. Barbara Smith, "Toward a Black Feminist Criticism," *All the Women are White, All the Blacks are Men but Some of Us are Brave: Black Women Studies*, ed. Gloria T. Hull, Patricia Bellscott and Barbara Smith (New York: Feminist Press, 1982), 166.
7. Joan Bischoff, "The Novels of Toni Morrison: Studies in Thwarted Sensitivity," *Studies in Black Literature*, 6, 3 (1975), 22.
8. Wilfred D. Samuels and Clenora Hudson-Weems, *Toni Morrison* (Boston: Twayne, 1990), 53.
9. Doreatha Drummond Mbalia, *Toni Morrison's Developing Class Consciousness* (Selingrove: Subsquehanna University Press, 1992), 89.
10. Denise Heinze, *The Dilemma of "Double-Consciousness,"* 12.
11. Robert Stepto, *From behind the Veil: A Study of Afro-American Narrative* (Urbana: University of Illinois Press, 1979), xi.
12. Alice Walker, *In Search of Our Mothers' Gardens* (New York, 1983),

261-62.

13. Cheryl A. Wall, "Zora Neale Hurston Changing her Own Words," *American Novelists Revisited: Essays in Feminist Criticism,* ed. Fritz Fleis-Chmann (Boston, 1982), 91-92.
14. Hazel Carby, *Reconstructing Womanhood: Emergence of the Afro-American Woman Novelist* (New York, 1987), 175.
15. Marilyn Sanders Mobley, *Folk Roots and Mythic Wings in Sarah Orne Jewett and Toni Morrison* (London: Louisiana State University Press, 1991), 9.
16. Whneema Lubiano, "Toni Morrison," *African-American Writers*, ed. Valerie Smith (New York: Scribner's, 1991), 321.
17. Toni Morrison, "Rootedness: The Ancestor as Foundation," *Black Women Writers 1950-1980: A Critical Evaluation*, ed. Mari Evans (Garden City, New York: Anchor Press, 1984), 334.
18. Denise Heinze, *The Dilemma of "Double-Consciousness,"* 7.
19. Karen F. Stein, "Toni Morrison's *Sula*: A Black Woman's Epic," *Black American Literature Forum*, 17-18 (1983-84), 146.
20. C.G. Jung, "Psychology and Literature," *Lodge*, 181.
21. Denise Heinze, *The Dilemma of "Double-Consciousness,"* 8.
22. Harry Reed, "Toni Morrison's, *Song of Solomon* and Black Cultural Nationalism," *Centennial Review*, 32 (Winter 1988), 50.
23. Sandra M. Gilbert and Susan Gubar, *Madwoman in the Attic: The Woman Writer and the Nineteenth Century Literary Imagination* (New Haven: Yale UP, 1979), 17.
24. Barbara Christian, "Layered Rhythms: Virginia Woolf and Toni Morrison," *Modern Fiction Studies,* 39, 3 and 4 (Fall/Winter 1993), 487.
25. Anita Desai, *Cry, the Peacock* (New Delhi: Orient Paperbacks, 1980), 9.
26. Lakshminarasaiah, "The Wounded Black Psyche under White Duress in Toni Morrison's Novels," *Indian Journal of American Studies*, 23, 2 (Summer 1993), 7-15.
27. Kalipatnam Rama Rao, *Yajnam Kadha Yajnam* (Hyderabad: Hyderabad Book Trust, 1982), 38.
28. Toni Morrison, "Nobel Lecture 1993," *World Literature Today,* 68 (1994), 6.
29. Toni Morrison, Interview with Claudia Tate, Taylor-Guthrie, 165.
30. Toni Morrison, "The Language Must Not Sweat: A Conversation with Toni Morrison," with Thomas LeClair, Taylor-Guthrie, 121.
31. Eusebio L. Rodrigues, "Experiencing Jazz," *Modern Fiction Studies*, 39, 3 & 4 (Fall/Winter 1993), 733-34.
32. Toni Morrison, *Playing in the Dark, Whiteness and the Literary Imagination* (Massachusetts: Harvard University Press, 1992), 15.
33. Wilfred D. Samuels and Clenora Hudson-Weems, *Toni Morrison* (Boston: Twayne, 1990), 142.

# Bibliography


## Novels

*The Bluest Eye*. London: Pan, 1970.
*Sula*. London: Pan, 1973.
*Song of Solomon*: London: Pan, 1977.
*Tar Baby*. London: Pan, 1981.
*Beloved*. London: Pan, 1987.
*Jazz*. London: Pan, 1992.

## Miscellaneous

"Recitatif" [short story], *Confirmation: An Anthology of African American Women*. Ed. Amiri Baraka and Amina Baraka. New York: Quill, 1983. 243-61.

*Dreaming Emmett* [play]. Performed 4 January 1986 by the Capital Repertory Theater in Albany, New York.

## Edited Collections

*The Black Boo*. Comp. Middleton Harris, et al [Ed. Toni Morrison]. NY: Random House, 1974.

*Race-ing Justice, En-Gendering Power: Essays on Anita Hill, Clarence Thomas, and the Construction of Social Reality*. Ed. Toni Morrison. New York: Pantheon,

## Essays

"To Be a Black Woman," *New York Times Magazine*, 28 March 1971, 8.

"What the Black Woman Thinks About Women's Lib," *New York Times Magazine*, 22 Aug. 1971, 14-15, 63-66.

"Behind the Making of *The Black Book*," *Black World*, Feb. 1974, 86-90.

"Rediscovering Black History," *New York Times Magazine*, 11 Aug. 1974, 14, 16, 18, 20, 22, 24.

"Reading," *Mademoiselle*, May 1975, 14.

"A Slow Walk of Trees (as Grandmother Would Say) Hopeless (as Grandfather Would Say)," *New York Times Magazine*, 4 July 1976, 104-5, 150-64.

"I Will Always Be a Writer," *Essence*, Dec. 1976, 54-56, 90.

Foreword. *The Harlem Book of the Dead*. By James Van Der Zee, Owen Dodson, and Camille Billops. Dobbs Ferry, NY: Morgan and Morgan, 1978, n.p "The Lesson of Cinderella's Stepsisters," Ms., Sept. 1979, 41-42.

"City Limits, Village Values: Concepts of the Neighborhood in Black Fiction," *Literature and the Urban Experience*, ed. Michael C. Jaye and Ann Chalmers Watts. New Brunswick: Rutgers UP, 1981, 35-43.

"Writers Together" (Address given at the American Writers' Congress, 9 Oct. 1981). *Nation*, 24 Oct. 1981, 396 ff.

"Memory, Creation, and Writing," *Thought*, Dec. 1984, 385-90.

"Rootedness: The Ancestor as Foundation," *Black Women Writers (1950-1980): A Critical Evaluation*. Ed. Mari Evans. Garden City, NY: Anchor-Doubleday, 1984. 339-45.

"A Knowing So Deep," *Essence*, May 1985, 230.

"Faulkner and Women," *Faulkner and Yoknapatawpha*. Ed Doreen Fowler and Ann J. Abadie. Jackson: U of Mississippi P, 1986. 295-302.

"The Site of Memory," *Inventing the Truth: The Art and Craft of Memoir*. Ed. William Zinnser. Boston: Houghton Mifflin, 1987. 103-24.

"On Behalf of Henry Dumas," *Black American Literature Forum*, 22 (1988), 310-12.

"Unspeakable Things Unspoken: The African American Presence in American Literature," *Michigan Quarterly Review*, 28 (1989), 1-34.

*Playing in the Dark: Whiteness and the Literary Imagination*. Cambridge: Harvard UP, 1992.

"Introduction: Friday on the Potomac," *Race-ing Justice, En-gendering Power,* vii-xxx.
"Nobel Lecture 1993." *World Literature Today,* 68 (1994), 5-8.

## Interviews

*Conversations with Toni Morrison.* Ed Danille Taylor-Guthrie. Jackson: UP of Mississippi, 1994.
*Toni Morrison: Profile of a Writer.* Videotape. Prod. and dir. Alan Benson. Ed. Melvyn Bragg. LWT/RM arts, 1987. 52 min.
*Toni Morrison.* Videotape. Part 3 of *In Black and White. Six Profiles of African American Writers.* Dir. Matteo Bellinelli—. Prod. RTSI-Swiss Television. California Newsreel, 1992. 27 min.

## Bibliographies

Fkes Robert, Jr. "Echoes from Small Town Ohio: A Toni Morrison Bibliography." *Obsidian,* 5, 1-2 (1979), 142-48.
Folsom, Tonya. "Toni Morrison Bibliography: 1990-1993." *Toni Morrison Society Newsletter,* 1.1 (1984), 8-11.
Middleton, David L. *Toni Morrison: An Annotated Bibliography.* New York: Garland, 1987.
Werner, Craig. *Black American Women Novelists: An Annotated Bibliography.* Pasadena: Salem Press, 1989.

## Books on Toni Morrison

Bjork, Patrick Bryce. *The Novels of Toni Morrison: The Search for Self and Place within the Community.* New York: Peter Lang. 1992.
Bloom, Harold, ed. *Toni Morrison.* New York: Chelsea House, 1990.
Carmean, Karen. *Toni Morrison's World of Fiction.* Troy, NY: Whitston, 1993.
Gates, Henry Louis, Jr., and K.A. Appiah, ed. *Toni Morrison: Critical Perspectives Past and Present.* Amistad Literary Series. New York: Amistad, 1993.
Harris, Trudier, *Fiction and Folklore: The Novels of Toni Morrison.* Knoxville: U of Tennessee P, 1991.
Heinze, Denise. *The Dilemma of "Double-Consciousness": Toni Morrison's Novels.* Athens: U of Georgia P, 1993.
Holloway, Karla F.C., and Stephanie A. Demetrakopoulos. *New Dimensions of Spirituality: A Biracial and Bicultural Reading of the Novels of Toni Morrison.* New York: Greenwood, 1987.
Jones, Bessie W., and Audrey L. Vinson. *The World of Toni Morrison: Explorations in Literary Criticism.* Dubuque, IA: Kendall/Hunt, 1985.
Mbalia, Doreatha Drummond. *Toni Morrison's Developing Class Consciousness.* Selingrove: Susquehanna UP, 1991.
Mckay, Nellie Y., ed. *Critical Essays on Toni Morrison.* Boston: Hall, 1988.
Otten, Terry. *The Crime of Innocence in the Fiction of Toni Morrison.* Columbia: U of Missouri P, 1989.
Rigney, Barbara. *The Voices of Toni Morrison.* Columbus: Ohio State UP, 1991.
Samuels, Wilfred D., and Clenora Hudson-Weems. *Toni Morrison.* Boston: Twayne, 1990.

## Books that Include Toni Morrison

Awkward, Michael. *Inspiriting Influences: Tradition, Revision, and Afro-American Women's Novels.* New York: Columbia UP, 1991. 57-95 passim.
Baker, Houston A., Jr., Elizabeth Alexander and Patricia Redmond. *Workings of the Spirit: The Poetics of Afro-American Women's Writing.* Chicago: U of Chicago P, 1991. 132-61.
Barthold, Bonnie J. *Black Time: Fiction of Africa, the Caribbean and the United States.* New Haven: Yale UP, 1981. 174-84.
Budick, Emily Miller. *Engendering Romance: Women Writers and the Hawthorne Tradition,* 1850-1990. New Haven: Yale UP, 1994.
Butler-Evans, Elliott. *Race, Gender, and Desire: Narrative Strategies in the Fiction of Toni*

*Cade Bambara, Toni Morrison, and Alice Walker*. Philadelphia: Temple UP, 1989.

Byerman, Keith E. *Fingering the Jagged Grain: Tradition and Form in Recent Black Fiction*. Athens: U of Georgia P, 1985. 171-216.

Campbell, Jane. *Mythic Black Fiction: The Transformation of History*. Knoxville: U of Tennessee P, 198. 136-53.

Christian, Barbara T. *Black Feminist Criticism*. New York: Pergamon, 1985. 47-80.

_____. *Black Women Novelists: The Development of a Tradition* 1892-1976. Westport, CT: Greenwood, 1980. 137-79, 239-52

de Weever, Jacqueline. *Mythmaking and Metaphor in Black Women's Fiction*. New York: St. Martin's, 1992.

Dixon, Melvin. *Ride out the Wilderness: Geography and Identity in Afro-American Literature*. Urbana: U of Illinois P, 1987.

Dubey, Madhu. *Black Women Novelists and the Nationalist Aesthetic*. Bloomington: Indiana UP, 1994.

Hernton, Calvin. *The Sexual Mountain and Black Women Writers*. New York: Anchor-Doubleday, 1987. 37-58.

Hirsch, Marianne. *The Mother/Daughter Plot: Narrative, Psychoanalysis, Feminism*. Bloomington: Indiana UP, 1989.

Holloway, Karla F.C. *Moorings and Metaphors: Figures of Culture and Gender in Black Women's Literature*. New Brunswick: Rutgers UP, 1992.

Kenyon, Olga. *Black Women Novelists*, 1970-1993. Lewiston, NY: Edwin Mellen, 1994.

Kubitschek, Missy Dehn. *Claiming the Heritage: African-American Women Novelists and History*. Jackson: UP of Mississippi, 1991.

Mobley, Marilyn Sanders. *Folk Roots and Mythic Wings in Sarah Orne Jewett and Toni Morrison: The Cultural Function of Narrative*. Baton Rouge: Louisiana State UP, 1991.

Rubenstein, Roberta. *Boundaries of the Self: Gender, Culture, Fiction*. Urbana: U of Illinois P, 1987. 125-63.

Smith, Valerie. *Self-Discovery and Authority in Afro-American Narrative*. Cambridge: Harvard UP, 1987. 122-53.

Walker, Melissa. *Down from the Mountaintop: Black Women's Novels in the Wake of the Civil Rights Movement, 1966-1989*. New Haven: Yale UP, 1991.

Werner, Craig *H. Paradoxical Resolutions: American Fiction since James Joyce*. Urbana: U of Illinois P, 1982. 88-96.

Wilentz, Gay. *Binding Cultures: Black Women Writers in Africa and the Diaspora*. Bloomington: Indiana UP, 1992. 81-98.

Willis, Susan. *Specifying: Black Women Writing the American Experience*. Madison: U of Wisconsin P, 1987. 83-109.

## Relevant General Articles

Abel, Elizabeth. "Black Writing, White Reading: Race and the Politics of Feminist Interpretation." *Critical Inquiry*, 19 (1993), 470-98.

Bakerman, Jane S. "Failures of Love: Female Initiation in the Novels of Toni Morrison." *American Literature*, 52 (1981), 541-63.

Bayles, Martha. "Special Effects, Special Pleading." *New Criterion*, 6.5 (1988), 34-40.

Berret, Anthony J. "Toni Morrison's Literary *Jazz*." *CLA Journal*, 32 (1989), 267-83.

Bischoff, Joan. "The Novels of Toni Morrison: Studies in Thwarted Sensitivity." *Studies in Black Literature*, 6 (1975), 21-23.

Byerman, Keith. "Remembering History in Contemporary Black Literature and Criticism." *American Literary History*, 3 (1991), 809-16.

Campbell, Josie P. "To Sing the Song, To Tell the Tale: A Study of Toni Morrison and Simone Schwarz-Bart." *Comparative Literature Studies*, 22 (1985), 394-412.

Clark, Morris. "Flying Black: Toni Morrison's *The Bluest Eye*, *Sula*, and *Song of Solomon*." *Minority Voices*, 4 (1980), 51-63.

Davis, Cynthia A. "Self, Society, and Myth in Toni Morrison's Fiction." *Contemporary Literature*, 23 (1982), 323-42.

Denard, Carolyn C. "Toni Morrison." *Modern American Women Writers*. Ed. Elaine Showalter. New York: Scribner's, 1991. 317-38.

de Weever, Jacqualine. "The Inverted World of Toni Morrison's *The Bluest Eye* and *Sula*." *CLA Journal*, 22 (1979), 402-14.

Edelberg, Cynthia Dubin. "Morrison's Voices: Formal Education, the Work Ethic, and the Bible." *American Literature*, 58 (1986), 217-37.

Erickson, Darlene E. "Toni Morrison: The Black Search for Place in America." *Dolphin: Publications of the English Department*, University of Aarhus, 20 (1991), 45-54.

Fisher, Jerilyn. "From under the Yoke of Race and Sex: Black and Chicano Women's Fiction of the Seventies." *Minority Voices*, 2 (1978), 1-12.

Foreman, P. Gabrielle. "Past-On Stories: History and the Magically Real, Morrison and Allende on Call." *Feminist Studies*, 18 (1992), 369-88.

Giddings, Paula. "The Triumphant Song of Toni Morrison." *Encore*, 12 Dec. 1977, 26-30.

Gobel, Walter. "Canonizing Toni Morrison." *Arbeiten aus Anglistik und Amerikanistik*, 15 (1990), 127-37.

Guerrero, Edward. "Tracking 'The Look' in the Novels of Toni Morrison." *Black American Literature Forum*, 24 (1990), 761-73.

Harris, Trudier. "Toni Morrison: Solo Flight through Literature into History." *World Literature Today*, 68 (1994), 9-14.

Hilfer, Anthony C. "Critical Indeterminacies in Toni Morrison's Fiction: An Introduction." *Texas Studies in Literature and Language*, 33 (1991), 91-95.

Holloway, Karla F.C., and Stephanie Demetrakopoulos. "Remembering Our Foremothers: Older Black Women, Politics of age, Politics of Survival as Embodied in the Novels of Toni Morrison." *Women and Politics*, 6 (1986), 13-34.

House, Elizabeth B. "Artists and the Art of Living: Order and Disorder in Toni Morrison's Fiction." *Modern Fiction Studies*, 34 (1988), 27-44

_____. "The 'Sweet Life' in Morrison's Fiction." *American Literature*, 56 (1984), 181-202.

Hovet, Grace Ann, and Barbara Lounsberry. "Flying as Symbol and Legend in Toni Morrison's *The Bluest Eye*, *Sula* and *Song of Solomon*." *CLA Journal*, 27 (1983), 119-40.

Hudson-Withers, Clenora. "The World of Topsy-Turvydom in Toni Morrison's Fiction: A Methodological Explication of New Black Literary Criticism." *Western Journal of Black Studies*, 10 (1986), 132-36.

Iannone, Carol. "Toni Morrison's Career." *Commentary*, Dec. 1987, 59-63.

Jones, Carolyn M. "*Sula* and *Beloved*: Images of Cain in the Novels of Toni Morrison." *African American Review*, 27 (1993), 615-26.

Lange, Bonnie Shipman. "Toni Morrison's Rainbow Code." *Critique*, 24 (1983), 173-81.

Lee, Dorothy H. "The Quest for Self: Triumph and Failure in the Works of Toni Morrison." *Black Women Writers (1950-1980): A Critical Evaluation*. Ed. Mari Evans. Garden City, NY: Anchor-Doubleday, 1984. 346-60.

Lee, Valerie Gray. "The Use of Folktalk in Novels by Black Women Writers." *CLA Journal*, 23 (1980), 266-72.

Lewis, Desiree. "Myths of Motherhood and Power: The Construction of Black Woman in Literature." *English in Africa*, 19.1 (1992), 35-51.

Lubiano, Wahneema. "Toni Morrison." *African American Writers*. Ed. Valerie Smith. New York: Scribner's 1991. 321-33.

Martin, Jacky. "From Division to Sacrificial Reconciliation in Toni Morrison's Novels." *Obsidian*, II, 5.2 (1990), 80-99.

McDowell, Margaret B. "The Black Woman as Artist and Critic: Four Versions." *Kentucky Review*, 7 (1987), 19-41.

Menke, Pamela G. "'Hard Glass Mirrors' and Soul Memory: Vision Imagery and Gender in Ellison, Baldwin, Morrison, and Walker." *West Virginia University Philological Papers*, 38 (1992), 163-70.

Mickleson, Anne Z. "Winging Upward Black Women: Sarah E.Wright, Toni Morrison, Alice Walker." *Reaching Out: Sensitivity and Order in Recent American Fiction by Women*. Metuchen, NJ: Scarecrow P, 1979. 124-53.

Miller, Adam D. "Breedlove, Peace and the Dead." *Black Scholar*, 9 (1978), 47-50.

Mitchell, Leatha Simmons. "Toni Morrison, My Mother, and Me." *In the Memory and Spirit of*

*Frances, Zora and Lorraine: Essays and Interviews on Black Women and Writing*. Ed. Juliette Bowles. Washington, DC: Institute for the Arts and Humanities, Howard U, 1979. 58-60.

Mobley, Marilyn S. "The Mellow Moods and Difficult Truths of Toni Morrison." *Southern Review*, 29 (1993), 614-28.

Morey, Ann Jannie. "Margaret Alwood and Toni Morrison: Reflections on Postmodernism and the Study of Religion and Literature." *Journal of American Academy of Religion*, 60 (1992), 493-514.

_____. "Toni Morrison and the Color of Life." *Christian Century*, 105 (1988), 1039-42.

Myers, Linda Buck, Neil Nakadate (response), Marco A. Portales (response). Richard L.Hernstadt (response). "Perception and Power through Naming: Characters in Search of a Self in the Fiction of Toni Morrison." *Explorations in Ethnic Studies*, 7 (1984), 39-55.

Osundare, Niyi. "Toni Morrison in Madison." *African Literature Association Bulletin*, 17 (1991), 18-19.

Owusu, Kofi. "Rethinking Canonicity: Toni Morrison and the (Non)Canonic 'Other.'" *Rewriting the Dream: Reflections on the Changing American Literary Canon.* Ed. W.M. Verhoven. Amsterdam: Rodopi, 1992. 60-74.

Petric, Jerneja. "Up and Down in the World of War and Peace: Toni Morrison's Use of Tropes in *Sula* and *Song of Solomon*." *Literature, Culture and Ethnicity; Studies in Medieval, Renaissance and Modern Literatures*. Ed. Mirko Jurak. Ljubljana, Slovenia: Mirko Jurak, 1992. 141-47.

Powell, Timothy B. "Toni Morrison: The Struggle to Depict the Black Figure on the White Page." *Black American Literature Forum*, 24 (1990), 747-60.

Pullin, Faith. "Landscapes of Reality: The Fiction of Contemporary Afro-American Women." *Black Fiction: New Studies in the Afro-American Novel since* 1945. Ed. Robert A. Lee. New York: Barnes and Noble. 1980. 173-203.

Rainwater, Catherine. "Worthy Messengers: Narrative Voices in Toni Morrison's Novels." *Texas Studies in Literature and Language*, 33 (1991), 96-113.

Randolph, Laura B. "The Magic of Toni Morrison." *Ebony*, July 1988, 100-6.

Rushdy, Ashraf H.A. "'Rememory': Primal Scenes and Constructions in Toni Morrison's Novels." *Contemporary Literature*, 31 (1990), 300-23.

Sargent, Robert. "A Way of Ordering Experience: A Study of Toni Morrison's *The Bluest Eye* and *Sula*." *Faith of a (Woman) Writer*. Ed. Alice Kessler-Harris and William McBrien. Westport, CT: Greenwood, 1988. 229-36.

Schroeder, Aribert. "An Afro-American Woman Writer and Her Reviewers/Critics: Some Ideological Aspects in Current Criticism of Toni Morrison's Fiction." *Arbeiten aus Anglistik und Amerikanistik*, 15 (1990), 109-25.

Schomburg, Connie R., "To Survive Whole. To Save the Self: The Role of Sisterhood in the Novels of Toni Morrison." *The Significance of Sibling Relationships in Literature*. Ed. JoAnna S. Mink and Janet D. Ward. Bowling Green, OH: Bowling Green State UP: 1992. 149-57.

Thomson, Rosemarie Garland. "Speaking about the Unspeakable: The Representation of Disability as Stigma in Toni Morrison's Novels." *Courage and Tools: The Florence Howe Award for Feminist Scholarship 1974-1989*. Ed. Angela Ingram. NY: MLA, 1990. 238-51.

Turner, Darwin T. "Theme, Characterization, and Style in the Works of Toni Morrison." *Black Women Writers (1950-1980): A Critical Evaluation.* Ed. Mari Evans. Garden City, NY: Anchor-Doubleday, 1984. 361-69.

Wade-Gayles, Gloria. "The Truths of Our Mother's Lives: Mother-Daughter Relationships in Black Women's Fiction." *SAGE*, 1, 2 (1984), 8-12.

Wagner, Linda W. "Toni Morrison: *Contemporary American Women Writers: Narrative Strategies.* Mastery of Narrative." Ed. Catherine Rainwater and William J. Scheick. Lexington: UP of Kentucky, 1985. 191-207.

Walther, Malin LaVon. "Out of Sight: Toni Morrison's Revision of Beauty." *Black American Literature Forum*, 24 (1990), 775-89.

Warner, Anne Bradford. "New Myths and Ancient Properties: The Fiction of Toni Morrison." *Hollins Critic*, 25, 3 (1988), 1-11.

Weems, Renita. "'Artists without Art Forms': A Look at One Black Woman's World of Unrevered Black Women." *Conditions: Five*, 2 (1979), 48-58.

Wilentz, Gay. "Toward a Diaspora Literature: Black Women Writers from Africa, the Caribbean, and the United States." *College English*, 54 (1992), 385-405.

Willis, Susan. "I Shop Therefore I Am: Is There a Place for Afro-American Culture in Commodity Culture?" *Changing Our Own Words: Essays on Criticism, Theory, and Writing by Black Women*. Ed. Cheryl Wall. New Brunswick, NJ: Rutgers UP, 1989. 173-95.

## Articles on Toni Morrison's Novels

### (i) *The Bluest Eye*

Alwes, Karla. "The Evil of Fulfillment: Women and Violence in *The Bluest Eye*." *Women and Violence in Literature: An Essay Collection*. Ed. Katherine Anne Ackley. New York: Garland, 1990. 89-104.

Baum, Rosalie Murphy. "Alcoholism and Family Abuse in *Maggie* and *The Bluest Eye*." *Mosaic* 19, 3 (1986), 91-105.

Bennett, Paula. "The Mother's Part: Incest and Maternal Deprivation in Woolf and Morrison." *Narrating Mothers: Theorizing Maternal Subjectivities*. Ed. Brenda O. Daly and Maureen T. Reddy. Knox-Villie: U of Tennessee P, 1991. 125-38.

Bishop, John. "Morrison's *The Bluest Eye*." *Explicator*, 51 (1993), 152-55.

Caputi, Jane. "'Specifying' Fannie Hurst: Langston Hughes's 'Limitation of Life,' Zora Neale Hurston's *Their Eyes Were Watching God*, and Toni Morrison's *The Bluest Eye* as 'Answers' to Hurst's *Imitation of Life*." *Black American Literature Forum*, 24 (1990), 697-716.

Dickerson, Vanessa D. "The Naked Father in Toni Morrison's *The Bluest Eye*." *Refiguring the Father: New Feminist Readings of Patriarchy*. Ed. Patricia Yaeger and Beth Kowalski-Wallace. Carbondale: U of Illinois P, 1989. 108-27.

Dittmar, Linda. "'Will the Circle Be Unbroken?' The Politics of Form in *The Bluest Eye*." *Novel*, 23 (1990), 137-55.

Doughty, Peter. "A Fiction for the Tribe: Toni Morrison's *The Bluest Eye*." *The New American Writing: Essays on American Literature since* 1970. Ed. Graham Clarke. New York: St. Martin's P, 1990. 29-50.

Fick, Thomas H. "Toni Morrison's 'Allegory of the Cave': Movies, Consumption, and Platonic Realism in *The Bluest Eye*." *Journal of the Midwest Modern Language Association*, 22 (1989), 10-22.

Gertster, Carole J. "From Film Margin to Novel Center: Toni Morrison's *The Bluest Eye*." *West Virginia University Philological Papers*, 38 (1992), 191-200.

Gibson, Donald B. "Text and Countertext in Toni Morrison's *The Bluest Eye*." *LIT*, 1 (1989), 19-32.

Gravett, Sharon L. "Toni Morrison's *The Bluest Eye*: An Inverted Walden?" *West Virginia University Philological Papers*, 38 (1992), 201-11.

Klotman, Phyllis R. "Dick-and-Jane and Shirley Temple Sensibility in *The Bluest Eye*." *Black American Literature Forum*, 13 (1979), 123-25.

Kuenz, Jane. "*The Bluest Eye*: Notes on History, Community, and Black Female Subjectivity." *African American Review*, 27 (1993), 421-31.

Lloyd, Margaret G. "A Thematic Approach to Teaching *The Bluest Eye*." *SAGE*, 6, 1 (1989), 59-62.

Miner, Madonne M. "Lady No Longer Sings the Blues: Rape, Madness, and Silence in *The Bluest Eye*." *Conjuring: Black Women, Fiction, and Literary Tradition*. Ed. Marjorie Pryse and Hortense Spillers. Bloomington: Indiana UP, 1985. 176-91.

Ogunyemi, Chikwenye Okonjo. "Order and Disorder in Toni Morrison's *The Bluest Eye*." *Critique*, 19 (1977), 112-20.

Pettis, Joyce. "Difficult Survival: Mothers and Daughters in *The Bluest Eye*." *SAGE*, 4, 2 (1987), 26-29.

Portales, Marco. "Toni Morrison's *The Bluest Eye*: Shirley Temple and Cholly." *Centennial Review*, 30 (1986), 496-506.

Rosenberg, Ruth. "Seeds in Hard Ground: Black Girlhood in *The Bluest Eye*." *Black American Literature Forum*, 21 (1987), 435-45.

Royster, Philip M. "*The Bluest Eye*." *First World*, 1, 4 (1977), 34-44.

Somerville, Jane. "Idealized Beauty and the Denial of Love in Toni Morrison's *The Bluest Eye*." *Bulletin of the West Virginia Association of College Teachers*, 9 (1986), 151-61.

Tignor, Eleanor Q. "Toni Morrison's Pecola: A Portrait in Pathos." *MAWA Review*, 1 (1982), 24-27.

Tirrell, Lyne. "Storytelling and Moral Agency." *Journal of Aesthetics and Art Criticism*, 48 (1990), 115-26.

Umeh, Marie A. "A Comparative Study of the Idea of Motherhood In Two Third-World Novels." *CLA Journal*, 31 (1987), 31-43.

Wong, Shelley. "Transgression and Poesis in *The Bluest Eye*." *Callaloo*, 13 (1990), 471-81.

## (ii) *Sula*

Abel, Elizabeth. "(E)Merging Identities: The Dynamics of Female Friendship in Contemporary Fiction by Women." *Signs*, 6 (1981), 413-35.

Banyiwa-Horne, Naana. "The Scary Face of the Self: An Analysis of the Character of Sula in Toni Morrison's *Sula*." *SAGE*, 2, 1 (1985), 28-31.

Barksdale, Richard K. "Castration Symbolism in Recent Black American Fiction." *CLA Journal*, 29 (1986), 400-13.

Bogus, S. Diane. "An Authorial Tie-Up: The Wedding of Symbol and Point of View in Toni Morrison's *Sula*." *CLA Journal*, 33 (1989), 81-93.

Bryant, Cedric Gael. "The Orderliness of Disorder: Madness and Evil in Toni Morrison's *Sula*." *Black American Literature Forum*, 24 (1990), 731-45.

Coleman, Alisha R. "One and One Make One: A Metacritical and Psychoanalytical Reading of Friendship in Toni Morrison's *Sula*." *CLA Journal*, 37, 8 (1993), 145-55.

Domini, John. "Toni Morrison's *Sula*: An Inverted Inferno." *High Plains Literary Review*, 3 (1988), 75-90.

Gabbin, Joanne V. "A Laying on of Hands: Black Women Writers Exploring the Roots of Their Folk and Cultural Tradition." *Wild Women in the Whirlwind*. Ed. Joanne M. Braxton and Andre Nicola McLaughlin. New Brunswick: Rutgers UP, 1990. 246-63.

Gillespie, Diane, and Missy Dehn Kubitschek. "Who Cares?: Women. Centered Psychology in *Sula*." *Black American Literature Forum*, 24 (1990), 21-48.

Henderson, Mae Gwendolyn. "Speaking in Tongues: Dialogics, Dialectics, and the Black Women Writers Literary Tradition." *Changing Our Own Words: Essays on Criticism, Theory, and Writing by Black Women*. Ed. Cheryl A. Wall. New Brunswick: Rutgers UP, 1989. 16-37.

Hoffarth-Zelloe, Monika. "Resolving the Paradox?. An Interlinear Reading of Toni Morrison's *Sula*." *Journal of Narrative Technique*, 22 (1992), 114-27.

Homans, Margaret. "'Her Very Own Howl': The Ambiguities of Representation in Recent Women's Fiction." *Signs*, 9 (1983), 186-205.

Hunt, Patricia. "War and peace: Transfigured Categories and the Politics of *Sula*." *African American Review*, 27 (1993), 443-59.

Johnson, Barbara. "'Aesthetic' and 'Rapport' in Toni Morrison's *Sula*." *Textual Practice*, 7, 2 (1993), 165-72.

Lee, Kyung Soon. "Black Feminism: *Sula* and *Meridian*." *Journal of English Language and Literature*, 38 (1992), 585-99.

Lewis, Vashti Crutcher. "African Tradition in Toni Morrison's *Sula*." *Phylon*, 48 (1987), 91-97.

Lounsberry, Barbara, and Grace Ann Hovet. "Principles of Perception in Toni Morrison's *Sula*." *Black American Literature Forum*, 13 (1979), 126-29.

Martin, Odette. "*Sula*." *First World*, 1, 4 (1977), 34-44.

Matza, Diane. "Zora Neale Hurston's *Their Eyes Were Watching God* and Toni Morrison's *Sula*: A Comparison." *MELUS*, 12, 3 (1985), 43-54.

McDowell, Deborah E. "Boundaries: Or Distant Relations and Close Kin." *Afro-American Literary Study in the 1990s*. Ed. Houston A. Baker. Jr., and Patricia Redmond. Chicago: U of Chicago P, 1989. 51-70.

_____. "New Directions for Black Feminist Criticism." *Black American Literature Forum*, 14 (1980), 153-59. Rpt. in *The New Feminist Criticism*. Ed. Elaine Showalter. New York: Pantheon, 1985. 186-99.

Middleton, Victoria. "*Sula*: An Experimental Life." *CLA Journal*, 28 (1985), 367-81.

Montgomery, Maxine Lavon. "A Pilgrimage to the Origins: The Apocalypse as Structure and Theme in Toni Morrison's *Sula*." *Black American Literature Forum*, 23 (1989), 127-37.

Munro, C. Lynn. "The Tattooed Heart and the Serpentine Eye: Morrison's Choice of an Epigraph for *Sula*." *Black American Literature Forum*, 18 (1984), 150-54.

Ogunyemi, Chikwenye Okonjo. "*Sula*: 'A Nigger Joke.'" *Black American Literature Forum*, 13 (1979), 130-33.

Ordonez, Elizabeth J. "Narrative Texts by Ethnic Women: Reading the Past, Reshaping the Future." *MELUS*, 9, 3 (1982), 19-28.

Reddy, Maureen T. "The Tripled Plot and Center of *Sula*." *Black American Literature Forum*, 22 (1988), 29-45.

Royster, Phillip M. "A Priest and a Witch against the Spiders and the Snakes: Scapegoating in Toni Morrison's *Sula*." *UMOJA*, 2 (1978), 149-68.

Schramm, Margaret. "The Quest for the Perfect Mother in Toni Morrison's *Sula*." *The Anna Book: Searching for Anna in Literary History*. Ed. Mickey Pearlman. Westport: Greenwood, 1992. 167-76.

Seidel, Kathryn Lee. "The Lilith Figure in Toni Morrison's *Sula* and Alice Walker's *The Color Purple*." *Weber Studies*, 10, 2 (1993), 85-94.

Shannon, Anna. "'We Was Girls Together': A Study of Toni Morrison's *Sula*." *Midwestern Miscellany*, 10, 2 (1982), 9-22.

Smith, Barbara. "Toward a Black Feminist Criticism." *In the Memory and Spirit of Frances, Zora, and Lorraine: Essays and Interviews on Black Women and Writing*. Ed. Juliette Bowels. Washington, DC: Institute for the Arts and Humanities, Howard U, 1979. 32-40.

Sokoloff, Janice M. "Intimations of Matriarchial Age: Notes on the Mythical Eva in Toni Morrison's *Sula*." *Journal of Black Studies*, 16 (1986), 429-34.

Spillers, Hortense J. "A Hateful Passion, A Lost love." *Feminist Studies*, 9 (1983), 293-323.

Stein, Karen F. "'I Didn't Even Know His Name': Names and Naming in Toni Morrison's *Sula*." *Names*, 28 (1980), 226-29.

_____. "Toni Morrison's *Sula*: A Black Woman Epic." *Black American Literature Forum*, 18 (1984), 146-50.

Wessling, Joseph H. "Narcissism in Toni Morrison's *Sula*." *CLA Journal*, 31 (1988), 281-98.

## (iii) Song of Solomon

Atlas, Marilyn Judith. "The Darker Side of Toni Morrison's *Song of Solomon*." *Society for the Study of Midwestern Literature Newsletter*, 10, 2 (1980), 1-13.

_____. "A Woman Both Shiny and Brown: Feminine Strength in Toni Morrison's *Song of Solomon*." *Society for the Study of Mid Western Literature Newsletter*, 9, 3 (1979), 8-12.

Awkward, Michael. "'Unruly and Let Loose': Myth, Ideology, and Gender in *Song of Solomon*." *Callaloo*, 13 (1990), 482-98.

Benston, Kimberly W. "Re-Weaving the 'Ulysses Scene': Enchantment Post-Oedipal Identity, and the Buried Text of Blackness in Toni Morrison's *Song of Solomon*." *Comparative American Identities: Race, Sex, and Nationality in the Modern Text*. Ed. Hortense Spillers. New York: Routledge, 1991. 87-109.

Blake, Susan L. "Folklore and Community in Song of Solomon." *MELUS*, 7, 3 (1980), 77-82.

Bowman, Diane Kim. "Flying High: The American Icarus in Morrison, Roth, and Updike." *Perspectives on Contemporary Literature*, 8 (1982), 10-17.

Brenner, Gerry. "*Song of Solomon*. Morrison's Rejection of Rank's Monomyth and Feminism." *Studies in American Fiction*, 15 (1987), 13-24.

Bruck, Peter. "Returning to One's Roots: The Motif of Searching and Flying in Toni Morrison's *Song of Solomon*." *The Afro-American Novel since 1960*. Ed. Peter Bruck and Wolfgang Karrer. Amsterdam: Gruner, 1982. 289-305.

Blusterbaum, Allison A. "'Sugarman Gone Home': Folksong in Toni Morrison's *Song of Solomon.*" *Publications of the Arkansas Philological Assn,* 10, 1 (1984), 15-28.

Butler, Robert James "Open Movement and Selfhood in Toni Morrison's *Song of Solomon.*" *Centennial Review*, 28-29 (1984-85), 58-75.

Coleman, James A. "Beyond the Reach of Love and Caring: Black Life in Toni Morrison's *Song of Solomon.*" *Obsidian,* II, 1, 3 (1986), 151-61.

Cooper, Barbara E. "Milkman's Search for Family in Toni Morrison's *Song of Solomon.*" *CLA Journal,* 33 (1989), 145-56.

Cowart, David. "Faulkner and Joyce in Toni Morrison's *Song of Solomon.*" *American Literature,* 62 (1990), 87-100.

De Arman, Charles. "Milkman as the Archtypal-Hero: 'Thursday's Child Has Far to Go.'" *Obsidian,* 6, 3 (1980), 56-59.

Demetrakopoulos, Stephanie. "The Nursing Mother and Feminine Metaphysics: An Essay on Embodiment." *Soundings,* 65 (1982), 430-43.

Duvall, John N. "Doe Hunting and Masculinity: *Song of Solomon* and *Go Down, Moses.*" *Arizona Quarterly,* 47 (1991), 95-115.

Evans, James H. "The Recovery of Sacred Myth: Toni Morrison's *Song of Solomon.*" *Spiritual Empowerment in Afro-American Literature*. Lewiston, NY: Edwin Mellen, 1987. 131-61.

Freiert, William K. "Classical Themes in Toni Morrison's *Song of Solomon.*" *Helios,* 10 (1983), 161-70.

Harris, A. Leslie. "Myth as Structure in Toni Morrison's *Song of Solomon.*" *MELUS,* 7, 3 (1980), 69-76.

Hubbard, Dolan. "In Quest of Authority: Toni Morrison's *Song of Solomon* and the Rhetoric of the Black Preacher." *CLA Journal,* 35 (1992), 288-302.

Imbrie, Ann E. "'What Shalimar Knew': Toni Morrison's *Song of Solomon* as a Pastoral Novel." *College English,* 55 (1993), 473-90.

Joyce, Joyce Ann. "Structural and Thematic Unity in Toni Morrison's *Song of Solomon.*" *CEA Critic,* 49 (1986-87), 185-98.

Lee, Dorothy H. "*Song of Solomon*: To Ride the Air." *Black American Literature Forum,* 16 (1982), 64-70.

MacKethan, Lucinda H. "Names to Bear Witness: The Theme and Tradition of Naming in Toni Morrison's *Song of Solomon.*" *CEA Critic,* 49 (1986-87), 199-207.

Marshall, Brenda. "The Gospel according to Pilate." *American Literature,* 57 (1985), 486-89.

Mason, Theodore O., Jr. "The Novelist as Conservator: Stories and Comprehension in Toni Morrison's *Song of Solomon.*" *Contemporary Literature,* 29 (1988), 564-81.

Middleton, Joyce Irene. "Orality, Literacy, and Memory in Toni Morrison's *Song of Solomon.*" *College English,* 55 (1993), 64-75.

Minakawa, Harue. "The Motif of Sweetness in Toni Morrison's *Song of Solomon.*" *Kyushu—American Literature,* 26 (1985), 47-56.

Naylor, Carolyn A. "Cross-Gender Significance of the Journey Motif in Selected Afro-American Fiction." *Colby Library Quarterly,* 18, 1 (1982), 26-38.

Pinsker, Sanford. "Magic Realism, Historical Truth, and the Quest for a Liberating Identity: Reflections on Alex Haley's *Roots* and Toni Morrison's *Song of Solomon.*" *Studies in Black American Literature.* Volume I: *Black American Prose Theory*. Ed. Joe Weiximann and Chester J. Fontenot. Greenwood, FL: Penkevill, 1984. 183-97.

Rabinowitz, Paula. "Naming, Magic, and Documentary: The Subversion of the Narrative in *Song of Solomon, Ceremony,* and *China Men.*" *Feminist Re-Visions: What Has Been and Might Be.* Ed. Vivian Patraka and Louise A. Tilly. Ann Arbor: U of Michigan P, 1983. 26-42.

Reed, Harry. "Toni Morrison's, *Song of Solomon,* and Black Cultural Nationalism." *Centennial Review,* 32 (1988), 50-64.

Rosenberg, Ruth. " 'And the Children May Know Their Names': Toni Morrison's *Song of Solomon.*" *Literary Onomastics Studies,* 8 (1981), 195-219.

Royster, Phillip M. "Milkman's Flying: The Scapegoat Transcended in Toni Morrison's *Song of Solomon.*" *CLA Journal,* 24 (1981), 419-40.

Samuels, Wilfred D. "Liminality and the Search for Self in Toni Morrison's *Song of Solomon.*"

*Minority Voices,* 5 (1981), 59-68.

Scruggs, Charles. "The Nature of Desire in Toni Morrison's *Song of Solomon.*" *Arizona Quarterly,* 38 (1982), 311-35.

Skerrett, Joseph T., Jr. "Recitation to the Griot: Storytelling and Learning in Toni Morrison's *Song of Solomon.*" *Conjuring: Black Women, Fiction and Literary Tradition.* Ed. Marjorie Pryse and Hortense J. Spillers. Bloomington: Indiana UP, 1985. 192-202.

Spallino, Chiara. "*Song of Solomon*: An Adventure in Structure." *Callaloo,* 8 (1985), 510-24.

Story, Ralph. "An Excursion into the Black World: The 'Seven Days' in Toni Morrison's *Song of Solomon.*" *Black American Literature Forum,* 23 (1989), 149-58.

Stryz, Jan. "Inscribing an Origin in *Song of Solomon.*" *Studies in American Fiction,* 19 (1991), 31-40.

Wedertz-Furtado, Utelinda. "Historical Dimensions in Toni Morrison's *Song of Solomon.*" *History and Tradition in Afro-American Culture.* Ed. Gunter H. Lenz. Frankfurt: Campus, 1984. 222-41.

Wegs, Joyce. "Toni Morrison's *Song of Solomon*: A Blues Song." *Essays in Literature,* 9 (1982), 211-23.

Weiximann, Joe. "Culture Clash, Survival, and Transformation: A Study of Some Innovative Afro-American Novels of Detection." *Mississippi Quarterly,* 38 (1984-85), 21-32.

## (iv) *Tar Baby*

Baker-Fletcher, Karen. "*Tar Baby* and Womanist Theology." *Theology Today,* 50, 1 (1993), 29-38.

Bell, Pearl K. "Self-Seekers." *Commentary,* Aug. 1981, 56-60.

Coleman, James. "The Quest for Wholeness in Toni Morrison's *Tar Baby.*" *Black American Literature Forum,* 20 (1986), 63-73.

Erickson, Peter B. "Images of Nurturance in Toni Morrison's *Tar Baby.*" *CLA Journal,* 28 (1984), 11-32.

Everson, Susan Corey. "Toni Morrison's *Tar Baby*: A Resource for Feminist Theology." *Journal of Feminist Studies in Religion,* 5, 2 (1989), 65-78.

Fishman, Charles. "Naming Names: Three Recent Novels by Women Writers." *Names,* 32 (1984), 33-44.

Hawthorn, Evelyn. "On Gaining the Double-Vision: *Tar Baby* as Diasporean Novel." *Black American Literature Forum,* 22 (1988), 97-107.

Lepow, Lauren. "Paradise Lost and Found: Dualism and Edenic Myth in Toni Morrison's *Tar Baby.*" *Contemporary Literature,* 28 (1987), 363-77.

Lupton, Mary Jane. "Clothes and Closure in Three Novels by Black Women." *Black American Literature Forum,* 20 (1986), 409-21.

Magness, Patricia. "The Knight and the Princess: The Structure of Courtly Love in Toni Morrison's *Tar Baby.*" *South Atlantic Review,* 54 (1989), 85-99.

Paquet, Sandra Pouchet. "The Ancestor as Foundation in *Their Eyes Were Watching God* and *Tar Baby.*" *Callaloo,* 13 (1990), 499-515.

Reckley, Ralph. "On Looking into Morrison's *Tar Baby.*" *Amid Visions and Revisions: Poetry and Criticism on Literature and the Arts.* Ed. Burney J. Hollis. Baltimore: Morgan State UP, 1985. 132-38.

Reyes, Angelita Diane. "Ancient Properties in the New World: The Paradox of the 'Other' in Toni Morrison's *Tar Baby.*" *Black Scholar,* 17, 2 (1986), 19-25.

_____. "Politics and Metaphors of Materialism in Paule Marshall's *Praisesong for the Widow* and Toni Morrison's *Tar Baby.*" *Politics and the Muse: Studies in the Politics of Recent American Literature.* Ed. Adam J. Sorkin. Bowling Green: Popular, 1989. 179-205.

Traylor, Eleanor W. "The Fabulous World of Toni Morrison: *Tar Baby.*" *Confirmation: An Anthology of African Women.* Ed. Amiri Baraka and Amina Baraka. New York: Quill, 1983. 333-52.

Walther, Malin LaVon. "Toni Morrison's *Tar Baby*: Re-Figuring the Colonizer's Aesthetics. *Cross-Cultural Performances: Differences in Women's Re-Visions of Shakespeare.* Ed. Marianne Novy. Urbana: U of Illinois P, 1993. 137-49.

## (v) *Beloved*

Anderson, Linda. "The Re-imagining of History in Contemporary Women's Fiction." *Plotting*

*Change: Contemporary Women's Fiction*. Ed. Linda Anderson. London: Edward Arnold, 1990. 128-41.

Askeland, Lori. "Remodeling the Model Home in *Uncle Tom's Cabin* and *Beloved*." *American Literature*, 64 (1992), 785-805.

Atlas, Marilyn Judith. "Toni Morrison's *Beloved* and the Reviewers." *Midwestern Miscellany*, 18 (1990), 45-57.

Bell, Bernard W. "*Beloved*: A Womanist Neo-Slave Narrative: or Multivocal Remembrances of Things Past." *African American Review*, 26 (1992), 7-15.

Bender, Eileen T. "Repossessing Uncle Tom's Cabin: Toni Morrison's *Beloved*." *Cultural Power/Cultural Literacy*. Ed. Bonnie Braendlin. Tallahassee: Florida State UP, 1991. 129-42.

Bowers, Susan. "*Beloved* and the New Apocalypse." *Journal of Ethnic Studies*, 18 (1990), 59-77.

Budick, Emily Miller. "Absence, Loss, and the Space of History in Toni Morrison's *Beloved*." *Arizona Quarterly*, 48 (1992), 117-38.

Christian, Barbara. "'Somebody Forgot to Tell Somebody Something': African-American Women's Historical Novels." *Wild Women in the Whirlwind*. Ed. Joanne M. Braxton and Andre Nicola McLaughlin. New Brunswick: Rutgers UP, 1990. 326-41.

Corti, Lillian. "*Medea* and *Beloved*: Self-Definition and Abortive Nurturing in Literary Treatments of the Infaticidal Mother." *Disorderly Eaters: Texts in Self-Empowerment*. Ed. Lilian R. Furst and Peter W. Graham. University Park: Pennsylvania State UP, 1992. 61-77.

Cummings, Kate. "Reclaiming the Mother('s) Tongue: *Beloved, Ceremony, Mothers* and *Shadows*." *College English*, 52 (1990), 552-69.

Daily, Gary W. "Toni Morrison's *Beloved*: Rememory, History. and the Fantastic." *The Celebration of the Fantastic: Selected Papers from the Tenth Anniversary International Conference on the Fantastic in the Arts*. Ed. Donald E. Morse, Marshall B. Tymn, and Osilla Bertha. Westport, CT: Greenwood, 1992. 141-47.

Davies, Carole Boyce. "Mother Right/Write Revisited: *Beloved* and Dessa Rose and the Construction of Motherhood in Black Women's Fiction." *Narrating Mothers: Theorizing Maternal Subjectivities*. Ed. Brenda O. Daly and Maureen T. Reddy. Knoxville: U of Tennessee P, 1991. 44-57.

Davis, Christina. "*Beloved*: A Question of Identity." *Presence Africaine*, 145 (1988), 141-50.

Demetrakopoulos, Stephanie A. "Maternal Bonds as Devourers of Women's Individuation in Toni Morrison's *Beloved*." *African American Review*, 26 (1992), 51-59.

Duvall, John N. "Authentic Ghost Stories: *Uncle Tom's Cabin, Absalom, Absalom*!, and *Beloved*." *Faulkner Journal*, 4 (1988), 83-97.

Ferguson, Rebecca. "History, Rememory and Language in Toni Morrison's *Beloved*." *Feminist Criticism: Theory and Practice*. Ed. Susan Sellers and Linda Hutcheon. Toronto: U of Toronto P, 1991. 109-27.

Fields, Karen E. "To Embrace Dead Strangers: Toni Morrison's *Beloved*." *Mother Puzzles: Daughters and Mothers in Contemporary American Literature*. Ed. Mickey Pearlman. Westport. CT: Greenwood, 1989. 159-69.

Finney, Brian. "Temporal Defamiliarization in Toni Morrison's *Beloved*." *Obsidian*, II, 5, 1 (1990), 20-36.

Goldman, Anne E. "'I Made the Ink': (Literary) Production and Re-production in *Dessa Rose* and *Beloved*." *Feminist Studies*, 16 (1990), 313-30.

Henderson, Mae G. "Toni Morrison's *Beloved:* Re-Membering the Body as Historical Text." *Comparative American Identities: Race, Sex, and Nationality in the Modern Text*. Ed. Hortense J. Spillers. New York: Routledge, 1991. 62-86.

Holloway, Karla F. C. "*Beloved*: A Spiritual." *Callaloo*, 13 (1990), 516-25.

Horvitz, Deborah. "Nameless Ghosts: Possession and Dispossession in *Beloved*." *Studies in American Fiction*, 17 (1989), 157-67.

House, Elizabeth B. "Toni Morrison's Ghost: the Beloved Who Is Not Beloved." *Studies in American Fiction*, 18 (1990), 17-26.

Inoue, Kazuko. "'I got a Tree on My Back': A Study of Toni Morrison's Latest Novel, *Beloved*." *Language and Culture*, 15 (1988), 69-82.

Jablon, Madelyn. "Rememory, Dream History, and Revision in Toni Morrison's *Beloved* and Alice Walker's *The Temple of My Familiar*." *CLA Journal*, 37.2 (1993), 136-44.

Jordan, Elaine. "'Not My People': Toni Morrison and Identity." *Black Women's Writing*. Ed. Gina Wisker. New York: St. Martin's, 1993. 111-26.

Keenan, Sally. "'Four Hundred Years of Silence': Myth, History, and Motherhood in Toni Morrison's *Beloved*." *Recasting the World: Writing after Colonialism*. Ed. Jonathan White. Baltimore: Johns Hopkins UP, 1993. 45-81.

_____. "Toni Morrison's *Beloved*: Re-appropriating the Past." *Women: A Cultural Review*, 4 (1993), 154-66.

Krumholz, Linda. "The Ghosts of Slavery: Historical Recovery in Toni Morrison's *Beloved*." *African American Review*, 26 (1992), 395-408.

Lawrence, David. "Fleshly Ghosts and Ghostly Flesh: The Word and the Body in *Beloved*." *Studies in American Fiction*, 19 (1991), 189-201.

Levy, Andrew. "Telling Beloved." *Texas Studies in Literature and Language*, 33 (1991), 114-23.

Liscio, Lorraine. "Beloved's Narrative: Writing Mother's Milk." *Tulsa Studies in Women's Literature*, 11 (1992), 31-46.

Lucas, Rose. "The Parturition of Memory: Toni Morrison's *Beloved*" *Australasian Journal of American Studies*, 10, 1 (1991), 39-47.

Mathieson, Barbara Offutt. "Memory and Mother Love in Morrison's *Beloved*." *American Image*, 47, 1 (1990), 1-21.

May, Leslie S. "'Eat Me, Drink Me, Love Me': Orality, Sexuality, and the Fruits of Sororal Desire in 'Gob(b)lin(g) Market' and *Beloved*." *The Significance of Sibling Relationships in Literature*. Ed. JoAnna S. Mink and Janet D. Ward. Bowling Green. OH: Bowling Green State UP, 1992. 133-48.

Mayor, Elsie F. "Morrison's *Beloved*." *Explicator*, 51 (1993), 192-94.

McKinstry, Susan Jaret. "The Ghost of An/Other Chance: The Spinster Mother in Toni Morrison's *Beloved*." *Old Maids to Radical Spinsters: Unmarried Women in the Twentieth Century Novel*. Ed. Laura Doan. Urbana: U of Illinois P, 1991. 259-74.

Mitchell, Carolyn A. "'I Love to Tell the Story': Biblical Revisions in *Beloved*." *Religion and Literature*, 23.3 (1991), 27-42.

Moody, Joycelyn K. "Ripping Away the Veil of Slavery: Literacy, Communal Love, and Self-Esteem in Three Slave Women's Narratives." *Black American Literature Forum*, 24 (1990), 633-48.

O'Donnell, Patrick. "Remarking Bodies: Divagations of Morrison from Faulkner." *Faulkner, His Contemporaries, and His Posterity*. Ed. Waldemar Zacharasiewicz. Tubingin: Franke Verlag, 1992. 322-27.

Page, Philip. "Circularity in Toni Morrison's *Beloved*." *African American Review*, 26 (1992), 31-39.

Park, Sue. "One Reader's Response to Toni Morrison's *Beloved*." *Conference of College Teacher's of English Studies*, 56 (1991), 39-46.

Perloff, Marjorie. "Great American Novel?" *ANQ*, 5 (1992), 229-31.

Reyes, Angelita. "Rereading a Nineteenth-Century Fugitive Slave Incident: From Toni Morrison's *Beloved* to Margaret Garner's Dearly Beloved." *Annals of Scholarship: Studies of Humanities and Social Sciences*, 7 (1990), 464-86.

Rhodes, Jewell Parker. "Toni Morrison's *Beloved*: Ironies of a 'Sweet Home' Utopia in a Dystopian Slave Society." *Utopian Studies*, 1 (1990), 77-92.

Ridley, Chauncey A. "Sethe's 'Big, Bad' Love." *Understanding Others: Cultural and Cross-Cultural Studies and the Teaching of Literature*. Ed. Joseph Trimmer and Tilly Warnock. Urbana: Nat. Council of Teachers of English, 1992. 153-64.

Rigney, Barbara Hill. " 'A Story to Pass On': Ghosts and the Significance of History in Toni Morrison's *Beloved*." *Haunting the House of Fiction: Feminist Perspectives on Ghost Stories by American Women*. Ed. Lynette Carpenter and Wendy K. Kolmar. Knoxville: U of Tennessee P, 1991. 229-35.

Rodrigues, Eusebio L. "The Telling of *Beloved*" *Journal of Narrative Technique*, 21 (1991), 153-69.

Rushdy, Ashraf H.A. "Daughters Signifyin(g) History: The Example of Toni Morrison's *Beloved*." *American Literature*, 46 (1992), 567-97.

Sale, Maggie. "Call and Response as Critical Method: African-American Oral Traditions and

*Beloved.*" *African American Review,* 26 (1992), 41-50.

Scarpa, Giulia. "Narrative Possibilities at Play in Toni Morrison's *Beloved.*" *MELUS,* 17, 4 (1991), 94-103.

Schapiro, Barbara. "The Bonds of Love and the Boundaries of Self in Toni Morrison's *Beloved.*" *Contemporary Literature,* 32 (1991), 194-210.

Schmudde, Carol E. "The Haunting of 124." *African American Review,* 26 (1992), 409-16.

_____. "Knowing When to Stop: A Reading of Toni Morrison's *Beloved.*" *CLA Journal,* 37, 2 (1993), 121-35.

_____. "Morrison's *Beloved.*" *Explicator,* 50 (1992), 187-88.

Scruggs, Charles. "The Invisible City in Toni Morrison's *Beloved.*" *Arizona Quarterly,* 48 (1992), 95-132.

Segal, Carolyn Foster. "Morrison's *Beloved.*" *Explicator,* 51 (1992), 59-61.

Sitter, Deborah Ayer. "The Making of a Man: Dialogic Meaning in *Beloved.*" *African American Review,* 26 (1992), 17-29.

Smith-Wright, Geraldine. "In Spite of the Klan: Ghosts in the Fiction of Black Women Writers." *Haunting the House of Fiction: Feminist Perspectives on Ghost Stories by American Women.* Ed. Lynette Carpenter and Wendy K. Kolmar. Knoxvillie: U of Tennessee P, 1991. 142-65.

Stave, Shirley A. "Toni Morrison's *Beloved* and the Vindication of Lilith." *South Atlantic Review,* 58 (1993), 49-66.

Todd, Richard. "Toni Morrison and Canonicity: Acceptance or Appropriation?" *Rewriting the Dream: Reflections on the Changing American Literacy Canon.* Ed. W. M. Verhoven. Amsterdam: Rodopi, 1992. 43-59.

Trace, Jacqueline. "Dark Goddesses: Black Feminist Theology in Morrison's *Beloved.*" *Obsidian,* II, 6, 3 (1991), 14-30.

Travis, Molly Abel. "Speaking from the Silence of the Slave Narrative: *Beloved* and African-American Women's History." *Texas Review,* 13 (1992), 69-81.

Traylor, Eleanor W. "Henry Dumas and the Discourse of Memory." *Black American Literature Forum,* 22 (1988), 365-78.

Turner, Margaret E. "Power, Language and Gender: Writing History in *Beloved* and Obasan." *Mosaic,* 25, 4 (1992), 81-97.

Wisker, Gina. "'Disremembered and Unaccounted For' Reading Toni Morrison's *Beloved* and Alice Walker's *The Temple of My Familiar.*" *Black Women's Writing.* Ed. Gina Wisker. New York: St. Martin's, 1993. 78-95.

Wolff, Cynthia Griffin. "'Margaret Garner': A Cincinnati Story." *Massachusetts Review,* 32 (1991), 417-40.

Wyatt, Jean. "Giving Body to the World: The Maternal Symbolic in Toni Morrison's *Beloved.*" *PMLA,* 108 (1993), 474-88.

## (vi) *Jazz*

Bawer, Bruce. "All that Jazz." *New Criterion,* 10, 9 (1992), 10-17.

Hardack, Richard. "'A Music Seeking its Words': Double-Timing and Double-Consciousness in Toni Morrison's *Jazz.*" *Black Warrior Review,* 19, 2 (1993), 151-71.

Mbalia Doreatha Drummond, "Women Who Run with Wild: The Need for Sisterhoods in *Jazz.*" *Modern Fiction Studies,* 39, 384 (Fall/Winter 1993), 623.

Rodrigues L. Eusebio, "Experiencing *Jazz.*" *Modern Fiction Studies,* 39, 384 (Fall/Winter 1993), 623.

Shourie, Usha, "The Morrison Music: Narrative Style in *Jazz.*" *Indian Journal of American Studies,* 23, 2 (Summer 1993), 59.

Leonard John, "*Jazz* (1992)." *The Nation,* May 25, 1992.

# Index